Rakim Told Me:

Hip-Hop Wax Facts,
Straight from the Original Artists

The '80s

RAKIM TOLD ME:
Hip-Hop Wax Facts, Straight from the Original Artists.
The '80s.

Published by Wax Facts Press, Somerville, MA. www.waxfacts.com.

ISBN-10: 0-9766225-0-5

Library of Congress Control Number: 2005921384

First printing, 2005

Cover design and layout: Matt Nicholas (www.mattnicholas.com)

Printed in Canada

Funky Fresh Thanks:

First and foremost to my beautiful and patient wife Margot, who is not only the most incredible female on the planet, but who is also a cold-crushing proofreader. To my dear pals Mitch Myers and Michelle Mercer, for support, aiding and abetting. To my family and closest friends, thanks for not talking me out of this. To Dave Tompkins, for his inability to write a boring sentence, and for supreme old-school wisdom and enthusiasm. To Matt Nicholas, for design skillz. To all the amazing MCs and producers in this book, my idols, who graciously gave me their time and let me nerd-out with them. And thanks to Hip-Hop, because there is always good to be found in it, somewhere, somehow, then, now and forever.

Long live 1988...

Table of Contents

Why the *hell* didn't hip-hop albums ever have liner notes ?!

Am I the only person who thinks this is wrong? I hope not. And if you're reading this, maybe you feel the same way I do.

I have always felt that listeners were robbed of context and background when they bought great albums from hip-hop's golden age. Jazz albums and rock albums frequently have extensive liner notes (the former more than the latter), talking in-depth about the performers and their history. Liner notes also occasionally try to contextualize what the artist is doing with comparisons to their peers in the modern day. But hip-hop albums never had liner notes. The best you could hope for back in the day was something beyond the LP – maybe a fluffy piece in *Word Up!* Magazine about Special Ed (with a fold-out poster!) that told you a little more about where he grew up and what kind of girls he liked to hang with. Or the occasional *Spin* or *Village Voice* profile. But for me, it wasn't enough in the first place and it was too ephemeral to start with. Magazines and papers fade away too quickly. I'm here to try and bring back the essence of your favorite hip-hop albums from back in the day, one platter at a time.

For the past decade, I've been very fortunate in my happened-upon journalistic career, in no small part because I do the "Classic Material" column in *XXL* Magazine (props to Elliott Wilson for initiating the column in 2000 and signing me up, and thanks to Ell and my current editor Bonsu Thompson for continuing to let me do it). Once a month I face the sometimes daunting task of tracking down a legendary rap artist or group and asking them specific questions about what is usually the first album they ever made.

There's a lot of secret history behind these records – not because of some vast anti-hip-hop conspiracy. But because, for whatever reason, only a select few people in the history of the artform have felt that this legacy was important enough to save in book form, for future generations. Highest props are due to Steven Hager, David Toop and Nelson George. They are the holy trinity in this regard, as far as I'm concerned.

Whenever I read a reference book or do archival or online research about an artist or album, what I usually get are facts that don't have quotation marks around them. From a journalistic standpoint, this is very dangerous information, since without confirmation from the artists themselves, how do you know it's true? Many times, in fact, artists ask me "Where the hell did you hear *that*?" about a fact gleaned from this kind of research (which is why I always ask). Also, to be honest, I don't really care what a writer has to say about an album or an artist. I care what the ***artist*** has to say. And that's why, even though I frame each story here with my narrative voice, I try and stay out of the way and let the legends themselves speak. If I do step into the frame more than is necessary anywhere in these chapters, I apologize. I am known to get carried away.

The longest "Classic Material" column I have handed in is around 1,100 words. Currently it's a couple hundred less. This count is definitely enough to tell the stories of these records, but it always leaves me with hundreds and usually thousands of extra words from the artists I talk to. There are incredible things I find out and can't share – because it doesn't work with the flow of the column, or because if I say just one or two sentences it would sidetrack the whole piece. These facts are trapped inside the transcriptions of every interview I do. They lay dormant in the "filing system" in my messy-ass room. But not anymore.

What you have here are *not* the complete stories about any of the 21 albums and artists covered in this book. They're the most that I could get out of these gentlemen and ladies when I was getting my column ready, usually under a tight deadline. And please make a note, before you start nerding-out and complaining about omissions: this is not a complete list of the "ultimate hip-hop albums of the 1980s." I wish N.W.A.'s *Straight Outta Compton* was in here. Same with albums by LL Cool J, Queen Latifah, Whodini, Kurtis Blow and Stetsasonic, to name a few. Each month provides new challenges for me to cover the albums I do, and sometimes I'm not able to get the people I want. I have no real complaints, though – this is an impressive collection of albums, if I do say so myself. And future volumes are lurking right around the corner.

If you've never heard these albums before, you might not swoon over the pages here. This book is not for bookstore browsers who want something "literary" to fill up a lonely night at home by the fire. This book is for people who love hip-hop and who worship these artists and albums like I do.

Aside from two subjects here (Ultramagnetic MCs and Boogie Down Productions' KRS-One), most of these chapters follow the same basic format. The first part of each piece is about the artist's history and the making of the album in question; the second part contains direct quotes from them about specific tracks on each album. As you may know if you read "Classic Material" in *XXL*, this is the basic way all of the columns flow, and I like the format. It cuts out superfluous words and gives you as much straight talk from the artist as possible. These are wax facts, nothing more, nothing less.

I've put a lot of work into compiling these stories and I hope that after reading these chapters you go right to your crates and pull out *The Great Adventures of Slick Rick* or *Life Is... Too $hort*. If it's been a while, then for god's sake, put down that Lil Jon album for a second and go back to the real deal.

Brian Coleman
Earth, 2005

Tea Kettle At The Edge of Panic

In 1988, an 18-year-old golf enthusiast in seersucker pants dubbed himself Uwe "Rhymes with Duvet" Blab, after the fire-headed German center who had honed a mean hook shot at Indiana while playing under the unfurled V-neck sweatered gut of Coach Bobby Knight. I don't know if Michael Jordan would admit it but the Bones McKinneys out there believe that Uwe's arc helped thump UNC-Chapel out of the Final Four that year, being '83, the year the NC State Wolfpack adopted Jonzun Crew's "Pack Jam" as the mantra for their championship season coached by the late great Jimmy V the Viper himself. "Look out for the OVC" was the code for Derek Whittenburg to launch that last second air ball so Lorenzo Charles could squeak it in. Who woulda thunk.

Regardless of all that, Uwe Seersucker might've been the only charter member of the Teenage Republicans who could recite all the words to Public Enemy's "Rebel Without A Pause" while casually barreling down Providence Road in a 77 Impala, drunk off a mixture of oatmeal and Coors Light that he called Cold Wheats.

"Simple and plain, give me the lane!" he'd yell.

"Let's get some Cold Wheats and listen to that tea kettle attack," he'd say.

The Tea Kettle Attack of course being the looped saxophone from a James Brown situation recorded back when Blab was blowing up diapers.

In 1988, a six-foot-three Japanese guy from Detroit walked into the "Senior Lounge" of a small private school in North Carolina, disabled the Smiths tape in the stereo (*Strangeways Here We Come*) and usurped it with "We Want Some Pussy," a song by 2 Live Crew, the pride of Broward County. He called himself DJ Flesh KK, inspired by 1974's *Flesh Gordon*, which according to critic R. Reginald is "...an unusual film, difficult to evaluate." Rarely was this 2 Live tape allowed to run its course since plaid-plastered Trigonometrist Stan Fry had an office on the adjacent wall.

But Stan eventually had to go eat lunch. So the tape of We Want Some Whoop-Whoop ultimately found its way to "Get It Girl," another popular 2 Live Crew song. So popular that a Mormon cheerleader in an acid-washed denim dress adopted it for a half-time routine. Saddle shoes make a great 808 on a parquet floor. Not to mention the hand jive. Their get was a git, like go on git! Nor is it easy to sync up 2 Live's arpeggioed "Gi" in a squad of ten. But they expertly performed it one night, stomp-stomp-clap, when the basketball team, a squad of zeros, had the scoreboard flipped on them in the biggest loss sustained in their otherwise unmemorable season.

In 1988, a 5-something fool in Alexander Julian pastel walked in late to Music Appreciation Class on "Offensive Lyrics Day." At the time, a football player, known to yell "Oskie! Oskie! Suzy!" on the field, was back-masking a Led Zeppelin album. All that "My sweet Satan" business.

If you were really good you said backwards lyrics forwards, in streams of assonance that kicked Pig Latin's ass up and down the field. Like when Sir-Mix-A-Lot went, "Kearf a tsuj s'ehs." Or when the Fresh 3 MC's said, "We're so fresh we don't have to rehearse, we can even rap to you in reverse."

And they did. Or at least we believed they did.

As "Offensive Lyrics Day" continued, someone else played "Sugar Walls." Another played Richard Pryor, triggering an unfortunate memory within the latecomer, one where he'd just seen Eddie Murphy *Delirious* and, after doing Eddie doing Mr. T doing the avid *Deliverance* outdoorsmen, was forced to run a mile in his civvies.

On pizza day for crying out loud.

Yet he somehow snapped out of his reverie long enough to contribute to the class. Thus Just-Ice's "That Girl Is A Slut" was successful in offending everyone in Music Appreciation, the administration and the whole dadblam state of North Carolina. (Not surprisingly he spent his Friday nights eating a frozen Tostino's pizza and watching Miami Vice.) Before being deported to the Dean of Discipline, the guy who paid $4.99 for "Put That Record Back On" and NOT "That Girl Is A Slut," was grabbed by an aspiring dental hygienist in white leather Capezios. "Why does Dana Dane sound like Slick Rick?," she asked.

I don't know, ma'am but in 1988 a beady-eyed history teacher who lived with his mother walked into a classroom in a powder wig and a judge's robe. His name was Eddy. The lights dimmed and Eddy thundered through Jonathan Edwards' "Sinners In The Hands of An Angry God." With a scowl. A big fat fucking scowl.

It wasn't looking good for the 2 Live Crew.

It wasn't looking good for Greg Tassos either. Greg Tassos had a demon brow and reportedly the best weed on campus. One day, after smoking an iffy knot of 'Triffid Sticky,' Greg Tassos stole a Ryder truck and drove that sucker across the quad and up to the door of Mary Todd's Shakespeare class, stormed in, said he was the anti-Christ and pointed at the clock and stopped it.

And then walked out mumbling something about how the Triffid Nebula is giving birth to a new family of stars.

Now that was some shit.

"Meteor shit!" said fungus-besieged farmer Jody Verill.

And Mary Todd, ever unflappable, was just happy that Greg Tassos made it to class at all.

That's what they call sticktoitness, she said.

Sticktuition, if you want to get fancy.

We admire the memory while sitting in a black Mercury Cougar listening to *Raising Hell*, wondering if Greg Tassos kept a bag of cheeba inside his locker, like RUN, before RUN changed his mind and decided to say he kept a microphone inside his locker, which was cool and all but you know RUN was still thinking cheeba, if not smoking it, when he performed "Here We Go" or whatever that riff was he co-opted for "Hollis Crew (Krush-Groove 2)," kind of like what Melle Mel did with "Superrappin'" and "The Message" if you think about it it's all too much to many people.

Meanwhile just up the road in Greensboro, North Carolina, the Bizzie Boyz were making random rap history though at the time they didn't know it.

And meanwhile, over in Fayetteville, North Carolina, Dizzie Fitzgerald was making random rap history though at the time he didn't know it.

And meanwhile once more, just a flea-flicker away from Fayetteville, over in Wilmington, North Carolina, where I once nearly drowned in the eye of a hurricane named after my dad ("Charlie"), Courageous Chief was making random rap history though at the time he didn't know and come to think of it neither do I, at this moment, because nobody can find that shit.

Philly, however was different.

In 1988, The Smiths fell again. This time to Schoolly D. The walls of Stan Fry really rumbled that day when the son of a bootleg food distributor threw on "Parkside 5-2." Fruity Whirls, Cheetah Chomps, Toastie O's, Oatie Oots. He could get it all. In *bulk*. "Same White Bitch Got Me Strung Out On Cane." One of the greatest song titles of all time.

Anyway the guy who played Schoolly D, he's the one who bought "You're Gonna Get Yours" the same day someone else we won't mention bought Lisa Lisa & Cult Jam's second tape. But this guy, he wore red Spot-Bilts, watched movies like *Mother's Day* and said things like Got Toe Mighty, which a week later became "Cotton Candy" even though, once upon an in vain, it was originally "Goddammit!" And he would say evil things just to be evil and even say the word evil after he said them, moving his eyes all funny at the same time. You know the type.

And he hadn't even heard a lick of Ultramagnetic MC's. *Critical Beatdown* was the first tape I fell asleep to in the late afternoon only to wake screaming my britches off in the darkness not knowing where the hell I was, fumbling around for my exoskeleton. If you fell asleep listening to some guy in a fur coat talking about eating your brains you'd wake up yawping too.

I didn't know how it'd gotten all the way over to Side 2.

Auto-Reverse was kind of new back then so things kind of had a mind of their own.

Dave Tompkins
Red Hook Dinosaur Crane
2005

“Many people tell me this style is terrific
It is kind of different
But let’s get specific”

KRS-One,
Boogie Down Productions,
“South Bronx”

SCHOOLLY D

Saturday Night: The Album

(Schoolly D / Jive, 1986/1987)

"I knew I was going to do this when I was 9 or 10 years old. I knew I wasn't going to be the weatherman or working in some office. I was either going to be some crazy painter or a musician," states Jesse B. Weaver, Jr., aka Schoolly D. Schoolly actually ended up doing both of his prophesized vocations, in a way. A musician for sure, and also a crazy painter – of street tales. He was the man who planted the seeds of gangsta rap, out of Philly, unequalled and incredibly influential in the mid-'80s rap world.

"I first started thinking I was gonna be a DJ, I used to spin records all the time," he says. "But there was like 20 DJs in the crew and like 10 rappers. So I went with rapping." The crew in question was the Park Side Killers aka The 5-2 Crew (named after their part of West Philly, Parkside Ave and 52nd Street), consisting of Royal Ron, Pimp Pretty, Disco Len, Mixmaster Mark and T-Ski Flash. "I was the last cat to be let in," Schoolly adds.

Immortalized in the songs "P.S.K. What Does It Mean?" and "Parkside 5-2," they were his musical family. Royal Ron was younger than Schoolly, but was a father to his style, the man who taught Jesse how to become Schoolly D. "Ron made me work hard at rapping," Schoolly recalls, "He put a lot of thought into his words, a lot of complex stuff. And when everyone was trying to be Melle Mel or Kurtis Blow, he told me to just be myself. He was also the first guy I knew with a [Roland] 909 [drum machine], and he let me borrow it." Aside from his lyrics, Schoolly's use of the 909 was one of his calling cards, and with his potent mix of subwoofer-shredding beats and lyrical mischief, Mr. D messed up rap music up forever.

Schoolly was born in the City of Brotherly Love, high schooled in Atlanta and soon thereafter back in West Philly. In 1984 he began his assault on the rap industry, at the age of 19, with his first two self-released singles, "Gangster Boogie / Maniac" and "C.I.A. / Cold Blooded Blitz" (both on his own Schoolly D Records). The combined four songs were an odd mix. "Maniac" was straight electro, with processed space-mutant vocals on the chorus and high-pitched keyboards. "C.I.A.," on the other hand, stood for "Crime In Action," an uplifting tribute to the artistic efforts of local graffiti writers. "'C.I.A' was me trying to be positive," Schoolly chuckles today. "A week after I put that out I was laughin' at myself. It sounded like every record I didn't want to do. It was so forced."

After his first singles that year, he sought advice from Philly rap radio goddess Lady B in a meeting that cemented his desire to go for self. He recalls: "I took 'Gangster Boogie' [a prototypical gangsta rap track] to her and she said 'Are you crazy? Go back and do something else, like Grandmaster Flash. You'll never get signed talking about guns and drugs. Not until you do something positive.' So I said 'Fuck that shit, I'll just keep putting records out myself.'" Schoolly's course was set – no more positive messages, and no more asking for peoples' permission or caring what they thought.

Schoolly's first DJ was a guy named DLB, who was featured on the first two singles, and then never heard from again, at least not on a Schoolly track. The reason? "He was a chicken! In the studio he could do anything, but when it came time to perform on-stage he always had cold feet. That muthafucka said he had tennis elbow and couldn't perform. And he don't even play tennis!" The problem of DLB's absence was solved quickly enough. DJ Code Money, just out of high school in 1984 and a family friend (Schoolly's older brother served in Vietnam with Code's father), "Just walked up to me and said that he wanted to DJ." And, like many other things in Schoolly's musical life, that was that. Code was a skilled DJ and an innovative one for the time. DJs were making names for themselves back in '85, but they were still mostly relegated to flashing out in-between verses only. Schoolly points out: "Code was one of the first DJs to scratch through a whole fuckin' record, not just on the chorus."

Schoolly's true musical calling card, the song that people remember him for even to this day, came in 1985 with the single "P.S.K. What Does It Mean?" and "Gucci Time." Both songs were cooked up in a classical recording studio, with the aid of a massive reverb chamber. Schoolly schools: "In 1985 there were *no* rap studios, not in Philly at least. So we had to go to a real studio, with this guy we called Jeff Cheesesteak. We recorded 'P.S.K.,' 'Gucci Time,' and 'Freestyle Rappin'' there. And the craziest shit was that they had a real reverb, not just a processing effect. It was these big fucking plates, they took up a whole room. It takes like 3-4 people just to move them around."

He adds: "Even years later I've tried to get that sound again, but I can't. People ask me how the fuck I got that sound [as heard on the booming "P.S.K.," for example] and I still can't duplicate it. One other thing with the recording back in those days is that we was *hiiiiigh*. It was like – puff puff – MORE REVERB! MORE REVERB! [laughs]. We stayed at that studio working and smoking all night, until like six in the morning, and when I woke up at one or two the next day I played it and was like 'What the fuck is this??!!?' But I played it for the crew and they went ballistic. It was instant. Those songs went everywhere in like six months."

Both cuts were combinations of booming drum programs and Schoolly's dusted, arrogant style detailing — in decidedly un-PC fashion, and laced with profanity — the alleged tales of his Park Side Killers neighborhood crew and Schoolly's own actions taking out biters. The rap world had never heard anything quite like it, and fans took notice, buying up copies anywhere they could. The demand was so large, in fact, that nationwide bootlegging was a major distribution avenue for Schoolly, albeit an unpaid one: "Those bootleggers made me big because when it came down to it, I didn't have the money to get the records out there. The person who helped me figure that shit out was Luke [Luther Campbell of 2 Live Crew and Luke Skyywalker Records], he took me all over Miami and showed me all the different bootlegged versions of my own records. It was crazy."

Schoolly even jokes that the infamous Vincenzo The Godfather of Vinyl (legendary in the annals of Philly old-school mythology) "Made 'P.S.K.' go gold because he bootlegged it so much." Schoolly claims that the "P.S.K. / Gucci Time" single "definitely went over 500,000" in sales, but since many of those weren't accounted for, he'll never be sure. Either way, it was good-enough cash and definitely a big splash for Schoolly on the national scene.

Success came quick, partially because of Schoolly's learn-on-the-fly business savvy (aided by eventual RuffHouse head honcho Chris Schwartz) and also because he continued to pave new ground in the rap world – gangsta ground which would eventually be emulated and expanded upon by N.W.A., Ice-T and the Geto Boys. By 1986 he was in the studio recording his debut LP *Saturday Night: The Album*, originally released on Schoolly D, and re-released with extra tracks as part of a "disheartening" multi-album deal with Jive. About his former label he says: "I signed with them partially to pay a lot of bills that we had, because distributors weren't paying me for the records I was selling. Jive didn't understand that I was an artist, not an entertainer. You can tell an entertainer what to do, but you can't do that to an artist. It insults them."

The artist part of Schoolly's work was no joke, especially with his productions, which favored the heavy kick of the Roland TR-909 drum machine, his weapon of choice. "My brother was a drummer, so I used to study him," Schoolly explains. "By 1985 I had mastered the 909. I'd stay up until five in the morning, just trying to get better at it. I was like drum machine crazy. The 727 had the best cowbell and percussion sounds, the 505 had the best hi-hats. At first I didn't want to use the SP-12 [Emu's newly-unveiled sampler, which could be used to sample drums instead of programming artificial ones], but when I saw that I could link up all my machines and use that, I went even more crazy."

His production methods might have been powerful and influential, but they weren't necessarily complicated. He remembers: "I'd do the drums first. Then we just sat there and smoked and drank until we got silly enough and drunk enough. Then the first thing that hit my mind, that was the song. We kept the tape rolling and we'd just do it over and over again and by the end of the night I'd have the song down on tape." After getting barred from the classical studio in Philly, they landed at a more rap-friendly recording haven: INS Studios in New York. His primitive recording techniques were soon upgraded there, as he relates: "The only way I knew how to record back then was like old James Brown style, all in the room at the same time. If you listen real close to 'P.S.K.' and 'Gucci Time' you can hear me hittin' the buttons [on the drum machine], rappin' at the same time, with Code cuttin'. But the cats at INS were like 'You don't have to do that, you know.'"

Schoolly's first real introduction to the world at large (thanks to legitimate distribution), 1987's Jive version of *Saturday Night: The Album*, was a major event in rap's teenage years. It was drenched in his unique vocalese, random, flippant and occasionally hilarious lyrical content (he admits to letting the music take over certain tracks because he "didn't have anything more to say"), DJ Code Money's influential scratches, and, perhaps most importantly, Schoolly's crisp conga-and-timbale-drenched drum programs. The album was well-received and almost immeasurably influential.

Schoolly says that a Jive decision had an adverse effect on his next album, the still warmly-received and definitely dope *Smoke Some Kill* (from 1988): "The extra tracks they added to the Jive version of *Saturday Night* [including 'Parkside 5-2,' 'Housing The Joint' and 'Get N' Paid'] were actually supposed to be for *Smoke Some Kill*. It was a total scam to reissue *Saturday Night* like they did, with those tracks, because it had already sold hundreds of thousands of copies. If those tracks would have come out on *Smoke Some Kill* like they were supposed to, it would have been an even better record."

In the end, *Saturday Night: The Album* was everything that Schoolly D was all about: funk, loose rhymes and attitude. It was the embodiment of his own personal philosophy, which he sums up like so: "Stick to your guns, because you're either gonna catch up to the world or the world's gonna catch up to you. If you're a true artist, just stick to your guns. I'm glad I did, because I love my freedom."

TRACKS (including "P.S.K." single and *Saturday Night* album)

Housing The Joint

Me and Spoonie Gee was going through a little somethin' back then. He made a record about me ["The Godfather"] saying I stole his style. So that was a response to that. Later on we did shows together and it was cool. I only performed that live once, and that was because Chuck D was on the bill, because he liked it so much. I got the idea for that song out in California when I saw Sly Stone on some talk show, and they played "Thank You..." when he came out. I got home, got that Sly record, booked some studio time, made the track, did the rap and recorded it all in one day. For some reason I just never felt comfortable doing that one live.

We Get Ill

That was a Bootsy [Collins]-inspired track. If you listen you can hear Bootsy's shit all over that track. It was going to be an instrumental originally. But everybody at the time was saying "We get ill" so I went back and did vocals over it.

Do It, Do It

That started in Code's basement. We were going to go and record "Saturday Night" in a couple days. We rarely did anything at Code's house, but he started just going back and forth with that Funkadelic ["You'll Like It Too"] break and I started rapping over it. He put the tape machine on record and we taped it. That was the first time we worked with Joe ["The Butcher" Nicolo]. We did it on three tracks, with the drum program, Code cutting and me rapping. Joe looked at us like: "Aren't you going to put anything else on there?" since we had 24 tracks to use. And we said: "Nope, that's it." That was his introduction to hip-hop. The big bad wolf stuff on there came from an old nursery rhyme record and Code cut that up as a message for all other DJs.

Dedication to all B-Boys

That's something I always really wanted to do, and it was inspired by the Commodores. I was doing the drum program and Code started singing "Young girls are my weakness" and it was just magic. That early shit was just magic. There are a lot of cuts at the end because people always wanted to hear as much as possible. I recorded records the way I heard records. Isaac Hayes always made long records, and you never got tired of it. Live also, people wanted to hear the long break at the end. Everybody who was part of the band got to do their thing, and Code was part of the band.

Get n' Paid

That was about shit we was going through at the time. You show up at these shows and everybody got a goddamn excuse. The promoter would say: "Yo, School, I'll be back. My grandmom's sick, but you just go on and by the time you're off I'll be back." Then after we're done it's like "Where's Jo Jo?" "Oh, Jo Jo left with two bitches right about when you went on stage." So we was like: "Gimme my money before I go on, or I ain't rappin'."

Dis Groove

That's when I first started fuckin' around with the 808, with the heavy, sub-low kick drum. Code came up with that concept. I was also messing around with the SP-12 [sampler]. I was sampling the 909 and the 808. I worked on that track for two days, then played it for Code and he started scratching over it. That was the first track I used the 808 and the SP-12 on. I was sampling all those 808s off of old Mantronix records before that. With that backwards tape stuff at the end, that was Joe and his tricks. He wanted to be part of things, so that's how he did it.

Parkside 5-2

5-2 is for 52nd Street. I had already done the drum program for that and we just sat in the studio smokin' and drinkin', like usual. I said "Parkside" and then Pimp Pretty said "5, 5....2" just like that. I talk about lots of my growing-up stuff in there. Royal Ron taught me how to rap, and always helped me keep my shit straight. Disco Len was the first

DJ in the neighborhood, and the guy who always had money. He was basically the guy who kept me from doing anything illegal. That had a lot of lyrics on it, for me. Sometimes with a song I'm just like: "You know, I ain't got no more to say." It's just that simple. Sometimes the music just speaks so strong that you don't need as many lyrics. Some songs are about what I got to say and the music is secondary. Some tracks, the music is in the front, on purpose.

B-Boy Rhyme and Riddle

That's me and a live drummer at the same time. Joe brought him in and wanted to experiment with it. Code just let the organ thing keep going. Right there it was just magic, and I just came up with the lyrics, ran in real quick, did the lyrics, came back and Joe's just lookin at me like I'm fuckin' crazy. The drummer was some cat from some group like Experimental Project or Product or something. He like burnt his eyelids off or something. On purpose. But I like the weird guys. It was all just one take. Shan had his Pumas and I had my Filas.

Saturday Night

That track was actually an accident. It was a fuck-up! We got to the studio to record that track and Code forgot the a/c cord for the 909, after I had let him borrow it. I wasn't going home to get that shit, and they had a drum machine there, so I programmed the beat into it. But by accident I hit some button and it made the kick and snare go to timbale sounds. I was like "Whoa! What the fuck is this shit?" But I just kept looping it. And we just put it on tape right there. I can't even remember the name of the drum machine, and I've never seen it again. The 909 program I did was the exact same, just without the timbales. A lot of that shit on that track actually happened. My mom didn't have a gun, but it *felt* like she had a gun. She did catch me plenty of fuckin' times trying to sneak somebody in the crib, and she fucked up my room and kicked some ass. It's truth, just a bit exaggerated.

It's Krack

I just wanted to make a statement, that's why I put in those keyboards. I wasn't just a rap producer, I was a *music* producer. So I did that instrumental to show off my other talents. That's me playing keyboards, and Code named it. Back in the day people was like: "Ahh, that shit is *crack*." Meaning it was hype like crack.

P.S.K. What Does It Mean?

"P.S.K." sold 100,000 copies in New York before they even knew I was from Philly. People were trying to figure out where I was from, because no one from Philly had made that impact before. It's really very simple, that drum beat. I came up with it sittin' at the dinner table at my mom's, with my 909 and my headphones on. And she's like: "We're trying to eat dinner, so take that shit and get the fuck away from the goddamn table." And I was like: "But Ma, I'm trying to create a masterpiece!" "Master yo ass!," she said. I used to always listen how they'd put together hi-hats in all the James Brown songs, and I just listened and listened and listened. It's similar to "Gucci Time" but "Gucci Time" was more about the hi-hats. Code did all the scratches on "P.S.K.."

With that track we was fucked up and we was high. It was the first big thing we did in a big studio, and it kind of made us nervous. When we recorded that, the engineer, Jeff Cheesesteak (that's what we called him), was all nervous, too, with eight black guys showing up. He was worried about motherfuckers stealing shit, which they did. I didn't know, but all my homies was upstairs cleanin' out all kinds of microphones. I made them bring the mics back, though. At about five or six in the morning, after so many takes, I was like: "Yeah, that's *right*." It made the speakers do this kind of sucking motion and that's when I knew it was right. The engineer, Jeff, was like: "What the fuck are you doing to my speakers??!!?"

Gucci Time

We recorded that one the same night as "P.S.K." DLB [Schoolly's original DJ] did the scratches for it. People used to bite my shit a lot, because we used to make mix tapes and sell them around town. We would sit in the room and just make tapes and copy them, we had like 8 tape decks running at the same time. I used some nursery rhyme shit with those lyrics, like P-Funk did on "Let's Take It To The Stage." I took a lot of my writing style from George Clinton and Richard Pryor. Pryor could be real mean, but he knew you couldn't get your point across unless you make muthafuckas laugh a bit. I was influenced by those two more than any rappers.

RUN DMC

Raising Hell

(Profile, 1986)

If there was one hip-hop group on top of the world at the end of 1985 it was most certainly Run-DMC, who had been on an unstoppable tear since their debut single, "Sucker MCs" in 1983. But even with gold and platinum albums under their belts (1984's *Run-DMC* and 1985's *King Of Rock*, respectively, both on Profile), the group still had more to accomplish. Darryl McDaniels, aka DMC, says today: "1986 was when Run-DMC really became Run-DMC. That's when we really gelled."

Raising Hell was only the cherry on the top of some of the best years a hip-hop artist or group has ever experienced. The group grew from modest beginnings in Hollis, Queens, with one main goal – to be iller than the old-school legends they worshipped. "Our whole thing," DMC says, "Was to be like the Cold Crush Brothers. To have the best show, the best rhymes and the best DJ, with more beats than anybody. Cold Crush were our idols, and all we wanted to do was be better than them. In 1983 Cold Crush were on their way down because they wasn't making powerful records. On 'My Adidas' we said that we took the beat from the street and put it on TV. That's exactly what we did. We didn't really think it was pioneering, we just did what rappers before us was doing on tapes. When a lot of the old guys, like Kool Moe Dee, Treacherous Three and Grandmaster Flash got in the studio they never put their greatness on records. Me and Run and Jay would listen to tapes in our basement and we'd say: 'They didn't do that shit last night in the Bronx! What the hell is this 'Birthday Rap' shit and 'What's your zodiac sign?'?! So we said that we weren't going to be fake. We ain't gonna wear no costumes. We're gonna keep it real."

Believe it or not, even though they had huge sales and even critical success with their first two albums, the group knew that they hadn't even begun to spread their wings, artistically. DMC explains: "Everything before *Raising Hell* was written when we was in the shower or on the way to the studio, or even at the studio. A lot of the rhymes on the first two albums was just stuff we had in our rhyme books from way back, and Russell [Simmons, the group's manager and Run's brother] let us put it on record. But we didn't want to make no more corny bullshit records. A lot of [tracks] on the first two, you like them, you can recite them because you've listened to the album a lot. But they weren't *dope*."

He continues: "We wanted to do an album where every record on there is our best. No throwaways. At the time we didn't think that [certain] tracks on the first two albums were filler, but after *Raising Hell* we looked back and saw them as that. We knew both albums could have been doper, especially after what we did in 1986. When we were making *Raising Hell* there were records we looked back at on the first two albums and said: 'We should never have made that one.'" With their change in attitude also came a change in format and songwriting: "Back then it was like: 'You rhyme, I rhyme, then Jay, you scratch.' But *Raising Hell* was Run-DMC working simultaneously. That's why the album came out so def."

After worldwide tours in 1984 and 1985 the group was ready to record their masterpiece, which they sketched out on the Fresh Fest 2 tour in 1985, after their film debut in *Krush Groove*. "We wrote that whole album on the road, that's why it was so dope," DMC says. "We would write a song every night after a great performance, so we had a lot of energy and momentum going."

There were also some changes within the Run-DMC camp at the time. For one, the group was starting to grow apart from producer Larry Smith, who had worked with the trio for their first two albums. DMC says that there wasn't any bad blood, it was just time to move on. "It was actually more him [leaving, as opposed to the group choosing not to hire him again]. He wanted to do a lot of musical stuff, more complex things, but we wanted to keep it raw. He wanted to do Whodini type of stuff. What he had for us, we didn't need anymore. It wasn't that we didn't want it, it's just that we had our shit down pat because it was us three on the road every night. It was like: 'We got dope shit and we're gonna use *our* shit this time, not yours.' Larry wasn't pissed, I don't think, we just all wanted to do something different."

Returning home to Queens after touring, in late 1985 they put themselves on lock-down at Chung King studios in Manhattan for three months. In place of producer Smith, a cocky new maverick was brought in: Rick Rubin. DMC remembers: "Rick came in because he had the rock thing, and we wanted to take rock to the left. We went to Rick's dorm room at NYU and he had like every rock record in the world. Plus he could play stuff on guitar. So we said: 'We need this guy, Russell.' Rick was that sound we wanted at that time."

Even though Rubin's and Russell's names were on the production marquee, DMC says that they oversaw and added to the music on *Raising Hell* more than created it: "Rick and Russell got production credit but we [the group members] really did everything. They just put their names up there so they could look big. Rick was very hands-on, no doubt about it, but we were in charge. Rick would give us ideas and we'd just run with it. Russell would sit back and say: 'Go left! Go right! Go Up! Go Down!' He directed everything."

After slaying audiences with the material on the road every night for months on end, the group that walked into Chung King had the eye of the tiger: "Our main goal with *Raising Hell* was to have the best tape [he emphasizes this, versus using "album," to show how they wanted it to be like the old days] of anyone else's being sold. People used to buy a lot of Cold Crush tapes, so we wanted to have the fullest cassette tape rolling around. And since we were huge at that point, we had the chance to put it on an album for everyone to hear."

DMC remembers recording the album vividly: "We did that album in like three months. Because every rhyme was written on the road and had been practiced and polished. We knew what we wanted to do. Rick was all music and instruments. Jay was music and DJing. And me and Run was lyrics. Run and I would tell them to change this thing and that with the music from time to time, because we was the ones rapping over it. Overall, we definitely had a game plan."

He continues: "Some songs were on the radio before the label even had a chance to figure out what they was gonna do with them. 'My Adidas,' 'Peter Piper,' and 'Hit It Run.' We took them right to the radio stations, as soon as they were recorded. Red Alert, Chuck Chillout and Mr. Magic. And they ate 'em up! Then, after we finished the album we did a show at the Apollo, for two nights. And instead of playing old shit we did the whole *Raising Hell* album. People went *crazy*, and they hadn't even heard the songs before. That's when we knew the album was dope. It was the proof we needed."

There were, of course, numerous highlights on *Raising Hell*. But none were more impressive than their first worldwide smash, "Walk This Way," a cover of the Aerosmith rock perennial, with group members Steven Tyler and Joe Perry on-board. That was exactly what Rubin's new rock angle brought to the table, and it's a big reason why the album ended up selling, as DMC says "Around six million, something like that. That's what they told us. Worldwide maybe like 10 or 11 million copies." Although "Walk This Way" was the second single, it was the album's first video, and most certainly a main reason why the single took off like it did. Why no video for the first single, "My Adidas" with "Peter Piper" on the flip? Simple, DMC says: "We was on the road too much, we didn't have time to do a video for it."

The group also continued to expand upon their duties as role models, especially with the song "Proud To Be Black," the album's parting shot. DMC says: "We knew that there was power in this music. We could teach, we could innovate, we could inspire and motivate. We made it cool to put messages in lyrics [he rhymes the first verse of "Sucker MCs"]. Nobody ever bragged about going to college! Especially in the 'hood. But we knew we could make education cool, we knew we could make a difference."

In the end, Darryl sums *Raising Hell* up like this: "It's definitely our best album. Everything about it was perfect to me. That album was everything that hip-hop was and wanted to be. It brought hip-hop to life, for every generation, every race, creed and color. No one could hate it. It stands as the only album we really *made*, and it made us the legends that we are today. Because it was a visual record. We did it live on stage every night, before we even went into the studio. Everything now and then was and is too one-sided. It wasn't broad enough. But that changed with *Raising Hell*. It was a record that everybody just *got*."

And in tribute to Jam Master Jay, the main musical force in the group and a sorely-missed hip-hop legend, DMC reminds us about his true greatness: "He was the first DJ to DJ for the rap cause. We didn't use no band, we didn't use no tape playback, we never had a DAT. Jay DJed vinyl, live. Without Jay there's no Run-DMC, and that's why we disbanded. We can't make records anymore, because Jay was the backbone of the group. He was every DJ then, today and in the future." He continues: "Hip-hop brings joy, happiness, enlightens people and makes them think. Jay did all those things, as a DJ, an artist and as a person. There will never be another."

TRACKS

Peter Piper

That was our collective favorite record on the album, because it was a rap/DJ record. Jay cut that all up live in the studio. We had been rhyming over that loop [Bob James' "Take Me To The Mardi Gras"] since before rap records was even made. We always used to just freestyle over those beats. But for the song on the album, we wrote those lyrics while we was on the road.

It's Tricky

That was a routine like the Cold Crush [Brothers] used to do, how they'd use a melody from another record and put their names and words in there. That was just based on [he sings Toni Basil's hit "Mickey"]. So I just changed the chorus around and we just talked about how this rap business can be tricky to a brother. It was our idea but Rick had a lot of musical input on that one. Him and Jay, both. With that video, we didn't know who Penn & Teller was. I have a line about my dad in there. When we'd go on the road my parents became celebrities in our neighborhood. They couldn't go to the market without getting recognized. They enjoyed it, they was famous, too.

My Adidas

That was the first single, with "Peter Piper." We were sponsored by Adidas, and that was definitely a big deal. But more to other people than to us. We was just intent on bustin' ass. We wore Adidas and then everyone started wearing Adidas, but we didn't want people to dress like us. We just wanted people to like our beats and rhymes. We got the sponsorship deal in 1985, the night we had everyone hold their Adidas up at Madison Square Garden. Someone at Adidas heard about us and sent a rep out to one of our shows, to spy. And he saw how big it was.

Walk This Way

One day me and Jay was in the studio and we was sampling Aerosmith and Rick said: "Yo, do you know who that is?" and we was like: "No, but we like this beat." Because we used to always rap over that beat in the 'hood. We didn't know the group name or anything. So Rick gave us the 411, the whole history of the band. We had our own rhymes over the beat, but Rick said: "No, do *their* lyrics." Jay was the person that knew that "Walk This Way" was going to be a hit. Me and Run had our doubts, we thought it was taking the rock and roll shit a little far. Because me and Run didn't want to use their lyrics, we thought that they was hillbilly gibberish. We was so pissed, but Jay was a visionary, he saw it. After Jay gave us a kick in the head we went in and laid down the [Aerosmith] vocals. If you listen to their version and our version, a lot of it is off, because we couldn't understand what they was saying. We just went by what it sounded like. We never got to do our own original lyrics because they knew that if we had, then we wouldn't have learned the Aerosmith lyrics.

When Steven Tyler came into the studio, Jay was cutting up "Walk This Way" and he said: "Here's what we used to do with your record." And Steve said: "Yo, when you gonna hear *me*?" And Jay looked up and said: "We never get to hear you. After this guitar riff it's back to the beginning." And Steve thought that was so amusing. Those guys were real cool. That record was a rebirth and a birth, because as a result you have Kid Rock, Limp Bizkit, Korn, all of those bands today. But that definitely wasn't our first rock/rap record. "Rock Box" on the first album was the best one we did. We always used to rock over rock beats in the street. We wanted to be hard, and rock was hard. Other groups didn't use as much rock because they didn't know [draws out and emphasizes next word] how. A lot of them still don't get it right.

After we did the video to "Walk This Way" we was like: "That's a wrap, we don't gotta make no more videos." That one let us know that we was more than just rappers, we were rock stars. So we didn't want to keep making videos, because it might spoil the greatness of that one. Any ones after that one was just because we wanted to make one, to go with a record. We were never able to do a better one. "Walk This Way" was serious and historical and everything else was comedy and fun. Some nights out on tour we'd have to play "Walk That Way" first because there were nothing but white people out there who had only heard that song. Then they'd buy the album and the next time we came to town they'd be yelling for "My Adidas."

Is It Live

The go-go flavor on there was because of Davy D. You remember Davy D, right? He was involved in production on that one. He had a lot of beats, and just as many records as Bambaata. He's not listed on the [*Raising Hell*] album but he was there. And he did a lot more on *Tougher Than Leather*. We loved go-go and we did shows in DC all the time. People get into a go-go trance, it's like voodoo down there.

Perfection

That was our drum record. This kid Styxx played drums on that, he was Run's neighbor's son. He was maybe 13 and he was dope. We wanted to make a song like "La Di Da Di" but we didn't want to bite. So instead of Run doing the beatbox like Doug E Fresh we got a drummer. A lot of people still love that record.

Hit It Run

That's Run on beatbox, like we did on stage every night. We started doing that live around 1985, just the same way as it came out on the album. That's probably my favorite track on the album, because I'm poppin *sooo* much shit on there! And with Run doing the beatbox [laughs]! That record just has a lot of energy, it's like our battle anthem, our park jam.

Raising Hell

That one definitely has a Beastie Boys influence on there. Because of Rick [who produced the Beastie Boys' *Licensed to Ill*], and also because they took stuff from us and we took stuff from them. We learned that punk rock is just as hip-hop as Afrika Bambaata is. And you can be silly and still be dope. Rick played guitar on there, and he was definitely getting his rocks off, especially towards the end [laughs].

You Be Illin'

Run thought of that one, he wanted to do a record like Prince, that type of funk and R&B. But we had to put some humor on it, so people wouldn't say: "What the hell are they doin', trying to be Prince?" We met Prince a lot of times, but we never performed with him.

Dumb Girl

That was what people in the South was doing, with the deep bass [imitates deep bass thump]. And down South there was a lot of girls. Back then there was a lot of dumb girls runnin' around, so we paid our ode to the dumb girls. We wanted to be humorous and not too preachy.

Son of Byford

That was just a beatbox routine we would do live on stage. It started as a freestyle but we did it all the time and we all wanted to put it on the album. That's my dad's name, so there you go. It was always that short [as it appears on the album]. People would go crazy when we did that shit.

Proud To Be Black

That song was influenced by Public Enemy, because we would hang around them all the time. They didn't have records out yet but we'd go to their radio station, WBAU in Long Island. Chuck was like a father, he would educate us. So we said: "Let's make a record that Chuck might make." We all also went to college and that record was more about education than being a black thing, really. We wanted to educate kids. 1986 was a perfect year for a song like that, for the transition. Because in the 'hood it was either be a basketball player or a drug dealer, back then. The world is bigger than just going to the party and having fun.

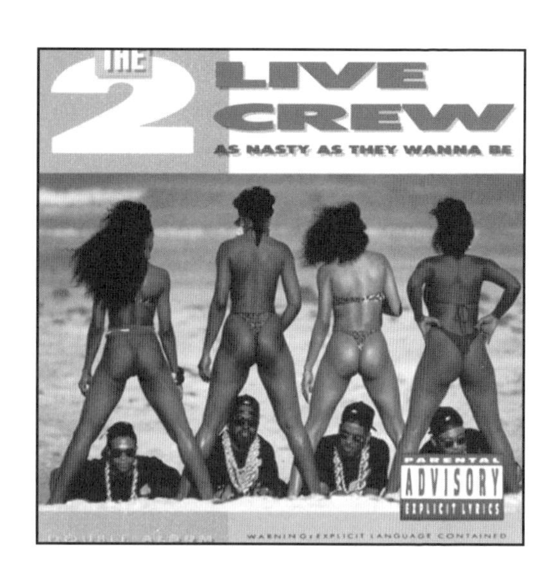

2 LIVE CREW
As Nasty As They Wanna Be

(Luke Skyywalker, 1989)

"I think a lot of our music got overshadowed by the girls," says legendary DJ Mr. Mixx of the 2 Live Crew. That may seem like the understatement of the year, but we should still take what he says seriously.

In the world of rap there has certainly been no group that did so much to bring females to the front of their lyrics (and, indeed, the front of their stages). But 2 Live Crew weren't a novelty act. Mixx continues: "The one big misconception about 2 Live Crew was that everybody was trying to make us out to be the nastiest guys on Earth. Before we was doing recordings, I was making mixtapes of the hottest rap records and I'd just scratch in a Dolomite or Eddie Murphy record in-between the breaks. So, basically all we was doing was comedy stuff to a beat. We was Eddie Murphy, Redd Foxx and Richard Pryor, just as a rap group." The group's figurehead, known these days as Uncle Luke, adds: "It was all just comedy, and then all the controversy started and we became misogynists all of a sudden. We was like 'We ain't doin' this to offend nobody!'"

Back in their heyday in the late '80s and early '90s, the quartet – DJ/producer Mixx, MCs Brother Marquis and Fresh Kid Ice and manager/hype-man/first-amendment poster child Luther "Luke Skyywalker" Campbell – were running shit. The group's label, Luke Skyywalker Records, was the first black-owned indie label to have two certified gold records. Master P couldn't have done his thang if 2 Live hadn't opened the door. "When I got in the record business, I wanted to be the next Quincy Jones," Luke says today. "Russell Simmons is still messed up to this day about what kind of money we was making back then, and as an independent label." Mixx says: "All this Master P and Puffy praise about them being groundbreaking entrepreneurs is all bullshit. None of them ever sold records to distributors directly. We did. We was a true indie label."

Although 2 Live Crew is still known today as a Miami group, their original incarnation (without Luke) was 3,000 miles away. The original members met in Riverside, California on March Air Force Base – Mixx and rappers Fresh Kid Ice and the Amazing V. Mixx recalls: "Me and Ice, the Chinese-lookin' dude, were in the Air Force. He worked outpatient records and I was a cook, in the hospital on the base. Amazing V was in the service, too." Medical records and the military base eventually gave way to an unrelated, but similar-sounding pursuit: bass records. The group put out two singles, in 1984 and 1985, on their own Fresh Beat label (distributed through West Coast powerhouse

Macola): “Revelation” and “What I Like.” Mixx describes their first two wax outings: “The group was marginal on the rap side, but the beats and the scratching was what people really went for.”

In 1985, Luke was a hotshot club DJ (his crew was dubbed Ghetto Style DJs) and promoter in Miami, known for making soon-to-be hit records popular in clubs like his homebase: Pac Jam, on 199th Street in Northeast Miami. “My whole thing back then was breaking records,” Luke explains. “If I liked a group I’d call up the artist and say: “Look, I’m gonna make your record hot. Give me three weeks and come down and do a show for me.’ The first group I brought down was T La Rock and Jazzy Jay. I would bring guys down and they would never have been on an airplane before in their life.”

In 1985, the Cali version of 2 Live Crew was one such group. Luke invited them to Miami in August, where they played their first show ever, at Pac Jam. Mixx remembers one extra reason that Luke was inclined to like the group: “There’s a lyric in our song ‘2 Live’ [the b-side to “Revelation”] where Ice says ‘Like Luke Skywalker / I got the force’ and when the record started catching on in Miami, Luke told people that it was about him.”

Mixx remembers that first show vividly, even today: “I had never seen that kind of stuff being done that Ghetto Style DJs [who did an opening set] did. They’d pull the music completely out and do their own phrases and choruses for songs. They weren’t doing any real scratching at all. They’d play all the latest hip-hop and reggae records, but they’d also play old-school breaks. They were really popular. Luke had an amazing sound system, too. 24 bass bins and almost no tweeters. Our first show was well-received, even though we didn’t have very much stage presence. My scratching was a big issue back then, though, in Miami. They weren’t seeing that in the South then. No one could do that stuff.”

The group returned, again at Luke’s request, on New Years Eve 1985, and were again received well. But shortly thereafter, the Amazing V left the group, choosing a safe military career over the less certain hip-hop route. Down one MC, Mixx knew just the person to fill the spot – a local Riverside, CA rapper that Mixx had always liked named Marquis Ross. The problem: Marquis had moved back to his hometown of Rochester, NY after graduating from Riverside Polytech High School. With help from LA’s Rodney O (of Rodney O & Joe Cooley fame), Mixx located Marquis and convinced him to come back to California to join the group.

With very little keeping them in California (Mixx had since left the service and Ice was thinking about leaving), Miami became the group's new home by the end of 1986. "We didn't have no kind of angle in LA, nothing going on, but things were hopping off in Miami, so we went there," Mixx says.

The last music they produced in California was a song that paid tribute to their new patron, Luke Skyywalker: "Trow The D[ick]." Mixx says of the song, which he claims is the first Miami Bass record of all time: "[Trow The D] was a dance at the time down in Miami, and in appreciation to Luke for getting us gigs, we wanted to do a tribute record. We took the dance they was doing and Chris [Fresh Kid Ice] wrote some lyrics. I did the music based on 'Dance To The Drummers Beat' [by Herman Kelly], which was a break that Luke and them always used to play, and I scratched in some Dolomite stuff. Ghetto Style DJs didn't produce the record, but they inspired it."

Luke tried to convince record labels in Miami to press the song up, including Pretty Tony's popular Music Specialists imprint, but they wouldn't. So Luke decided to go for self, and the Luke Skyywalker Records empire began. Mixx claims that "Trow The D" went on to sell 200,000 records, a mind-bogglingly large number for a start-up indie. Luke explains how this was the group's rebirth and the start of the true 2 Live Crew era: "Our first real single, 'Trow The D[ick],' kind of started all the sex stuff, combined with the fact that Mixx and I both had a thing for comedians like Redd Foxx and Rudy Ray Moore [aka Dolomite]. In order to be different, we couldn't be coming like Run-DMC and all them New York rappers, so we did the adult comedy thing."

"There was no turning back at that point," Luke continues, "Because in the music biz you can't put out one record independently and expect to get your money from that one record. I had to put out another record, because they [distributors] wanted a steady flow." The label's second release was an answer record, recorded by Luke's cousin Anquette, called "Trow The P[ussy]." "She had never rapped before in her life," Luke laughs. "After those two records I was like: 'Yeah, let's do this.' It was another challenge for me, and I like challenges. I started that label out of my mother's wash house, and those records were sold out of the back seat of a Honda."

By all accounts, early 2 Live Crew shows weren't anything to write home about. The MCs were serious, they did their lines, Mixx blew minds with his innovative turntable skills, and they left. Luke, watching these from the wings, slowly went from manager to on-stage instigator. He explains: "When I got involved, I didn't really want to be in the group, I was just trying to help them out. Their live show wasn't no different than any other rap group out there, they'd just walk up and down on stage and do their songs. And when I went on the road with them, the shows really started to get boring to me. So I was like: 'All right, let me get up here and start some shit.' So I'd get up there and do what people today call a hype-man. Before me there wasn't no hype man."

Mixx recalls: "Luke came to the front of the stage after a while, since Marquis and Fresh Kid Ice weren't really messing with the crowd. So Luke and other dudes from Ghetto Style DJs would jump on-stage when we would perform 'Trow The D' and do the dance and pull girls up on stage to dance with them. That's how the group got to be how everybody knows it now. Eventually, Luke or Marquis would pull a girl out of the audience and got onto humpin' on her and that always broke the ice with the crowd. And a lot of times girls would come up and want to challenge us, thinking they had more game than 2 Live Crew. That definitely made every show unpredictable."

The group continued building on their "adult comedy" niche throughout 1986 and 1987, with growing fan response. Mixx explains: "All our sex stuff basically came from how the girls were dancing at the parties we'd play, along with the comedy records I had. We were just having fun and reacting to the crowds. For example, they used to do that 'We want some pussy' chant in all the parties, so we just made it into a record [a single off the *2 Live Crew Is What We Are* album]."

The group's first two albums, late 1986's *2 Live Crew Is What We Are* and 1987's *Move Somethin'* [both on Luke Skyywalker] were huge hits in the South and West of the U.S., each going gold (again: on an indie label, with indie distribution). It should be noted that *Move Somethin'* and *As Nasty* both had corresponding "clean" versions, to dispel any misconceptions that all they wanted to do was pollute the minds of our nation's youth. Mixx says: "We was the first group to have the Parental Advisory stickers on our records, after our first album got in the hands of a 14-year-old, in 1987. The kid's mother made a stink, called the distributor, Tipper Gore got involved and those stickers got made." Luke relates a sad fact: "Even after we did those clean versions we still got flack. People said that we were doing the clean versions just so people would want to buy the dirty versions. We couldn't win!"

As popular as their first two albums were, their third full-length, *As Nasty As They Wanna Be*, was the big one, both in sales and in controversy. As with all 2 Live Crew records, it was recorded quickly, at Luke's recently-inaugurated Luke Studios, purchased from Miami production legend Pretty Tony. Luke describes the group's basic and effective production dynamic: "I would have an idea about a song and go to Mixx and he'd put the music together, then maybe I'd give the guys [Marquis and Ice] the idea for the lyrics." Mixx always had a cache of tracks waiting to be matched to a lyric or concept. He says: "I was always doing tracks, so none of our albums took long to record." Samples were never an issue either, as Mixx explains: "Back in the day we never cleared no samples [laughs]. What ended up happening is we didn't clear 'em, and then we just got sued. We was selling so many records and making so much money that it was better and easier to just pay the settlement than to clear that shit in the first place!"

One interesting side-note: contrary to what fans might have assumed, when the group got in the studio, it wasn't a party-time affair. Luke says: "When those guys got to the studio it'd be all business. If I was recording by myself in there, it got crazy. You name it, it went on in there. I got a lot of song ideas by stuff I'd see in those sessions [laughs]! But with the group, it was boom-boom-boom, knock the tracks out. Mixx agrees: "The studio was the only place where we actually had any real peace, believe it or not. We all had our own friends, too, so that was really the only time where we would all get together."

After quick work in early 1989, the album was released in June. It built slowly but surely, driven by the lascivious, bass-driven singles "Me So Horny" and "C'mon Babe," and as the new decade turned, things started to get crazy in a way that no one could have predicted. "We had sold 1.3 million records by March, 1990, independently," says Mixx. "And then that Sheriff [Broward County, FL, Sheriff Nick Navarro] started attacking the group. He tried to tell stores not to sell our record and even filed a suit against us, for obscene material being sold. Not just to minors – just being sold, period!"

The group had fought in court before to protect their right to be as nasty as they chose, but things came to a head that spring, as Navarro's men arrested Luke, Marquis and Fresh Kid Ice after a show in Hollywood, Florida. Luke recalls: "We went to court about it being legally obscene and we lost. Then we performed in Hollywood, FL after the judgment and the Sheriff said: 'If you perform any of those songs [on the album], we'll arrest you.' We didn't really think they'd do it." Luke and Ice got arrested later that night, driving home in Luke's car. Mixx and Marquis rode in a van with the group's female dancers, to hide. Marquis turned himself in the next day. "I didn't get arrested because I didn't say any of the lyrics," Mixx explains.

And as much as the controversy helped to sell even more records (Luke estimates that the record has gone quadruple platinum to this day. "It's still selling, and it probably always will," he grins), Luke has some regrets, since it clouds his and the group's important legacy: "In the end I'd rather that all that stuff *hadn't* happened," he says today, "Because I'd be more appreciated as an executive in the record industry. I think I'd be a lot more successful. I would have done my industry a lot more of a service if I hadn't gone through all that. To this day I still get black-balled. But we learned after a while that we couldn't beat the machine. We just had to do our own thing, regardless of what people said that we were."

More than arrests, more than lucrative record sales and even more than all the ladies that walked through the doors of Luke's compound or on the group's stages, the 2 Live Crew were about having fun, and that is what *As Nasty As They Wanna Be* is all about. "We were a group that controlled our own destiny," Luke reminds us. "That's the most important part, because [there] wasn't no major label. We could say what we wanted to say and we sure as hell did!" Mixx adds: "In this game we're really undefeated in what we've done. The only people that really defeated us were ourselves, with Luke and me falling out. It's been a 10-12 year hiatus, but we're talking again."

TRACKS

Me So Horny

Mixx: We was in DC recording with Trouble Funk and Marquis was watching *Full Metal Jacket* in the hotel, on TV. And we saw that part where the girl says "Me so horny" and he said: "Man, we gotta do something with that shit!" So as soon as we finished the session and got back home, I rented the movie and sampled that [vocal] piece from the girl. I already had the music track programmed, so we put the two things together.

Luke: At the time *Full Metal Jacket* was hot, but we really chose to lead with that song [as the first single] because I knew that people would bug out when they heard a song called "Me So Horny."

Mixx: That's actually not our biggest hit of all time, even as big as that song was. We're best known for "We Want Some Pussy." That's by far our most recognizable one.

C'Mon Babe

Mixx: That was originally supposed to be the first single from the album, and was the first record we actually did for the album. But once we recorded "Me So Horny" it became a toss up. Luke went with "Me So Horny" because it had more bite to it. On "C'mon Babe" that's not a porno flick, it's sampled off one of my old comedy records, by this dude Wavy Gravy.

Luke: That was actually a better song than "Me So Horny," from a lyrical standpoint, the delivery and rap style. That was stronger in that way.

Put Her In The Buck

Luke: I don't know who came up with that one. But I'll tell you what – you get me a bottle of liquor and I'll come up with hooks and concepts and all kinds of shit!

D.K. Almighty

Mixx: That was a Kraftwerk sample on there. I knew the Fearless Four version of that Kraftwerk song ["Rockin It"] but I liked the original better.

Dirty Nursery Rhymes

Mixx: We wasn't thinking about Schoolly D when we did that, but Schoolly was one of the few guys from the North that we was cool with. He used to come down and do shows for Luke, and he was a very cool dude.

Break It On Down

Mixx: That was some more Trouble Funk go-go on that one. Go-go wasn't really big in Miami, I was just a big Trouble Funk fan.

2 Live Blues

Luke: A lot of the songs from that record [*As Nasty As They Wanna Be*] were derived from other songs, like rock or reggae or whatever. That one was our blues song. We were just trying to do some different stuff on there, and still keep it on the sex tip.

I Ain't Bullshittin'

Mixx: A lot of the big tours that went out at the time didn't want us to headline, even though we was sellin' more records than the headliners in some places. But they were booked out of New York, and they wasn't giving Luke a fair shake, because they didn't take us seriously. We were the first one to sell records in that kind of volume out of the South, period. They figured it was dance music, not rap. MC Shan came down to Miami early on and would trip out because he was from the land of rap and everyone was paying attention to these so-called country bumpkins from Florida. Most New York guys were like that.

Luke: That's a classic, people like that shit to this day, because I was calling people out on that. MC Shan, I don't even remember what he said that pissed me off, but I fucked him up on that record. Everybody was talking shit about us. I mean, a lot of people claim they know all about discrimination and all that, but the people that really know about it are from the '60s, who had to go in segregated bathrooms, go around the corner to get the food at the restaurant they weren't allowed in. We really felt like that with other rappers when we'd meet them or tour with them. Us and N.W.A. bonded together on the road, 'cause we was both outcasts. A lot of people seemed to think that if you wasn't from New York, you wasn't shit.

The Fuck Shop

Mixx: I went to high school with white cats and I knew that Van Halen record by hanging out with them. Luke liked that Guns 'N' Roses guitar riff, so he brought that one in, too. We always had rock-oriented records, like "We Want Some Pussy" from the first album and "S&M" from the second.

Luke: I was like: "Let's do a rock and roll song" and I'd like this song or that song and I'd tell Mixx and he'd come back with something great.

"The Fuck Shop" was just another name for a hotel, everybody had their favorite that they'd go in, wherever we were. Whenever we went on the road it became a fuck-fest [he says this very seriously]. One thing about us is that we never had to worry about going to jail for raping or nothing like that, because they pretty much knew what was gonna happen when they came in the room with us. It could be any hotel, as long as we had a bed to lay on.

If You Believe In Having Sex

Luke: My whole thing as an artist and on-stage was that kind of thing, call-and-response stuff, shouting to the crowd. And the other guys in the group would do everything else. All our chant-type songs, that was all me.

Get The Fuck Out Of My House

Mixx: I was experimenting with house music on that one. The Jungle Brothers' "Girl, I'll House You" came out before that, and a lot of our records would get mixed with that by DJs, since a lot of our records were up-tempo. That was really just us fuckin' around, though, and Luke saying some old bullshit [laughs].

Luke: That was me talking about some girl. I had this one chick that was lazy, didn't want to do nothing. So I came home from Chicago and had heard some house tracks and wanted to do something different, some house-styled shit.

Reggae Joint

Mixx: Reggae was just big in Miami, and all those songs we sampled on there were big hits in the reggae scene there. Luke used to play a lot of reggae stuff at his jams, with Ghetto Style DJs.

Bad Ass Bitch

Mixx: That's Trouble Funk on that one, playing live. It was cool working with them. We was one of the first and only rap groups, aside from some New York cats, to use their stuff.

Luke: I was a big fan of go-go, 'cause I stayed in DC for a while, back when I was younger. I was out-of-control and my mother sent me to DC to live with my brother who was in the Army. I was going to the Cap [Capital] Center, hearing Trouble Funk and Rare Essence and all that shit. It was great to record with them. I always wanted to put out a go-go record on my label, but never did.

Mega Mixx III

Mixx: With that third one [mega-mix – he did one on every 2 Live Crew album] I actually had a musical theme to go with, based on Bambaata's "Renegades of Funk." I found out where he got that chorus from and built off of that. Each one of those Mega Mixxes I did got more complex. They were getting easier to do, though, because I'd line all the records up in advance and just run through 'em.

MC LYTE

Lyte As A Rock

(First Priority / Atlantic, 1988)

Hearing it when it hit in 1986, you'd never know that East Flatbush, Brooklyn's MC Lyte (Lana Moorer) was only 16 when she came out with her classic ode to the woes of both crack and fickle male love: "I Cram To Understand U," released initially on independent First Priority Records. "I was originally just called Lyte," she says today. "But when I got the record back it had MC Lyte on it. Lyte is some positive word-play. Truth is the light. The light shall lead you out of dark passages. Light was one of the many forces created by God. That kind of thing."

Some people didn't even know what sex the MC who rhymed the lyrics was: "Whcn 'Cram' came out, no one had seen a picture of me, and they all thought I sounded like a little boy," Lyte intones. But Lyte was all woman, and a very strong one at that, which she proved on wax and on stage.

On the subject of her earliest years, she says: "I was actually born in Queens, by accident. My mom was out visiting my grandfather and I decided it was time to come out." Born in Far Rockaway, she soon returned to Brooklyn, where she spent the '70s and '80s.

Of course every kid in Brooklyn was eating and breathing hip-hop by the mid-'80s, but Lyte showed more talent and more ambition than most. She says: "In junior high I used to bang on the lunchroom tables and rap. In 1984 I had a couple of songs written already and went to [DJ] Clark Kent's house and did a song in the basement called 'I Cram To Understand You.'" This was the beginning of her recording career, although the song in question wasn't to appear for two more years, and in a different form. She explains: "The final version of it was with Audio Two's production. Clark didn't produce the original song, he just played an instrumental of someone else's record, and I just rhymed the lyrics over that."

The First Priority label where Lyte had her debut wasn't a random connection. In fact, it was a family affair, owned by former club promoter and entrepreneur Nat Robinson, who also happened to be Lyte's stepfather. Producer and rapper Milk D of the Audio Two was Nat's son, and Lyte's half-brother. She says: "Nat formed the label for Milk and Giz (the Audio Two's DJ) and he came to me and said: 'Do you want to give it a go?' And I said: 'Sure!' Me, Milk, Giz, the Alliance, MC Peaches and UBL kind of just created our own little world. The First Priority Family."

She adds: "Milk lived in Bed Stuy and I lived in the 90s [in Brooklyn].

Even though we weren't in the same house, we hung out a lot and grew into the music together." So Milk's production wasn't just a great musical match – it was brotherly love. The "Cram" track itself, which followed directly after the Audio Two's smash "Top Billin'," was a loose, funky storytelling rhyme that was impossible to resist.

Success came quickly for Lyte and the Audio Two, and they were soon standing shoulder to shoulder with the rap stars they admired. "I did a lot of clubbing when I was young," Lyte recalls. "It was OK then to be young and be at the Latin Quarter or Union Square. There were big high school crowds there. I saw Salt 'N Pepa and Boogie Down Productions perform at Union Square, and Public Enemy and Jazzy Jeff & The Fresh Prince at Latin Quarter. Then in 1986 I was performing at Latin Quarter, too, after 'I Cram' came out. It was wild."

Lyte and the funky and off-kilter Audio Two were both signed to Atlantic in 1987, through the auspices of First Priority, and both dropped their debut full-lengths in 1988. Believe it or not, it wasn't as easy as it should have been to get Atlantic on-board with Robinson's female star-in-waiting. Lyte recalls: "Atlantic didn't actually even want to sign me. But my dad said: 'If you want Audio Two, you have to sign Lyte.'" It was nepotism at its best, but Nat wasn't trying to force bad goods on Atlantic to pad the deal. Actually, it was quite the opposite, as future record sales would show.

After the signing in 1987, Lyte and the First Priority family got right to work. "I had 'Cram' and 'Take It Lyte' done already, and a bunch of rhymes, and they had a bunch of beats," she recalls. "So it was basically just fitting the right lyrics to the right production. It only took a couple of months to get everything done. By the time Atlantic actually signed me, they were behind it and ready to roll." With extra work by Stetsasonic's Prince Paul, EPMD's DJ Scratch and The Alliance (King of Chill, K-Swift and DJ Skill) filling out the production roster, a classic was born, released in early 1988.

With males surrounding her and working with her, Lyte wasn't exactly all alone in the rap biz, but then, as now, it wasn't the easiest road on the less-represented side of the gender divide: "I think it was a big deal then, and I think it's still a big deal for a female MC to be accepted and liked. Every woman who has been able to stay in the game has come from a certain camp. Men who come out and make it put their stamp of approval on these women, like Eve from Ruff Ryders, Foxy from The Firm. You don't have to have it, but it's definitely a selling point."

Regardless of her gender, Lyte's style was undeniably fresh. With a husky tone, a strong will and flow, and a maturity and intelligence far beyond her teenage status, *Lyte As A Rock* was a quick-selling new entry in the hip-hop sweepstakes. It yielded singles like the aforementioned "I Cram To Understand U," "Lyte As A Rock," the brutal and dope Antoinette/Hurby Luv Bug attack "10% Dis" and Lyte's own personal favorite, "Paper Thin."

"People loved that album because it was something different," Lyte explains today. "I wouldn't change anything about that first album. It came out exactly as it was intended to be. It's my baby. You know, the first one. I've matured intensely in comparison to the content on that record, of course, but my peers in the biz still love that record. In some ways it was ahead of its time." She adds: "When the record came out there was a lull in female MCs, and in innovative hip-hop in general. So that's why I think it was such a breath of fresh air to people. The timing couldn't have been more perfect. 'I Cram' had done its run and people wanted to know more about who I was."

And for those who always wondered about who was on the cover of the album: "That was my DJ, K-Rock, my bodyguard Big Foot, and me. It was a really good thing that Big Foot was big, but he was just my road manager, actually. On the cover, the concept was that K-Rock was being enticed by the woman on the side of the picture. Basically we wanted to give him something to do during the shot. He was the loverboy of the First Priority family anyways, so it made sense. And me, I'm all about the business."

TRACKS

Lyte vs. Vanna Whyte

That was a concept that King of Chill came up with. He had this great beat and decided on that scenario. So I was like 'OK, cool' at the time, but that's one that I would have left off, in hindsight. That was a combination of my DJ, K-Rock, and DJ Scratch doing the DJ stuff. They worked on that one together. That was the only time I ever worked with Scratch. All that equipment I'm talking about was Chill's dream equipment. I didn't know any of that stuff. But he had a longing for all of those items.

Lyte As A Rock

The original version of that song was by Audio Two, but the album version and the one the video was done to a remix that King of Chill did, which had a house vibe to it. The original was a little more on the basic hip-hop vibe. The video for that was fun, but I remember it was really grueling: it was like 6 am to 6 am. The premise was me going through a timewarp, and fitting into any era that I was in. That was the second video we did. "Paper Thin" was the first one.

I Am Woman

Yes, "I am woman, hear me roar......" I think Hellen Reddy did the original version, right? Once again that was King of Chill's concept. He felt it was a powerful statement and I agreed. He made up the track and together we started formulating the lyrics. I was 17 when we recorded that.

MC Lyte Likes Swingin'

I had wanted to do something with [Kool & The Gang's] "Hollywood Swinging," so I adapted it and sang it. I don't remember if I made up the chorus like that and gave it to Prince Paul [who produced it] or he gave me the beat and I made the chorus after. I worked that song out with Paul in the studio and then I did some shows with Stetsasonic after that.

10% Dis

The Audio Two had spoken with Hurby Luv Bug about getting a female act and doing an answer to "Top Billin'" called "Stop Illin'." Hurby kept putting it off, and then next thing we knew we were in the car and heard the song "I Got An Attitude" [by Antoinette, produced by Hurby] using the same kicks and snares [as "Top Billin'"], and she flipped Milk's lyrics also. They [Milk and Giz] didn't want to dis a female MC so they said "You have to do it." We went into INS two days later and did it. It was pretty easy – we just sat there and thought of the worst things we could possibly say about somebody [laughs]. It's titled that because that's only 10% of what I could have said. I didn't even know Antoinette. It was strictly a war on wax. She tried to dis me back but the hype on me was so big that they didn't care if she had a rebuttal to it. I think she was from Queens. We actually had a battle once at The World. I won. Even then it was understood completely that it was just business.

Paper Thin

That blends in samples from Al Green. My mom used to play lots of Al Green when I was growing up. What I'm saying on that track hits close – it's *me*! It was how I felt. I'm not gonna use you for your money, I'm too strong and independent for that. That's my favorite track on that album.

Lyte Thee MC

That was my alias. King of Chill used "Superstition" [by Stevie Wonder] on it. I love that song. It reminds me of the young MC Lyte. I think they actually sped my voice up on that one. Chill did all the drum programming on that.

I Cram To Understand U

I still get people to this day who come up on the street and ask me about Sam, but he was a totally fictitious character. None of that stuff happened to me. I mixed in elements of reality, but in 1981 I was 11 years old and wasn't going anywhere near Empire Blvd. [the Skating Rink, in Brooklyn]. I didn't go there until I was 14. It was a roller rink, every Sunday it *was* hip-hop. They had Kurtis Blow and New Edition perform there but mostly it was just roller skating and great music. Milk heard that rhyme before he made that beat up, so he knew how he was going to do it. I did it a capella to show him what it was all about. We recorded a first "draft" of that at Clark Kent's house in 1984, over some instrumental that was already out, and two years later Milk made that track to the same lyrics.

Kickin' 4 Brooklyn

I love that song because it's for Brooklyn and the beat is just so original to me. Milk had a sense of making a track sound exactly like you wanted it to sound. That song was a rhyme I had written a while back, even the hook. We called our home Planet Brooklyn. Me and my producer, King of Chill, decided that it made it sound like such a remote piece of land. At the time my whole life was Brooklyn.

Don't Cry Big Girls

We got sued for that, royally [laughs]! Back in those days you didn't get sample clearances. It was Frankie Valli or the Beach Boys or someone like that. It came down to whether we'd pull it off the shelves or give the people what they were asking for, and we did the latter. I think Milk came up with the sample first and I thought it was a cool idea and wrote the lyrics.

ERIC B & RAKIM

Paid In Full

(4th & Bway / Island, 1987)

"I came in the door, I said it before / I never let the mic magnetize me no more."

When you hear the intro and those first lines, your whole body starts to shiver. You're instantly transported to New York, 1986. Those lines are so ill that your mom could say them and they'd still move a crowd. And they don't stop for the duration of Eric B & Rakim's unsinkable classic "Eric B Is President." A song like that only comes along maybe twice a decade, and few of them stay with you like the duo's master tome. They set off a lot of things in 1986 – an onslaught of raids on the James Brown sampling archive; a rebirth of anti-party, pro-scientific lyricism; and a 500% rise in purchases of dinosaur-choking gold medallions across the tri-state area.

Interestingly, William Griffin, Jr., the youngest of three Griffin brothers and better known to hip-hop as Rakim, didn't figure their booming single (first released on Zakia Records, b-sided with the also-mind-blowing "My Melody") would change hip-hop the way it did. "I had no idea it would impact like that, but maybe that's because I'm my own worst critic," Rakim Allah says today, adding: "I had already been rhyming for so long at that point that I wasn't looking to pursue a recording career. To be honest, at the time I was hoping to play football at Stony Brook [University, in Long Island], since my cousin had a scholarship there. I played quarterback and had met with the coach there. He told me to get my grades up and we could talk." Luckily for hip-hop fans, fate turned Rakim away from the gridiron and gave the duo a monster hit.

Although he had deep family roots in Brooklyn, William Jr. was born and raised in Wyandanch, NY, and came up through an established hip-hop scene that wasn't as flashy as New York's, but skills were most certainly required at the door. "Wyandanch played a big influence in my life," he says. "There was always block parties and DJs at the park. DJs like Pleasure, Nelson PR, DJ Motor and DJ Maniac. These guys were around like back when I said in 'Microphone Fiend' that I was too small to get on the mic. There were a lot of parties in the school gyms. We had a lot going on." He adds, talking about his New York experiences: "I had lots of family in Brooklyn and cousins in Queens, so I used to go to their cribs and go to the park, in Jamaica [Queens]. I'd also make sure I always saw the Cold Crush Brothers. [Grandmaster] Caz was a big influence on me. We'd go to DJ battles in New York all the time, Mike & Dave Productions. I remember joining in on a rap convention back then, I think it was on 127th Street. Biz Markie was there, I remember."

Aside from his cousins and local friends who introduced him to the hip-hop life, he also had an important musical influence in his family: legendary R&B vocalist Ruth Brown, his aunt. “She used to keep her eye on me, babysit me,” he says, also adding that he saw her perform on several occasions in his youth. “Being in that environment, watching her do what she do, that kept me grounded once I got on for myself.” Did the old-school music legend approve of her nephew making hip-hop? “Once she heard my first record she called me up to let me know how much she liked it. She told me to keep doing my thing and to stay focused. She definitely appreciated it, because, especially what I was doing, it was about poetry and rhythm. She respected that.”

Back in his earlier teens, before he picked up a mic and started dropping supreme knowledge, young William started out behind the turntables, as Kid Wizard (he says he started using Rakim in late 84 or early 85). “I started DJing before I was rapping and I didn’t know which one to do, so I did both. Back then you had to do everything. You had to breakdance, beatbox, all that,” he recalls. “But after a while a lot of crews were trying to recruit me on the mic, even when I was too young to even hang out. Plus it was always easier to get on the mic than it was to get on somebody’s turntables. Once I started rapping, a lot of people forgot I could even DJ. They started realizing that I had more skill than anyone in the area, and they wanted me.”

Rakim talks about his early microphone influences: “Melle Mel was always using big words and ill rhythms, but he’d break it down and get a little political, too, like ‘White Lines’ or the joint he did on *Beat Street*. He was scientifical with it. Kool Moe Dee and Caz [from Cold Crush] were conscious and lyrical with their skills, and witty, too. I knew that Melle Mel and Caz and Moe always put something into their work, and every time I sat down to write a rhyme I always wanted to make sense and show that I went to school and I took language and social studies and that I knew how to write a book report. That’s the way I took my rhymes, because of those guys. Listening to them coming up was the best thing that could have happened to me.”

Around 1985, as his MC skills were beginning to hit full stride, he made an important trip to DJ Maniac’s (a friend of Ra’s older brother, Stevie) crib: “I went over to his house and made a tape, so when I went to college and cats start yappin’ off about how great they were, I could put in my tape and shut all that talk down. So I had 90 minutes with different beats and me rapping on the whole thing, all the way through.” That tape was soon heard by an up-and-coming DJ and producer named Eric Barrier through a mutual friend – future record exec Alvin Toney, from Wyandanch. Eric B was engineering mobile broadcasts for New York's WBLS-FM at the time. Rakim says: "Eric was looking for an MC, and Alvin brought him to my crib and we played him the tape that me and Maniac made." The rest, as they say, is history.

"I told Eric that I wasn't really interested in the rap game, but I said that if he popped something off I'd be a special guest," Rakim explains. Eric wasn't so casual about what might go down. He knew they had chemistry and something big could be made of the situation. As such, he started shopping rough demos around, and didn't have to go too far before he found their first home: Robert Hill's Zakia Records. "I think that's the first place that Eric took our music to," Rakim says. "Zakia was right around the corner from his mom's place. She lived on 124th Street, and Zakia was between 124th and 125th, on Adam Clayton Powell [Blvd]. They liked what they heard and we did a deal with them." With Zakia behind them ("Robert Hill ran the label and took care of studio costs," Ra says), they went in the studio and the duo was born – the single even reflected The R's request for "special guest" status: "Eric B *featuring* Rakim."

The Marley Marl-overseen single (technically and nominally, Eric B produced it, but Rakim claims that Marley's input truly made it what it was), was recorded in late 1985 and hit streets in early 1986. It straight-up sideswiped the hip-hop world, boasting a new sound, a slower tempo and Rakim dropping quotable line after quotable line. Rakim says of the new sound back then: "Whenever I heard a slow track, what would click in my head was that I could put more rhythms and more words into it. I could triple up on words, take the rhythm, syncopate it and take you where you've never been before. That was my little trademark. When a track is fast there are only so many rhythms and so many words you can throw in four bars."

After the single's success, it wasn't hard to find suitors for an album deal. "4th & Bway kind of bought Zakia," Rakim explains about the biz angle back in '86 and '87. "It was kind of a joint venture. Robert Hill ran into some .... [pauses] ... business problems, he got into some trouble with the law. But whatever he was doin', it didn't effect me. So our deal with 4th & Bway was nothing bad for my career. Either way, sometimes you don't need a major label to get you where you need to be."

The group also benefited from running with a talented crew back in '86 and early '87. "At first we was running with the Juice Crew," Rakim recalls. “We was doing shows with Shan and Marley and Fly Ty was booking us. Eric knew Mr. Magic from WBLS and Kool G Rap used to live around the corner from him in Queens, so that’s how we got in with them at first. The Juice Crew guys kept me on my toes. When you hear some hot shit, like what Kane and G Rap was doing back then, you can’t wait to go home and try to top it.”

As anyone who recalls from promo shots and album covers back in the day, Eric B & Rakim, like many of their peers, wore gold on a level with Mr. T. Ra says: “Me and Eric never really competed with wearing gold, because we knew if one of us bought something, the other one would go up the block and buy something, too. If I came through with a piece, he’d go out and get another piece. Eric was getting a new piece like every two weeks. The biggest piece I ever bought was like $14,000 back then. A necklace, with diamonds in it. Someone went into this shop and ordered it and then got locked up. It was like $18,000 but they were stuck with it, so I got it for less.”

During the pre-*Paid In Full* period, when not shopping for jewelry, the two also hooked up new management, which Rakim says went down right as the album was nearing completion: “After a while my brother Ronnie took me to Russell Simmons. Ronnie used to play in Kurtis Blow’s band and used to tour with him, way back when Run [from Run-DMC, who started out as “Kurtis Blow’s Disco Son”] was touring with them, so he knew Russell. Rush signed us up for management.”

After 4th & Bway signed-off on a full album, the duo quickly dispatched eight more classic cuts (six vocals and two DJ workouts) and the ultimate classic *Paid In Full* was born. “That album to me was like experimenting. We went to the studio, we laid the beat down, I took the notebook and did the rhymes right there. And that was a wrap. Today I like to perfect and shape it a little bit more. But back then that rawness was what was good about it. We just went in there, we wasn’t shootin’ to do a single, we wasn’t trying to cross over. I was just going into the studio doing what I would do before going to a block party. Give me a beat, I’m gonna write some rhymes to it and I’ma say this shit tonight. Everything now is more like tunnel vision. If you ain’t talkin’ about what everyone else is talkin’ about, it’s a different language.”

As untouchable as the group’s first classic was, Rakim states: “Those were just beats and rhymes that I would always do out in the park.” He also says that although Eric B got credit as sole producer, Ra did a good portion of the work in the studio. Rakim says: “Most of the tracks on the first and second albums, I done those myself. No question. Back then Eric B wanted to be the businessman, so I said: 'OK, you can take care of business, I'm going to stick with this notebook right here, just let me know what's poppin'.' So by not getting involved, he was right there telling them [at the record label] to print whatever he wanted them to print on the album cover. That was my mistake. Because if we did 10 tracks on the album, I did like seven of the beats myself. A lot of times they was just old park records. I had a record collection, I had turntables, I had all the breakbeats."

Even though Rakim tends to downplay the depth of thc first album, when pressed he admits to its lyrical importance: "Lyrically I took things from the nursery rhyme frame of mind, writing things that rhymed and sounded good, and put the ghetto on it. So that people could feel like they was involved. I just wanted people to see what I was talkin' about, wanted them to see the scenery. So they could put themselves in my place and live out what I was saying. The things I spoke about was things we did in the street, and we wanted people in the street to relate to them."

He adds, casually: "I wasn't planning on the rap game, but after the first single the door opened and I walked in."

TRACKS

I Ain't No Joke

That was the first single we did for the album itself, and the first video we ever did, too. That sample was just another James Brown record that I used to rhyme off. At first we was going to sample more of it but then we decided to have Eric just scratch [the horn riff] in. I used that song a long time before I met Eric, so that's another Rakim banger right there. With the drum programming on the album, our engineer Patrick Adams did a lot of that. I just spoke with him the other day, actually, he's a real talented cat. I'd basically just take my breakbeats and ideas in and he'd sample it up and put the [Roland TR-] 808 on it. Patrick was the guy who first turned me onto the 808. We'd dress up the beats. I titled the song that way because that's how I wanted people to perceive me on the mic. Back then I tried to think of slogans that somebody would want to put on the side of their car, or say all day. So that was like the ultimate.

My Melody

That was the first song we ever made. We did that one and Marley Marl made it sound like it was supposed to sound. He played a big role in that record. I always used to rhyme off "Standing On The Top" so we used that. We replayed it on keyboard, Marley did a lot of scratchin', Eric did some scratchin', too. MC Shan helped engineer it, when we finished the mix at the crib. After Marley's help on that first single we took it and ran with it.

If you notice, that song was like five verses and they was like 28 bars long. Those was all just different rhymes I had, and most of them was on that tape I made with DJ Maniac back in '85. So I took 'em and put 'em on one joint. Then I wrote one more verse in the studio, the one with "Marley Marl synthesized it." But those were some of my favorite older verses and I took them and shaped them into that track. That version on the album is a little different than the single that came out on Zakia. I guess back in the day they would change the single up and remix it for the album so you'd buy both. It was a squeeze play.

"Eric B Is President" definitely got more play than "My Melody" because it was more of a dance track. "Melody" was more of a listener type of track. But I got more love for the lyrics on "Melody" than "President." When I see people in the street today, they always talk about what I said on "Melody." I say: "Writin' my name in graffiti on the wall" on there. I wrote Kid Wizard or Wiz Kid or whatever saying was hot for that week. Graffiti always just amazed me. Back then we covered all the elements and graffiti was an important part of it. I used to write my rhymes in graffiti, fucking up the school hallways and shit like that.

I Know You Got Soul

Eric B brought in that drumroll [Funkadelic's "You'll Like It Too"] and I always used to rhyme off that James Brown track [Bobby Byrd's "I Know You Got Soul," produced by James Brown]. Those drums Eric brought were a real good idea because that just set it off.

Move The Crowd

My brother Steve did the music for that track. My oldest brother Ronnie played piano and Steve played sax and some piano. If I wasn't sampling something, like on there, we would play it on keyboards, and Steve was my keyboard player. That beat I think was Chick Corea "Return

To Forever" and the horns were James Brown. We put it all together. My family's musical background at the crib was crazy. My mom played jazz all day and my pops played smooth shit. My mom sang in Brooklyn sometimes, opera and jazz. She was definitely a big influence to me.

Paid In Full

When we got the deal with 4th & Bway we got the check and it said Paid In Full on it, so we was lookin' at it and Eric said: "Yo, that's what we're gonna name the album." I wasn't sure about it at first, but that idea definitely worked. It was a statement. With that track, I always used to rhyme off that Dennis Edwards ["Don't Look Any Further"] in the park. Eric put that beat up under the bassline. I think that was Patrick Adams [their engineer] replaying the bassline. I really dug the [Coldcut "Seven Minutes of Madness"] remix of that song [which appeared on the 12" release]. When we did it, it wasn't even 16 bars, it was kinda plain. I was gonna write another verse but Eric was like: "Yo, that's it. You said it all right there." But when they put the remix on it, it added a bit of flavor to it, and they put the universal sound in there, so I was feelin' it. The remix was done in London. We didn't hire them to do it, they just did it. But we ended up using it in the end.

As The Rhyme Goes On

We did that in-between, after the two singles were done ["Eric B Is President" and "I Ain't No Joke"]. I used to say that rhyme over a more up-tempo beat, then I added more to it when we recorded it. But that's just an old freestyle that I used to rock.

Chinese Arithmetic

That's all Eric B cutting on there. Eric did most of the turntable stuff, of course, but I did all the cuts on "Musical Massacre" [from 1988's *Follow The Leader* album]. Those are all Ra. I did the track, wrote the rhymes. We got nominated for a Grammy that year and I didn't think that we was gonna win and we had one more track to do for our album [*Follow The Leader*]. Eric wanted to go to the Grammys and I wanted to finish the album. So I did it all, including the scratches. I heard that he was mad at first but I guess he figured that people would think it was him, so he didn't mind. I had fun doing that shit.

Eric B Is President

We laid “My Melody” down and then Marley was like: “We need a b-side.” I went home and played with a little something on my turntables, got the “Funky President” out, did the rhymes to it and it was ready. I used to always rhyme off of [James Brown’s] “Funky President” back in the day, I grabbed it of my moms’ shelf. That woman’s voice at the beginning [of the album version] was just a stock record with different sayings on it, like they used for the London [Coldcut remix of “Paid In Full”] record. That was a cool way to set it off on the album version. We put that track way at the end of the album because that single had been out for a long time, people had already heard it.

The first time I heard that song on the radio I was walkin’ home one night at about 10 o’clock, to get ready for school the next day. And this kid was sitting in his car and the song is playing and the kid is nodding his head. Back then people used to always steal my tapes, so I went over to the car and I said [his tone gets more aggressive]: “Where the fuck you get that tape from, man?” And he looked at me and said: “Yo, this shit is on the radio.” He didn’t know who I was, and he was an older motherfucker on the block and I was running up on him. But I had the best walk home that night. Like: “This shit is really real, Ra.” That was crazy. We knew that track was larger than life when they started playing it on the radio during the day. Back then we didn’t have hip-hop all day on the radio, so prime-time was when they played a joint from noon to 1. We jumped in the car one afternoon to drive to New York and we heard it on the jump off. That let me know: “All right, Ra, it’s getting serious.” Frankie Crocker [WBLS’ legendary program director and personality] played it. Shit like that. That song is still one of my favorites to perform live. Everybody gets their Whop on, it’s still a classic joint. I always try to save that towards the end of a show, if not last.

BIZ MARKIE

Goin' Off

(Cold Chillin' / Warner Bros, 1988)

“A lot of money is given out for albums these days,” says Biz Markie. “But it wasn’t about money back then. It was about integrity, and about being able to say: ‘Yo, my album is *dope.*’ That’s the reason that *Goin’ Off* is the top for me. The hunger was there, and the album had so many different elements to it.”

New-jacks who have come up in the rap world past the ‘90s have had it pretty easy, at least compared to their predecessors. Back in the ‘70s and ‘80s peeps had to pave their own way. And no one showed that more than the diabolical Biz Markie, who brought more humor to hip-hop than it had ever seen. He made heads laugh and dance, but he also made them see themselves. Biz was Everyman. The class clown. The guy in the corner who had to work harder to get heard.

Biz Markie (born Marcel Hall) entered the world in 1964 in Harlem. His family moved to Brentwood, Long Island (home to fellow hip-hop pioneers EPMD) at age 10, and a couple years later he began honing his MC skills in earnest. “I got turned on to rapping in like 1978 from people around my way in Brentwood,” he says. “I’ve been beatboxing since I was a kid, but I started rapping in ’78. I was known as a rapper in Long Island, I had my own dances and stuff like that. I was in contests and doing parties. Uptown, Brooklyn, Long Island. Anywhere I could get on.”

He continues: “I was always trying to get into crews. One of the first ones I was in was from CI [Central Islip, Long Island] called Midnite Express. It was Kevin D, Rapper A, DJ Casper and Subie Gee. I was seeing live stuff in my area back then, but it was different. The Long Island sound was different than the New York sound, definitely. When we did stuff, at that time it wasn’t about shows in clubs. We was doin’ house parties, school parties, center parties, going to Bayshore, Long Island to do American Legion Halls. This was in the early ‘80s, when I was in 11th and 12th grade.”

Biz kept active on the party and battle scenes in New York and Long Island all throughout the early 1980s. But as people who know his legend are aware, his big connection was with Marley Marl’s Juice Crew. Biz got in on the ground floor, first meeting the man in 1984. He recalls: “I wanted to be down with Marley *bad*, all that time. I used to go up to Queensbridge [Projects] and sit out in front of Marley’s house for like 6, 7, 8 hours. Then he’d tell me to come back tomorrow. My man Phil Rodriguez hooked me up with MC Shan, and when I went to Queensbridge to see Shan one day, he wasn’t home. I went into this park and started battling everybody and beatboxing, and I took everybody out. This is when Nas and Prodigy [of Mobb Deep] was like real little kids, way back."

Marley started knowing Biz's name from then on out and from what he heard of Biz, Marley was also warming to his wacky but hard-to-ignore style. Biz's real entrée into the Juice Crew world was through his work with Roxanne Shante: "In 1985 I was down with Shante. I was her beatboxer because Marley and Shante wasn't getting along, so he wasn't going out as a DJ for her. Plus he was on the radio [with Mr. Magic's "Rap Attack"] so he wasn't going out to do shows. I would go out [to perform] with her and do all her records, just doing human beatboxing." Biz's first appearance on wax was on Shante's Marley-produced "The Def Fresh Crew" single, released on Pop Art in 1986.

Around the same time, Biz met another future Juice Crew rapper that he would have a long association with: Big Daddy Kane. Biz says: "I met Kane in 1984, in Brooklyn. Me and him battled in the street, in front of McQuarrie Mall. I was actually substitute teaching at Kane's school back then, at Sarah J. Hale High School in Brooklyn. The kids was so crazy at that time. I was about 21, not much older than them. I wasn't trying to be a teacher, I just had a whole bunch of different schemes back then [laughs]. Anything for a dollar."

In '86, after his work with Shante and after being down with Juice Crew members and showing his talent and determination, Biz got his first shot on wax: the Marley Marl-produced *Inhuman Orchestra* EP (Prism), which included the legendary tracks "Make The Music With Your Mouth, Biz" (with the song's risible chorus hook sung in falsetto by his longtime friend, TJ Swan) and "The Biz Dance." The EP was loose and goofy, showcasing Biz's sense of humor as well as his rapping and unique beatboxing skills.

Biz describes his working relationship with the soon-to-be-legendary Marl: "Me and him made some great music together. I'd bring in a record and say: 'Yo, can you do something with this?' And he'd hook it up on the drum machine, put this in here, add this, bah bah bah and the beat is done. Marley taught me how to work in a studio and put a beat together. Everybody to this day thinks Marley was the mastermind. He can definitely hook up a beat, yes. But he usually had to have somebody tell him what to do with the beat. Either way, I learned a lot of studio stuff from him, so it was a good relationship."

The record was a big hit across the tri-state area, and Biz's career was on its way, along with fellow Juice Crewers Shante, Shan and Kane, who Marley was producing concurrently, in a swirl of incestuous musical activity. In fact, Kane ghost-wrote some of Biz's rhymes back in those days. Biz says: "For those early singles, I would tell Kane the concept and the subject and he would just write it up. I had him do it because I wanted to get in the game, and he was a great lyricist. It was a trade-off thing, too – I gave him the beat for [Kane's single] 'Ain't No Half Steppin'. Stuff like that."

1987 was a busy year, spent performing, guesting on other peoples' records (like Big Daddy Kane's "Just Rhymin' With Biz") and releasing his smash "Nobody Beats The Biz" single. And while Marley's Juice Crew, including Shante and especially Shan, was battling with Boogie Down Productions and DJ Red Alert on wax (with BDP's "South Bronx" and "The Bridge Is Over" and Shan's "Kill That Noise"), Biz didn't get too involved. "It didn't bother me that they were battling because I was cool with Scott La Rock and KRS [One]. I was like a Pope, I was like Switzerland. I didn't have no beefs. And I think that's why my first album was one that hit even more than other Juice Crew records. Everybody liked it, because it wasn't a dis record."

In actuality, the Bronx vs. Juice Crew beef *did* reach Biz, and his first single in 1987 was even a result of it. "Back then this group on B-Boy [Boogie Down Productions' label] called The Brothers did a song that said some stuff about me [assuming he means Akiem The Rhythm Maker's "I Got Rhythm" from 1987]. I wasn't that mad about it, but I went home and wrote 'Nobody Beats The Biz' and since my record was so big, no-one listened to their record."

In the fall of 1987, Biz's popularity had merited a full-length, and so work on his debut, *Goin' Off*, commenced at Marl's newly-built home studio in Astoria, Queens. Biz remembers: "It didn't take more than two or three weeks to record everything for that album, it was quick. I had the funk and I knew what I wanted out of the album, so it was easy. The hardest thing was tracking down certain records that I needed. I went to Downstairs Records a lot for that." Biz's cousin and DJ, Vaughan Lee aka Cool V, as Biz says: "Was a main part of that album, too. He was there in the studio every day and did all the cuts on there, I'm pretty sure. Fly Ty [label manager for Cold Chillin'] came in and out. Kane was there, too. If I needed something written, he'd do it within two minutes, right there."

The album hit in February 1988, and it began the 1988 and 1989 ruling of Marley Marl's Juice Crew syndicate (Biz, Big Daddy Kane, MC Shan, Roxanne Shante and Kool G Rap & DJ Polo). Biz explains the album's success: "I'm a simple person. If the beat is funky with something on top, then that's it, that's all I need. That album was big right away when it came out because I had a couple records out already, and people wanted more. It was really just like I had another single when the album came out. Back then I had to wait until the last single started to die down before I released another hit."

And as for whether there was any inner-crew competition or jealousy: "There wasn't any competition within the Juice Crew, at least as far as I was concerned. My record wasn't harmful. I was my own separate person, and I was the clown so, you know, people don't take the clown as seriously. I was humorous, so I wasn't a threat." And regarding Cold Chillin's new partnership with Warner Bros (which began in 1987), Biz says that didn't change anything either: "Being on Warners or just through Cold Chillin' didn't make a difference, since I was never that promoted anyways. I was always my own promoter, since people never seemed to worry that much about me. They put more emphasis on Shan, Shante and Kane. It wasn't a big deal. I'd just have to work a little extra harder to get noticed."

TRACKS

Pickin' Boogers

I wanted to do a record like that because I knew a lot of people that used to pick boogers. I used to know a kid named Anthony Hussey, and he used to pick his boogers, back in the day.

Albee Square Mall

I went to the Albee Square Mall [on Fulton Street in Brooklyn] every day. I used to get food for free, clothes on credit without a credit card. And that was before the song. After the song I paid for everything 'cause I had money then. They loved me there after that song. All my Brooklyn boys in there would look out for me to make sure nothin' happened. I can't really hang out at any malls now. It's like, 'Hey, ain't you....?" I guess Laurel Mall, around the corner from my house [in Laurel, MD] is one I'd hang out at. TJ Swann was on that song [singing the hook] with me 'cause Swann always used to hang with me at the mall. Swan's great on that track, but I think "Nobody Beats The Biz" is his best song. He was my best friend from around the way, in Long Island. I've known him since like 1982. Working with him actually happened accidentally. We would just sit in the car or walk from the train station and he'd just sing while I did the beatbox. Since he was with me through my early struggles in the rap game I put him on, since he was my boy. And it worked. He had a draw, too, since the girls all liked him.

Return of the Biz Dance

That version was different than the original ["The Biz Dance," from the *Inhuman Orchestra* EP]. The beat that Marley did was so funky that I wanted to do a rhyme to it, and I didn't know what else to do so I did another Biz Dance track. The Biz Dance itself is still the same today as it was back then. I taught everybody the Biz Dance. I can't even tell you how many people.

Vapors

I wrote that song so I would be like Rod Serling. How he'd have different stories, like on the Twilight Zone. I wanted to show four different lives. And I wanted to show the good and the bad in those lives. Every single thing on that song was true. That's still one of my classics, and I still perform that one to this day. I have to. If I don't, they'll fight me. Snoop covered that song and I was always really happy about that cover. "Vapors" was always really big in LA, bigger than it was in New York. That was probably the biggest record I ever had on the West Coast. It told a story and West Coast loves stories. I love Snoop's version because he still kept the funk in it. Plus he changed the words up. It was a compliment.

Make The Music With Your Mouth Biz

The first version I had of that I used the "Pink Panther" beat. But I didn't like it so I didn't use it. I told Marley how I wanted the beat to go. I wanted the 808 bass sound to be deeper, but his button got stuck so it ended up with less bass. Marley did a remix of the song for the album, a dub version of the original. I don't know why he did that. I wasn't there for the mastering of that album. I wanted the "Make The Music" original on the album, not that version. But I had no control at that time. It was my first album. I knew that song would be a big record because people out there was just waiting for something new. There was an anticipation.

Nobody Beats The Biz

That's a remix, too, different than the single. I don't know why they did that either. The words ain't different, mostly just the way the song starts. I brought in that Steve Miller sample, because it was rock and I knew that stuff. I wanted it to just be Steve Miller but Marley had the Lafayette Afro Rock band sample [for the drumbeat]. I think Marley had the Lafayette track from Jabby Jab [unsure about spelling], and the record itself was really scratched up. So I called all over to get a better copy. I called Bambaata, I called Flash, I called everybody. I think Flash told me the name of it, so I knew that from him. I looked all over and I found a store on Utica Avenue that had African records. So I slept in front of the store and I bought every copy they had of that record there when they opened. I brought it back to Marley and he hooked it back up. I think the Wiz [the Nobody Beats The Wiz electronics store, whose jingle is modified for the chorus] might have sued us, but I don't know nothin' about that. They sold my records in their store either way. Marley might have done the cuts on that track.

This Is Something For The Radio

That wasn't a filler track, I liked that one. It was like three or four in the morning when I did that. I did a version of "Vapors" like that, too, with me talking and not rappin'. I just wanted to act like I was drunk [slurs speech for affect]. They recorded it while I was playin' around. And after I heard it it was cool. I said: "Keep it."

Cool V's Tribute To Scratching

We had a record called "Cool V's Scratchstrapiece" that was supposed to go on the album, with all Michael Jackson records. But it never made the album. You gotta hear it, it's incredible. Michael Jackson wouldn't clear the stuff. It was the second-to-last record we did for the album. Cool V was an incredible DJ. He was fast, accurate and he would not mess up. He was like a record. Besides being my cousin, he was just really good. An accurate DJ is the best one you can have.

DE LA SOUL

3 Feet High And Rising

(Tommy Boy, 1989)

1989 was a hugely transitional year for hip-hop. With incredibly strong *albums* by artists like Public Enemy, Boogie Down Productions, N.W.A. and various Juice Crew members, things were beginning to break wide open, nationally. And in that important year there was no album more unique, groundbreaking and important to the game than De La Soul's debut. Three Long Island teenagers – Posdnuos, Trugoy (now known simply as Dave) and DJ Maseo – and their wily, open-eared producer Prince Paul blew a lot of minds before the decade ended.

"I still stand in amazement at how timeless that album feels," says Pos today. "It was a capsule of our innocence," adds Dave, continuing: "I can hear four individuals who didn't give a damn about the rules and just went in and had a good time." Tommy Boy founder and owner Tom Silverman agrees: "That album is so important because it threw out the rulebook. At the time, hip-hop was starting to define itself as being one thing, with all the bragging, the way people dressed, even the sound. These guys said: 'No, you don't have to sound like that.' It opened up the door for self-expression at the time. They were the start of the third generation of hip-hop." Rules, straight-ahead beats and hip-hop's usual tough-guy posturing were rarely followed as they created 23-tracks of giddy, goofy, and occasionally serious rap music.

Although born in Brooklyn (Dave and Maseo) and the Bronx (Pos), all three De La members were raised through their high school years in Amityville, Long Island, about twenty miles to the East of New York City's five boroughs. Being close enough to have contact with hip-hop as it burgeoned, but also far enough away from urban congestion and stress, they agree that it made all the difference. Pos says: "Being where we were, there was just more room for you to try different things. It's a different mind-state. In LI you had your own four walls that weren't attached to anyone else's four walls. There wasn't the city congestion." Dave adds: "Hip-hop was something that we had the opportunity to digest from afar. We were influenced by it, but we developed our own style. If we had all grown up for all our years in the Bronx, De La Soul definitely wouldn't have been the same."

Dave and Pos first hooked up together in a local Amityville group called Easy Street around 1985, neither of them up-front as MCs: Pos DJed (as DJ Soundsop – Posdnuos is that name reversed) and Dave (as Jude, his middle name) beatboxed. "I was in 10th grade and Dave was in 11th," Pos recalls. "We all had a love for hip-hop." The group, which also featured main MC Ant and someone who went by Huggy Ro, didn't last long, but it cemented the artistic partnership between Pos and

Dave. Pos says: "Even back then, me and Dave knew that regardless of what happened, we'd still be working together. We just knew that the vibe we had was good. We helped to push each other, creatively." Dave remembers: "Pos and I clicked personally, and we were more serious than the other guys in that group, so we broke with Easy Street and got down with Charlie Rock, who was a good friend of mine. We didn't have a name, we were just starting to put music and concepts together."

Charlie was a well-known DJ in town, and the two learned a great deal from him. More importantly for their future, though, Charlie brought someone else into the fold: DJ Maseo. Maseo was a more recent Amityville transplant, having moved from Brooklyn to Amityville about two years earlier. Even within that short time, he had made a name as one of the best DJs in town, playing house parties and neighborhood park jams. Charlie, who was busy on the party circuit, saw the chemistry that Mase had with the two ex-Easy Streeters, and soon enough the De La Soul trio was set in stone. Pos says: "By 1986, De La Soul was in place. We had performed at high school functions and people around town were starting to know the name a little bit."

The final piece of the puzzle was no less important: Amityville's most popular DJ, and a budding producer at the time, Prince Paul. Aside from his local rep, Paul was also known for being part of the ground-breaking live hip-hop band Stetsasonic. "Paul did a lot of house parties around the way and was a great battle DJ," says Pos, "But I never even knew that he produced. I just knew that he DJed a lot and that Stetsasonic were incredible." Paul did have dreams of producing, but he wasn't getting heard on that front in Stet, who had several great, and older, producers in the group. So when he heard De La's roughest of rough demos, a lightbulb flashed. Pos remembers: "Mase would play these really gritty tapes we made in our house on Mase's drum machine for Paul, and he liked them."

Paul's budding genius behind the boards was just waiting to be unleashed, and he put it to work in his role as "mentor" – De La had great ideas, they just needed a push. As Dave says: "Prior to Paul even becoming involved, we had already made songs like 'Potholes In My Lawn' and 'Plug Tunin'.' When Paul came on board, he just added on to what we already had." At first Pos says he was concerned about someone new in the fold, but he got over it quickly: "I always knew that Paul was a good guy, but I was just concerned about what he was going to do with something that was very close to me, my music. When I saw how he thought and what his ideas were, though, we were all really gung-ho." Dave adds: "Paul could really stretch records out. We'd let him add just one more thing, and it was always the cherry on top. There was never a time when Paul didn't make a song better, where he didn't find exactly what was missing."

Paul himself says of the opportunity: "With Stetsasonic, a lot of the ideas I had for production were just too juvenile for them, since they were more serious. De La was more my age, more my style. And on that first De La record, it was a situation where I felt in total control for maybe the first time. That was pretty amazing for me. I was like: 'Really? You guys are actually listening to *me*?"

Paul and the trio worked on a three-track demo (including the songs "Plug Tunin'," "Freedom of Speak" and "De La Games" [which would eventually turn into "Daisy Age"]) in 1987 and, with fellow Stet-member Daddy-O, brought De La through a bidding war and into the arms of Tommy Boy Records. "We had three songs and – literally – a book full of ideas," Dave says. Pos recalls: "Daddy-O [from Stet] and us were both shopping our stuff at the same time [Daddy-O was shopping a solo deal for himself], but the labels were having more interest in De La than in Daddy's stuff. That's when Daddy-O started to come more on board with De La."

Tom Silverman remembers meeting De La for the first time, back in their demo-shopping days: "Those guys were freaks compared to everyone else in hip-hop back at that time. It was like they were brothers from another planet. They also had more raw intelligence than just about anyone else out there." About the bidding war, Pos remembers: "It was pretty surprising, we couldn't believe it. Pretty much any place that Paul and Daddy-O took our demo to was interested in giving us a deal." Since Paul and Daddy-O were already on Tommy Boy with Stetsasonic and they trusted the label and were impressed by Silverman and his Tommy Boy partner Monica Lynch, they went with them. Dave says: "We went with Tommy Boy just for the comfort of knowing that Prince Paul was there. And the enthusiasm was also a bit greater there, as well. Monica Lynch saw our vision and was down for it. Tommy Boy gave us a lot of love from the start, and gave us room to do whatever we chose to, creatively."

They signed with Tommy Boy in the fall of 1987, a couple months after Pos had graduated high school (he was already enrolled in Five Towns College in Dix Hills, Long Island, where Prince Paul also took classes), and, as Pos says: "Started work right away." Their first single, "Plug

Tunin'" was released first thing in 1988, followed by "Potholes In My Lawn." Both singles did well, and Tommy Boy green-lighted them for a full album, which is when the real fun began. Pos says: "The album didn't take that long to record because a lot of the ideas were already gathered in our mind, even before we got signed."

Dave agrees, looking back: "We definitely went right into the studio [Calliope Studios] once we got signed. I would say that we probably had ideas for six or seven more songs than actually made the album, too. We probably created 28 or 30 altogether. There are a lot of songs that have never been released, they're just sitting on tape, still." Their recording budget was $28,000, which included all recording costs, sample clearance fees and payments, and their own advances. "They got lower advances," says Tom Silverman, "But as a result, after the album blew up they got paid massive royalty checks. They bought houses for all of their parents after that."

All four men involved in the production agree that the work done on the album made it a truly exciting time for them, and the discoveries they were making in the studio were creating a tangible energy. "Whatever idea was brought to the table, we'd all just expound on it," says Dave. "It didn't matter who brought it. It could have been us four, it could have been my sister. It was all about enjoying music and enjoying creating more music." He adds, about their, and Paul's vague producerly roles on the album: "I didn't have a concept of what a producer was until I learned more about the game. The way I was introduced to production was with us. People working on something together. It was awkward back then seeing, for example, Paul do something for MC Lyte, where he did the whole beat and maybe someone else wrote her rhymes. I was like: 'Wow, that happens?' From the start, with us, it was like every man puts in their ten cents and let's make this into a dollar."

Many times the unexpected turned into fodder for whole songs. Pos says: "Prince Paul taught us that you need to leave open the surprise of a mistake, because it could turn around and be great. Paul's a genius that way. He's not afraid to scrap a record and start from scratch and try something else totally different. We learned early in the game from Paul not to always sound the same. We called Paul 'The Mentor' because we really did learn so much from him. A lot of things he had in his head, he tried for the first time with us." He adds: "A lot of ideas came from us just joking around. I'd crack a joke and next thing you know we're doing a game show. We learned, mostly from Paul, that you don't always need to map things out. You can make mistakes. That was important. And the zaniness of the album, overall, definitely came from Paul." Dave adds his own Paul praise: "Paul isn't intricate. It's simple with him. But he makes it sound like it took him a lifetime to figure it out. He can make a record that much better. Especially when you think that a track is already done."

After their studio lockdown and carefree audio pranks, De La and their mentor had something amazing to give to the world, *3 Feet High And Rising*, which they released in early 1989. Critically acclaimed across the board and eventually platinum-bound, the album was a phenomenon to say the least. Samples from obscure Johnny Cash to well-known Hall & Oates informed the musical landscape they created, and lyrically they traded between lines that were sometimes serious and sometimes so abstract they didn't make a whole lot of sense. Dave says today: "Maybe it was our warped character, but we didn't really want people to understand it all. Sometimes we were trying to make it difficult, because it would make people always want to know more."

"I knew that the album was either going to do absolutely nothing, or it was going to be really, really big," Tom Silverman says today. "It was either going to miss the mark totally, or be gigantic. It was just so different that it couldn't possibly land anywhere in the middle. I loved it when I heard all the tracks, and when they did the *final* version, when they put all the interstitial pieces in, it made it even more of a masterpiece."

Musically the genius was indisputable, but the group's live show wasn't exactly a selling point at first, according to Silverman: "When I first saw them live, they were one of the shittiest live bands ever. The record was selling about 10,000 copies a week for a while, which was really big back then. And then they went on the Fresh Fest tour and a week after that the record just stopped selling. They were getting booed off the stage, from what we heard. But I have to give them ultimate credit, because they responded to that by becoming the best live group in hip-hop. Over a year they made their show absolutely bullet-proof. At this point they're like the Grateful Dead of hip-hop."

There was one and only one major turning point once *3 Feet High and Rising* was released, and it came to be both a blessing and a curse for the group: the huge smash single, "Me, Myself And I." Silverman says: "Originally the attention on the album, which was a lot, was from press and college radio, which will always only give you so many sales. Press was definitely easier than radio, since they were so different. But without 'Me, Myself And I' it's very clear that the album wouldn't have done more than 100,000 units, instead of the platinum-plus that it achieved. We needed a focal point single for radio and that was it. We needed a spoonful of sugar to help the medicine go down."

According to Dave and Pos, group members eventually came to dislike not only the "Me, Myself And I" single, but also the hippy image that they had inherited, partially because of the way they were and partially because of the way that they were sold to America. "To call them hippies wasn't overly accurate, really," says Silverman, "But it was an easy way to explain to people why they were different. They *did* have a hippy-ish attitude when I first met them: they dressed in cotton clothes, Guatamalan stuff. Their style was more of a non-style, really." It wasn't necessarily anyone's fault, and it made them a lot of money, but there was a reason why their second album was called *De La Soul Is Dead*. Pos says: "We were really sick of all the hype after a while. When we handed in the album to the label, we were already elsewhere, musically. And *3 Feet High* was in the marketplace for so long. We were really just tired of it and that's why we reacted like that."

No matter how the group came to see and deal with their new-found fame, there is no disputing the greatness of the album, and they still, of course, look back on it fondly. "I can look back on that record and say that *3 Feet High* is art to its fullest. It's the record that I'm most proud of," says Dave. Pos adds: "That album was just a great stepping stone for us, and I'm so happy to know that some place in our career we made something that was so timeless and had such innocence. We had no idea that it would be so popular and lasting. Success to us was hearing Red Alert and Chuck Chillout play our records on the radio. So, for it to go that far outside of New York was mind-blowing."

Silverman says: "Aside from the U.S., that album was also important because it was the first hit hip-hop album on the international scene. It was the first album to do more than 500,000 units in Europe, way more than even Run-DMC. Musically it was just more accessible to people over there who were rock & roll fans. It had a European feel to it, somehow. It just wasn't seen as a dark, American rap record." He adds: "*3 Feet High* is the one that people talk about more than any other Tommy Boy album, which is saying a lot. It's incredible just to know that you were involved with something like that."

TRACKS

Intro

Pos: The gameshow concept was one of the last things we did, in mixing. I think Paul might have come up with the idea. Al Watts [gameshow announcer] was just one of the engineers where we were mixing. To this day, that's the way that a lot of sessions roll. If you're there, whether you're the engineer or someone we invited to hang out, you could wind up being on our album. We were doing skits back when we used to make tapes back at the crib, before we even met Paul. So we just fell right into that.

The Magic Number

Pos: The name of the album came from a Johnny Cash tune called "Five Feet High And Rising," which we used, when it says: "Three feet high and rising" right at the very end of that track, where it's that collage of all the different cuts. You hear it right before the song is about to go off. Dave's father had that record.

Change In Speak

Dave: That was the album version of "Freedom Of Speak," which was the b-side to our first single ["Plug Tunin'"]. It was definitely a declaration about us, like: "We've landed, we're here." But it wasn't boasting, like: "We're the shit." It was more letting people know that there's room for a change, and this is what we're all about.

Pos: The music on there was from a Mad Lads record, and then we used that Cymande ["Bra"] thing in there. I pretty much put that song together, I guess. We weren't as aware as it might have seem seemed about what ground we were breaking, lyrically.

Jenifa Taught Me (Derwin's Revenge)

Pos: That was our second single, and we used another 45 from my father's collection on there. I looped it up on a pause tape. I actually didn't even own recording equipment until *De La Soul Is Dead*. That single was really more of a double a-side, with "Potholes On My Lawn" on the other side. We didn't want "Potholes" on a single alone, though, because we thought it was too slow. But we did the video for "Potholes."

Dave: Derwin [mentioned in the song] is a friend of ours, who we used to crack on, like: "You never get no girls." He loved the song, of course. It put him on the map [laughs].

Ghetto Thang

Dave: Being more serious, like we were on that song, was just part of what we've always done. We've always touched on serious topics here and there, whether it's "Millie Pulled A Pistol On Santa" or "Baby Phat," as much as people might not think of that as a serious record. It's just part of us. In the midst of the fun, let's talk about important stuff as well.

Pos: We never worried about putting a serious song like that on an album, after something like "Jenifa." We really were content putting what we wanted to on that canvas. We didn't care if one thing was very different than the rest.

Transmitting Live From Mars

Dave: That's the one that the Turtles sued us for. It startled us at the time, because we were clueless about how severe it could get. Tom Silverman just pushed "Go" on the record without clearing everything. The attacks, especially the Turtles one, started coming after the record went gold. Steely Dan sued us, too.

Silverman: That Turtles suit cost Tommy Boy about $100,000 total, and De La had to bear about $50,000 of that amount. We had some "errors and omissions" insurance. The problem was that although we cleared 35 samples on the album, the Turtles one wasn't on the list that the group gave us, because it was one of the interstitial pieces, it wasn't even a real song, just an interlude. That was a bad situation, and demoralizing.

Take It Off

Dave: Lyrically on that track it was like: "Clear the way, let's gravitate towards some newer things, let's evolve, let's turn the soil over." And to this day we still have skits like that, that we share amongst ourselves.

Tread Water

Dave: When I heard the music, I just thought of that concept. A storyline with animals, just strolling down the line. And I used that happy-go-lucky rhyme style.

Potholes In My Lawn

Silverman: We did an $800 video for that song. It was done with a hand-held 8-mm camera and they were on these motorized scooters.

Say No Go

Pos: That was another single off the record. It sampled Hall & Oates' "I Can't Go For That." We never met them [Hall & Oates], but I was like: "Yo, if you need me to come and explain it to them, I will" to the business affairs people, in case they had trouble clearing it. More because I was just a fan. "Say No Go" was one of my favorite records on the album. I put most of that together, and Paul and Mase added some things.

Plug Tunin' (Last Chance To Comprehend)

Pos: "Plug Tunin'" was on our three song demo that we shopped to labels with, and it became our first single. The arrangement was always the same, Paul added the Liberace record on top. We didn't really worry if people would understand it or not, we was just happy to be doing a single. A lot of creative stuff was being done on singles at that time. With that track, we had always had the rhymes and the routine. I had found the music for the main part from an old 45 of my father's, I paused it up on a tape and had my rhyme and the chorus already mapped out. And Dave loved it. We took it to Mase and he put the drum pattern to it. When Paul heard it and we decided to deal with him I was really concerned with what he was going to add to it. But he added the "Night Themes" beat [Manzel's "Midnight Theme"], the main looped beat, that Cypress Hill used for "How I Could Just Kill A Man." He added that James Brown cut, the Billy Joel piano. Definitely the things he added to it made it 120 percent better than what we did.

Dave: We didn't always know that "Plug Tunin" would be our first single. It's the first thing we did and it was almost all we had when we got signed. Tommy Boy was so excited about it that they just wanted it *out*. It was an era when groups were still doing singles, so an album wasn't even talked about at that point. Not that many albums were still even coming out.

Buddy *(with Jungle Brothers and Q-Tip)*

Dave: I recall just being in Mase's den, sampling something on a little keyboard and I started doing that "meanie meanie meanie meanie meanie" thing. Then we just thought of the word "buddy" instead of the word "body." We didn't get specific about what we loved on a woman, so we just kept it vague. Then we was in the studio and just wanted to invite some people on there. The closest people to what we was doing at the time was the Jungle Brothers and Tribe [Called Quest]. And Latifah [heard on the 12" remix] was a labelmate, on Tommy Boy. So it just became a family affair.

Pos: That was done mid-way through the sessions. We always had the style we wanted to do for that song, and the beat we wanted to use. We would always see the Jungle Brothers in clubs we went to, hanging with Red Alert and all that. But we never met them until we did a show together, with Finesse & Synquis. We met Q-Tip through the Jungle Brothers.

Delacratic

Dave: That's Wize of Stetsasonic on beatbox there. I don't know why I didn't do it [since Dave started out as a beatboxer]. I was probably too shy.

Me Myself And I

Pos: That song was the second-to-last record we made for the album. From our understanding of where rap was at the time, we definitely never thought it was going to be such a success. After the first two singles, we realized we had to put "Me Myself And I" out. Like: "It ain't my favorite song, but people seem to be gravitating towards it and Tommy Boy could get a lot of things done with this song. So let's do it." We put it pretty far back in the album sequence, though.

Dave: When Mase played the track, I came up with what the song would be about right away. I actually wrote Pos' first eight bars. It was just like: "I'm being me. Enjoy the music. If you like it, then don't worry about how I'm dressed."

Silverman: I loved that song when I first heard it, but I can't even say that I knew it would be such a huge hit. I think that video pretty much encapsulates the entire message of that whole album. The anti-gold-chain sentiment. Maseo claims responsibility for that record being made. Paul didn't even want it on the album. It was so commercial, and they didn't want anything that obvious.

Pos: I loved the original [Funkadelic's "Knee Deep"] but I was like: "Yo, unless we're really hooking it up more than this, I don't really have much interest in doing this." A lot of the reviews that came out on the first two singles were saying that we were hippies, so with that video we were just trying to remind people that we were just trying to be ourselves. We took the vocal style and cadence on that from the Jungle Brothers' "Black Is Black." That's why we put in that Q-Tip sample [from "Black Is Black"].

Silverman: Using that "Knee Deep" sample on that track really helped De La Soul get over on the West Coast, when not many East Coast groups were getting over back then. If it wasn't for that track, LA might not have really gotten with the album at all.

Dave: We thought it would be something that people reminisced on, rather than being such a huge smash hit. Like: "Wow, they used 'Knee Deep,' I always loved that record." We definitely didn't think that it was going to be a platinum single. We started realizing how big it was becoming when our regimen was just non-stop. We were everywhere. We were on a big LL [Cool J] tour. The single started the fire and set up the album.

This Is A Recording 4 Living In A Fulltime Era

Pos: I just realized, talking to you, that that song was the last track we did for the record. For a long time I was thinking it was "Me, Myself And I." Right when it was done I went back and tried to put that together because I was like: "Yo, we don't have nothing, in my mind, that sounds 'street' or whatever." Like: "We got all these crazy-ass songs that we love, but is anyone gonna really like any of this?"

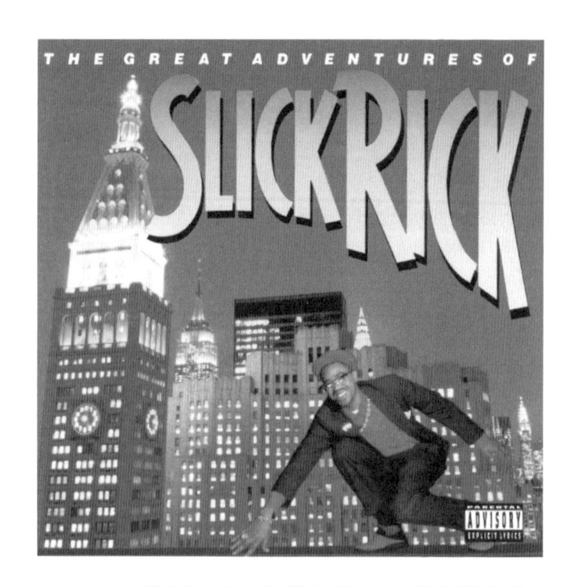

SLICK RICK

The Great Adventures of Slick Rick

(Def Jam, 1988)

No one will ever forget the almighty Slick Rick, in part because of the four nonsensical words that started his illustrious MC career: "La Di Da Di." Released as the B-side of Doug E. Fresh and the Get Fresh Crew's 1985 smash hit "The Show" (on Reality / Danya) the famed vocal has endured even longer than its flip. Sampled by dozens of producers, covered by lyrical ascendant Snoop Dogg, cut up by DJs ad infinitum, and memorized by most of the America old and/or schooled enough to remember the hip-hop explosion of the '80s, it's Rick's defining rhyme, and still part of his stage show.

The British-born and Bronx-raised Rick (Walters aka Ricky D) had storytelling skills from a very young age. He says: "When I was growing up in the Bronx, everyone was into rapping. In junior high it was the big thing. We all used to bang on the desk and say raps and such. I guess I must have stood out. And once you stand out at something, you're probably going to end up pursuing it." Although many of his friends (including fellow storytelling master Dana Dane, with whom he went to high school, graduating in 1983) reveled in flowing off the top of the dome, Rick always preferred the lyric book. "I was never the type to say freestyle raps," he explains. "I usually tell a story, and to do that well I've always had to work things out beforehand."

Rick met Doug E Fresh in 1984, when Doug was a judge at an MC contest. Rick says: "He liked my style and he started carrying me around with him. We used to do the early versions of 'La Di Da Di' during his shows, with him doing beatbox and me rapping. Stuff like we was doing back then was never done before. Two guys with no instruments, just microphone and mouth. The crowd liked that song a lot, so we decided to make a record of it. To everybody's surprise, it did really well." As for his fans still loving that cut today, even after all the other classics that Rick has churned out, he says: "Sure, I'm glad that the public likes 'La Di Da Di' still. I'm shocked that they do, honestly. I could understand more if they liked 'Children's Story' or 'Mona Lisa,' because 'La Di Da Di' is kinda slow. But if it makes the public happy, I'll do it all day long."

With his on-stage and on-record rhyme skills, which specialized in entertaining and frequently bawdy stories, Rick became a major attraction as part of Doug's high-energy stage show in 1985 and 1986. And in a move that disappointed Doug E Fresh fans, Rick left at the apex of his popularity to pursue a solo career. There have been different stories of Rick's leaving, many which focus on the paltry royalties he is rumored to have received from his part in "La Di Da Di." But Rick says: "I wasn't mad. I was a guest on Doug's ship, I wasn't an artist that was signed. The Get Fresh Crew was around before I was. I was a guest appearance, like Chill Will and Barry B as DJs. After the success of 'La Di Da Di' I figured it might be better to branch off and let Doug take control of his ship again, instead of us disputing over how to break up the pie. I was feeling like I should have gotten at least 35-40 percent for royalties, but I can't really knock him. It was his ship. And I was still doing OK. Hell, it was better than working as a mail clerk."

After setting out on his own, it wasn't hard to find record company suitors. He was signed in 1986 for an album on Def Jam, since he was also being managed by Russell Simmons at the time. Recording the album itself wasn't a lengthy task, but Rick fell prey to some record label delays. He says: "There were conflicts with different producers and the label saying how they envisioned me and me not agreeing with what they thought was hot. We had our little conflicts, so that stretched shit out a little longer. In the end, the label held some things up. Russell and Lyor [Cohen, at Def Jam] had their visions, I had mine."

The album recording itself started in 1987, even though the album didn't hit until late 1988. "It was hard for me to make a whole album," Rick says. "I was just a kid on the street who said one popular rap and that was it. Now it became a situation where you had to make twelve songs and it's all on you. It was a new experience and I didn't want it to sound wack. Plus you had to deal with a record label and their opinions and politics and all that. Most people were still just making singles back then, and I had never even envisioned making an album, so it was pretty crazy."

After an almost two-year absence from the hip-hop scene, Rick returned with the monumental album *The Great Adventures of Slick Rick*. Impressively well-produced by Rick himself with help on six tracks from Hank Shocklee and Eric Sadler (two-thirds of Public Enemy's legendary Bomb Squad) and one from Run-DMC's Jam Master Jay, it's a wild ride through Rick's psyche, veering from highfalutinly moral to hilariously bawdy, with everything in-between. Just a look and listen to the songs and you quickly remember how important the album was: "Children's Story," "Mona Lisa," "Hey Young World," "Indian Girl," "The Ruler's Back," "Teenage Love."

Its greatness was shown to the world in time, but it didn't happen overnight. "The hype built slowly," Rick recalls. "When 'La Di Da Di' and 'The Show' was out, I was way up there, I was very popular and known. But there was a gap between then and the time when 'Children's Story' [the album's first single] came out. I had to regain that momentum and that hype again. During that time I wasn't performing at all. I was so used to performing with Doug, and I was like: 'How am I gonna do 'La Di Da Di' in a show without him?'"

Rick also had to build his confidence back up a bit, after being out of the limelight. "When the album came out I just figured it was another rap album, like everybody else's. I knew I liked a lot of the songs and they made me dance, but that was about it. I think when you're younger what you want to do is just hear your record on the radio. That's just a great feeling. So that's all I really wanted. You're not thinking about how big it's gonna be, saleswise or any other way. My main thing was just that I didn't want to rhyme on no wack beats. I wanted to rhyme on stuff that was fun and that was hype. And I think I accomplished that."

Just as "La Di Da Di" had begun Slick Rick's career, *Great Adventures* cemented his place in hip-hop history. Rick's words, thoughts, lyrical execution and smooth, high-brow British-tinged flow were – and still are – absolutely unique. "I think *Great Adventures* made its mark because my personality came through, and the album had direction, to some degree," he says today. "It was almost like a diary. 'When I was 19, this is what happened and this is what I learned from it.' That kind of thing. Now I'm 34 [in October 1999]. It's all just writing down life experiences as you go on. I just put them in rap form."

Rick says in conclusion, about how the album was received then, and how it endures today: "Any time you've got something that isn't too preachy and has a positive point of view, it's going to last longer than if you're just having fun and doing straight party rhymes. People definitely remember that time in their life today, back in 1988. They remember hearing those songs for the first time back then, and I'm glad those were good times for them."

TRACKS

Treat Her Like A Prostitute

Jam Master Jay actually did the music for that [crediting on the album says Rick produced. Rick may be confusing this with "The Ruler's Back," which does actually credit Jam Master Jay for production]. It was something that me and Doug used to do, with the beatbox. We used to do it live and people used to just *snap*. The punchlines would always liven up a party. That was the only older song I did for the album. All the rest of them on there was new. That was like real-life experiences and then making them humorous to a certain degree. I just figured that that was how it goes. It was more my outlook on life at the time. I wasn't trying to be disrespectful to no *good* women.

The Ruler's Back

"Teenage Love" was the first song that we did for release as a single, but "The Ruler's Back" was actually out before it. I put it out there to [DJ] Red Alert [then of New York's Kiss 98 FM] on a cassette. It started to play so much that the label got mad at me [laughs]. We had a version of the track that was a little more bouncy, but we didn't get to drop that one. With the keyboard playing on there and other songs, it was definitely nothing too complex. Just a one-finger thing. I would just envision bringing in a whole orchestra, but do it one track at a time. Stuff like that is done in layers.

Children's Story

We got a little more creative with that one, with the sound effects. We tried to make it a visual picture, especially with the ending. The "Knock em out the box, Rick" was like the climax, big party part. We did the overlapping vocals because we wanted to keep the effect that was on [Doug E Fresh's] "The Show." I saw that scene in real life, so I just put it on paper and added a little fiction to make it more interesting. I didn't see the people get shot, but I saw the people go to jail and ruin their whole life.

The Moment I Feared

That was my track, I produced it. I don't know how they [Hank

Shocklee and Eric Sadler] got credit for that. But that's another thing. It was a story of me envisioning myself – you know how when you're young you envision yourself being with the drug dealer's girl. And you just imagine yourself falling into a story like that.

Let's Get Crazy

I didn't really like that one. That was just filler. I didn't even write all of that shit. It was like somebody wrote it and I just fixed the raps so they didn't sound so crazy or whatever.

Indian Girl (An Adult Story)

That was a story that had a funny ending. We were just having fun. I didn't work on that one for *too* long. When that song and "Treat Her Like A Prostitute" came out you had people saying they were bad and vulgar and all that. At the time I was writing them I wasn't thinking of being disrespectful to any religion or to women in general. I was just a young guy who was having fun. I figured "Indian Girl" would be humorous to other people just like it was to me when my friends were sitting around telling stories.

Teenage Love

The version I myself had done for that song was a more dancey type of track, you could definitely dance to it more than listen to it. But they [assumedly: Def Jam's Russell Simmons and Lyor Cohen, and producers Shocklee and Sadler] envisioned doing it the way it came out. That song was just expressions of what I went through in high school. You know, getting my heart broken and all that type of stuff. The rap wasn't written to follow the [LL Cool J] "I Need Love" trend, but the music was done for that type of feel. I think it was a good idea to make it more of a ballad. It would have been something to see how that song would have turned out [if they had released the original version]. But it's too late now. It would have had to come out at the exact same time, to see which one the public would have responded to more.

Mona Lisa

That was a dance track, to dance and have fun. We put a little "Walk On By" [by Dionne Warwick. Rick sings his own version in the song] at the end. If that kind of thing sounds good with a nice dance track then there's nothing wrong with that! It just fit in there somehow.

Kit (What's The Scoop)

That's me pretending to be Michael Knight from Knight Rider, with the car, and putting an adventure on wax.

Hey Young World

I wanted to put down a positive message with a reggae twist. It was a statement from my point of view. Seeing people going the wrong route and trying to explain to them that it's not the route to go. I wasn't trying to be too preachy.

Teacher, Teacher

That was another filler track. I wasn't really feeling that one. That was there just to make the album reach twelve [songs]. It was empty, it had no soul to it. I didn't put no effort into that song.

Lick The Balls

That was supposed to be a little more aggressive. Talkin' shit. Braggadocious. I liked it, to some degree. That was the one that Eric Sadler made that I thought wasn't so bad. Bringing in Sadler and Shocklee was the label's thing, they decided they would make it a hot album. It was pretty smooth working with them, overall. I liked "Lick The Balls" but the rest of the stuff they did I wasn't feeling as much.

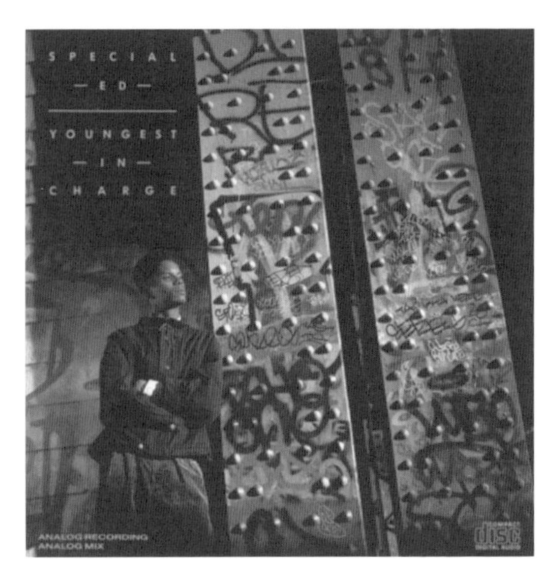

SPECIAL ED

Youngest In Charge

(Profile, 1989)

"I started out from battling, all my rhymes and all my styles," says Edward Archer, aka Special Ed, on the phone from his current home in Los Angeles. "I had to battle everywhere: in school, on the street, on my block. If someone asks you if you rhyme and you say yes, you'd better be able to rhyme. And I always said yes. I was lucky that I was talented at writing and I used that energy in a good way."

Unless you heard the album title before hearing the record itself, you'd never guess that the lyricist on the mic had just passed his Sweet-16 when his debut hit in 1989 (and was only 14 and 15 when he recorded it). But to producer Hitman Howie Tee, he could have been 5 or 50: Ed had immense talent that was not to be denied. "His lyrics, his storytelling and just his whole rap style impressed me," says Howie today (also in LA). "Anytime I threw a beat on, he knew how to ride it. When he first tried out for me, that album was born. It was just one long rhyme after that [laughs]. It just kept going and going."

Howie, who hailed from Schenectedy Ave in Brooklyn's Flatbush section, was the elder statesman of the duo by many years. He started out in the early '80s with the group CDIII, who released the single "Get Tough" on Prelude in 1983. "I was a DJ, too," he says, "I'd do all kinds of block parties, graduations, whatever. In Brooklyn, mostly." He was also down with the Kangol Kid from UTFO, which led to an important, albeit uncredited, studio adventure for Howie in 1984: UTFO's worldwide smash "Roxanne, Roxanne." "Full Force was taking UTFO into the studio to make the record 'Beats and Rhymes,'" Howie recalls. "Kangol wanted a b-side, so he came by my crib, since I had equipment in my basement, and we banged out the beat [for "Roxanne, Roxanne"]. When they got to the studio to do the final I couldn't go because I had a session with CDIII, so I gave Kangol my 808 [drum machine] and my sampler. He programmed his beat and I did Dr. Ice's beat. Educated Rapper always sounded good on 'Big Beat' [by Billy Squier] so we made sure he was on that one. And that's how the structure of that song came about."

Unfortunately, because he wasn't in the studio and likely because Full Force didn't want to break up the production credits more than they already were, Howie didn't receive anything for his work. But, he says: "As a payback for what I did on 'Roxanne, Roxanne' Full Force made me The Real Roxanne's DJ." It might not have been what he deserved, but it kept him busy and gave him some performance cash for 1985 and 1986. Howie, a master drum programmer, also did beats for UTFO's first album and for Lisa Lisa & the Cult Jam. He and Kangol had a group they produced on their own called Whistle, known for the track "Just Buggin'," from 1985, on Select.

By 1988, in his mid-20s, with an impressive production resume, Howie had yet to hit it big as a producer. That changed one day when a familiar-looking kid named Ed, from East Flatbush, walked into his garage. Ed, the youngest of five brothers and the only member of his family not born in Jamaica, was only 14 when he met Howie, who was ruling his neighborhood hip-hop scene. "Howie was the first dude that I knew of to have a crew and make mixtapes in his garage," Ed remembers. "Before I even thought of rapping I saw him across the street when I'd visit my cousin and see him cutting up records and making tapes with his crew."

Ed was, of course, advanced for his age at the time, in hip-hop and otherwise. "I'm just very focused and I'm talented," Ed says. "A lot of mature people come from where I'm from. We've all got New York states of mind that force you to grow up quick. But some people take that energy and apply it to the wrong things." Ed applied his confidence and his way with words to hip-hop at a young age. "What really brought me fully into rap music was Run-DMC. When I saw that they were so real and sold so many records, I said: 'I can do that. I've *been* doing that.' So I just started writing my own stuff, constantly." He continues: "My style really took shape in junior high. Before that I wasn't confident enough. But then I became an MC. Before that I was just writing some shit on the low. When I got into high school at Erasmus [Hall, in Brooklyn] that was when the big battles started. During my first year there was this dude Prince who was the nicest. So I challenged him and we battled under the arch at Erasmus and I burnt him. He was in 11th grade and I was 9th grade, and I took his name [meaning: Prince lost so he couldn't use it anymore]. It all really jumped off from there."

He adds: "My name, Special Ed, didn't come until around that same time. I used to use Eddie Love, Ed Ski, Eddy Ed and stuff like that. But my boy Eric Green from the neighborhood gave me the name. When I was young I was a little wild, following my brothers around and all, so my boy came at me with that name due to my wild personality. I was never in the special education program at school, of course, but I guess he thought it sounded good, so I went with it."

Howie and Ed were introduced by Ed's cousin Jennifer, who arranged for Ed to come to his spot and audition. Ed recalls: "When I got to be around 14 I told Jennifer that I wanted to get down with Howie Tee, because I knew that he was really doing it. He was the *man* in the neighborhood when it came to making music. I asked Jennifer because I didn't want to just walk up on these grown-ass people and demand shit. Luckily I made a good impression." Howie remembers that first meeting quite well: "I knew Ed since he was probably about 10, because Jennifer lived on my block. One day she came to my house and said: 'My cousin Eddie wants to rap for you.' And because he's Jamaican, I thought he'd do some chanting/DJ type of stuff ["DJ" used in the Jamaican sense, which is akin to an American MC]. Ed surprised me by asking me to put 'Impeach The President' [by the Honeydrippers, a classic breakbeat] on, and that's where it started."

Ed was the MC that Howie had been waiting for, and both of them had nothing to lose in taking a shot at getting Ed in the game. Ed had a novelty edge since he was so young, but he also had high-level skills, certainly more than any other MCs his age at the time. After they worked together a bit more in Howie's basement, it was clear that their chemistry was fully in place, and an album was recorded on a Howie's 8-track in 1987 and early 1988.

Although Howie was fully in control on the production front, Ed had plenty of input, which the elder producer seemed happy to use. Ed says: "I would go through records with him, pick stuff out and then he would chop it up and loop it and make it into a hit. Howie even offered me production credit on the album because he knew that I was deep into the music, even if I didn't know how to work the equipment. I had ultimate respect for him because he did that, but I declined, since he was the real producer on the album."

"The *Youngest In Charge* album was all recorded in my mom's basement, on an 8-track," Howie says. "Half of the 8-track was the board, and half of it was the reel to reel. It was an all-in-one. And it was actually a 7-track, I guess, because I needed one track to synch up my drum machine, to add extra beats to certain tracks." Howie had to work with Ed to form his rhymes into actual hip-hop *songs*. He explains: "Ed never had hooks and never knew how to break his rhymes up into bars, so I had to show him how to do that. As he rapped, as soon as he reached 16 bars I had to tell him to stop. And then I'd come up with the hook."

Recording the album wasn't the problem. That went quickly, since Howie had dope beats for days and Ed had overflowing rhyme books from years of work. The hard part was *selling* the album to labels.

Howie ran into many roadblocks shopping it. "We had the whole album recorded and then I shopped it for a year. To this day, I still don't know why it was so hard to shop that record," Howie says. "A lot of people just wasn't feeling Ed. They weren't hearing what we was hearing. Island, Jive, Polygram, they all passed. We went by Def Jam and Russell [Simmons] actually wanted to buy Ed's lyrics for Slick Rick, because he liked Ed's storytelling! Luckily Corey Robinson at Profile took a chance and signed it. They was looking for their next big rap group, since Run-DMC wasn't selling as well."

Ed had a more zen approach to the process. He says: "It wasn't that tough for me to deal with the fact that no one was picking up the album, because I didn't expect the world, I just wanted to get a start. All my hopes and dreams were in the future, but they just came quicker than I thought they would. When everything started happening it was just a blessing to me."

Once Profile came on-board, it was a pretty easy process – the album as it appears is almost exactly like the 8-track version that Howie had shopped to them, even down to the order of the songs. Howie recalls: "I didn't even know about that kind of stuff back then. We didn't think about the sequencing at all. The way the songs went onto the reel after we mixed them was how they were sequenced on the album." Ed notes that Profile did have one stipulation, considering Ed's young age – no hard stuff: "I couldn't even use some of the stuff with profanity and harder rhymes that I had written, with new tracks we wanted to put on the album. Profile turned down some of the harder rhymes that I had. So I actually had to adjust myself, since I lot of my rhymes were written hard like that, even then, at 15 years old. For example, I had a song called 'The Mission' that Profile refused to put out. It was recorded, but never appeared."

One thing was never in question, even though some may have been surprised: Ed wrote all his own rhymes. Howie says: "Nobody ever wrote a lyric for Ed, never one. They were all his. Nobody ever even gave him any ideas. When the record came out, people definitely noticed Ed for his talent, not because he was so young." Ed adds: "Everybody always asked me if I really wrote my own rhymes, because I was so young. And I'd be like 'Fuck you, I'll write a rhyme about *you*, right now.' It never really bothered me, though, since I knew the real deal."

Even considering the novelty of Ed's youth, the album stands very firmly on its own as a hip-hop classic, the ultimate in late '80s New York brag swagger, with hits like "I Got It Made" and "Think About It," which showed off Ed's battle stances, and also Howie Tee's masterful, never-endingly catchy productions.

"That record showed the world that kids are people, too," says Ed. "That I can do this, and do this well, with skill. I might be young, but don't judge my intelligence level or my ability. It was like me having a corporate job at 15. I accomplished something beyond what people expected." It was important for Howie, too. He says: "For me, that was the album that introduced me as a producer. Even though I was doing other things, like UTFO and the Real Roxanne, people didn't really know who was behind it. But that album was all me."

Howie adds: "People weren't even saying that it was a classic at the time, but it definitely came to be known that way. I knew it was a classic back then. We had that record for a year and I still liked everything about it after all that time. None of it sounded outdated, even after all the shopping we did and all the time that passed. I could have changed things, but I didn't want to. The production was solid, and the storytelling and Ed's rap style was just amazing."

"That album was all done as a demo, and on an 8-track reel-to-reel," Ed reminds us. "And it came off, which just goes to show you that you don't need multi-million dollar studios. You can do it with anything. Making good music is the bottom line."

TRACKS

Taxing

Ed: That was always my favorite track, but I don't know so much if it still is, because I'm so far advanced now. I can definitely hear my energy back at that time on that track. I think that was the first track we recorded for the album.

Howie: There was a Beatles sample we wanted to use, but no one could sample the Beatles back then. We still liked the feeling and wanted to use it, so Questar [Welsh, the album's engineer] played it on guitar, and changed up the melody a little, so that we didn't get in trouble.

I Got It Made

Ed: That single came out in 1988 and took off immediately, as soon as radio got it. It was in rotation right away, and I couldn't believe it. Right around then I played the Apollo, one of my first shows. I was in high school and at the Apollo and it was blowing my head. That song was just a mental joint to me, to tell people about the level that I was on. When they shot the video for that song it was freezing outside, like my whole face was frozen! That's why I've got my hands in my pockets in most of the shots. We had a low budget for the video so I guess that's why we was outside. I really love that video, though. Chica Bruce did that one, and also did the video for "Think About It."

Howie: That's definitely one of my favorites on the record. It was the first single, came out in April 1988. Profile took a while to put the album out after the single. That's just how they wanted to do it. People gravitated towards those lyrics and that track right away. Like with Ed saying things like "alligator soufflé" and all that. Once it came out the general public definitely understood and loved that record, even if the labels hadn't. I wasn't even around when they did that video. That was more Profile's thing. I was recording Chubb Rock's record at the time. There was a mix of that track called the "Businesslike Mix," with a totally different beat. I made that one, too, and I called it that because it was more R&B-ish to me, more relaxed and laid-back. It was the b-side of the single, because the label just wanted a remix. Ed used to battle kids in the hallway of his junior high school and those rhymes were the ones that he used in those battles. He didn't have any rhyme books, he just had all his stuff memorized!

I'm The Magnificent

Ed: I'm gonna keep it real, I didn't really like that song, even from the very beginning. I loved the lyrics, but the beat was just too commercial for me. I like street beats, and that was just too springy for me. When Howie remixed the track, I liked it. The second version was great.

Club Scene

Howie: That was the only song where Ed didn't already have rhymes written, he had to write those for the song right then. We wanted an up-tempo type of track. We did that one while we were mixing the album. Back then in the clubs there was a lot of up-tempo stuff, so I wanted to get some of that going on Ed's album. I didn't intend for it to be a single, I just wanted to make it available if anyone wanted to hear something like that from him. The female rapper on there is Dee Dee Scott, my daughter's mother. She did background singing on hooks and stuff like that on other parts in the album.

Ed: I always liked that track. That hip-house style was really big at the time and I wanted something for the house music fans. When I was younger I'd go to the Shelter and Limelight [dance clubs in Manhattan] and hear that stuff.

Hoedown

Ed: That was just a story I had about some hoes, so we just kind of put a whole bunch of rhymes together. When I heard those banjo samples Howie had, I knew we could use those lyrics on that song. Howie put it together nice. Profile didn't mind too much even though I was so young, because it was about girls and not violence. I was definitely nice with the ladies at 15, on a whole other level of the game.

Think About It

Ed: Those were a lot of battle rhymes I had used in past battles, and I switched up a couple styles on there, lyrically. Chica Bruce did the video for that track, and that one took me to a whole other level when it came to videos. People today are still like: "Yo, what was that video with the Hovercraft?" There was two guys chasing me all over the place in a car, in a boat, and then I hopped in a Hovercraft like James Bond. I escaped in a helicopter at the end. That was pretty high budget at the time.

Ak-Shun

Ed: That song was just a dedication to my homey, my DJ. I'd known him for so many years, we used to cut class in junior high and go make tracks. If you're gonna ride with me and be my DJ, then you're going to have your own song.

Howie: Akshun was Ed's DJ, but I did some of the scratching on the album, stuff that we did before I even met Akshun, before he came into the group. I met Ed first, without Akshun.

Monster Jam

Howie: I was definitely a big go-go [music] fan, so that's where that flavor came from. We replayed that over. Spanador, whose name is Alex Mosely, the guitar player from Lisa Lisa and Cult Jam, played that.

The Bush

Ed: That's a dedication to where I come from: Flatbush, Brooklyn. Brooklyn is always just on some next shit. It's some straight "Take what you want" shit. Back in 1988 and 1989 it didn't matter as much where you came from because it was becoming more worldwide, the hip-hop scene. But I've always represented Brooklyn.

Fly M.C.

Ed: That was just one rhyme [laughs]! It might seem like it is, hearing it today, but it's not Slick Rick influenced, because I wrote that before Rick got on. I wrote that in my house and I remember kickin' it to my brother Wayne and he flipped out. That was a very old rhyme before we recorded it.

Howie: That was the first track we did when we started recording the album. That's one of my favorites. I just love the stories he tells on there.

Heds And Dreds

Ed: That was some last minute shit, I just wrote that in the studio while we was there, like we had some extra tape or something. We did that one at Questar's place.

Howie: We also did that one late in the album process, when we were mixing the rest of the record. I wanted to have something on there that showed Ed's Jamaican roots, so we did that one. It obviously came very naturally to him.

ULTRAMAGNETIC MCs

Critical Beatdown

(Next Plateau, 1988)

"Other groups were just plain weed. We were more like angel dust."

No one would dispute the fact that legendary lyricist Kool Keith has a way with words. But instead of rhyming this time, he's a capella, over a cel phone from either New York or Los Angeles (he won't say), referring to the group that gave birth to his hall-of-fame status: the South Bronx's Ultramagnetic MCs.

Keith isn't finished yet. "If you were at a show and someone lit up [Angel] Dust [aka PCP], you'd be like: 'Wow, who's smoking that shit?' It was foreign. That burnt plastic smell, the embalming fluid. People would just walk away. And that's what we were: the Dust of the Industry."

Don't get it twisted: Keith's metaphor is meant in the most positive way. He's talking about the legacy of one of the most respected and least understood groups in the history of hip-hop.

"Dust" is known for producing "aural and visual hallucinations and an altered perception of time and space." That was an astute diagnosis for fans who became engulfed in the Ultra universe of the late '80s. It was a sonic world known for hard beats, left turns and outer-space stylings. "Ultra was all about never, ever being 'normal,'" says head producer, group patriarch and Keith's "straight man" lyrical partner Ced-Gee. "We was always out of the norm, yesterday and today."

"Our stuff was somewhat catered to the dust smokers," Keith continues, never one to leave a provocative point unattended. "We definitely stuck out that way."

Ultra stuck out in many ways. Musically for sure. Their aloof, hyper-intelligent "astronauts of hip-hop" image was a major calling card. But the real reason was because of the whole package, and what it yielded. In 1988 they made a universally-revered and undeniably classic album for as much money as their peers were spending on the sound system in one of their new cars.

Public Enemy, Eric B & Rakim, Ice-T and Boogie Down Productions had major labels (Columbia, Universal, Sire/Warner and Jive/RCA, respectively) on their side. In the music industry, game had finally started to recognize game. Conglomerates that had been concerned only with pop stars started to scoop hip-hop masters from the streets, realizing that they'd slept on the rap world too long. And artists started to finally see some money from the artform they'd put so much sweat equity into.

Ultramagnetic didn't have major label loot. Signed to growingly-popular and artist-friendly, but shallow-pocketed indie label Next Plateau, they carried their equipment on their backs and rode for hours during hazy nights and even hazier mornings on empty, graffiti-splashed trains, from the Bronx to the outer edges of Queens. They drank beer out of cans and ate pizza out of cardboard boxes. And they never once complained about it. Because they were a team, and they were onto something great. That something great was *Critical Beatdown*, their masterwork. One of the greatest hip-hop albums of the '80s. Arguably of all time. They did a hell of a lot, with very little.

BEAMING ABOARD THE "STREET STAR TREK"

The most popular reason to listen to the Ultramagnetic MCs, if you were a true hip-hop fan, was because you never knew what was lurking around the next corner. The beats were unassailable: hard and amazingly innovative. Even danceable, in their own angular way. Lyrically, though, is where the roller coaster started gaining speed. The words on any Ultra track were pure rope-a-dope. One second you're hearing a brag that doesn't make you think too deeply, impresses you but doesn't shake you up, and fits in nicely with any other innovative 1988 track. That was Ced-Gee. Even despite the technical content in his rhymes, he was still the straight man.

The next moment you are faced with a rhyme like this:

I'ma pull out your ears 'cause I'm sick
Travelin' hard
Ill, off, another lunatic
Smackin' germs, eatin' bugs, bitin' mouse
Roaches wander
But I'm travelin'
Onto Bellevue
'Cause I'm sick
-- "Travelin' At The Speed Of Thought"

And there was Kool Keith. The unstable element. The guy who would turn your head all the way around and then twist it back. Keith had a lot of competition in the lyrical innovation department during the Golden Age, but he still stands alone. You could take a complex lyrical peer like

Rakim and dissect his lyrics, translate them into English. With Keith it was more like you needed a clinical psychologist to help you get to the essence. Rapper Special Ed, another late '80s genius lyricist, explains Keith in this way: "He was on a whole other plateau, he was writing rhymes for people to figure out. Stuff that was so deep in his mind that you had to work to decipher it. You'd have to listen to an Ultramagnetic track five to ten times to understand what he was really trying to say, and see if it made sense." He adds, with a satisfied smirk: "And most of the time it did."

When Ced and Keith combined – music and lyrics, Earth and Jupiter, fire and water – the power of the Ultramagnetic MCs was impossible to ignore. As Keith says today: "Back then we were definitely convinced that we were on the U.S.S. Enterprise. We were the Street Star Trek."

In 1988 it can be argued that no album used the combination of imagination and top-level studio skills to as much advantage as the 15-track platter *Critical Beatdown*. Featuring lyricist Keith (Keith Thornton), producer/MC Ced-Gee (Cedric Miller), DJ Moe Luv (Maurice Smith) and occasional co-producer and hype man T. R. Love (Trevor Randolph), the group was both street-raw and futuristically complex.

UN-REALITY RAP

The album's cover, the first experience that most listeners had with the group, pointed out an interesting juxtaposition between the real lives of Ultra members and the lyrics on their tracks. Standing in front of a brick building with jailhouse bars, straddling crumbling debris, four hardcore b-boys, all dressed to the nines in street chic, sneer with determined and confident stares. The lanky Ced, laced with a gold rope adorned by a crab, is wearing a shiny, gold-plated, long-sleeve shirt with "Ultra Magnetic" spilling out over two lines. T.R. and Moe scowl from stage right. The only comic relief amongst the assembled ruins is Kool Keith's sun-wincing countenance, framed by a sideways, very out-of-place Budweiser hat. The group shows their determination and their style, but they're not standing in front of a rented luxury car or other item of conspicuous consumption. They are in their element, standing in the streets that they walk every day.

As a recent reissue of the album (on Roadrunner) shows in the liner notes, the original, previously unseen, un-cropped photos actually have them standing on top of three assumedly dead bodies, or at least vanquished foes. Keith explains: "Those guys were supposed to represent images of different rappers that were out at that time. Nobody specific, just different scenarios. They were composites, different pieces of the industry." Ced adds: "We was beating down the competition. I mean, the album was called *Critical Beatdown*, so it's not like we were going to be in front of a Rolls Royce. We were there to make our mark, not look good." It should be noted that Eric B & Rakim are sitting on the hood of a Rolls Royce, most assuredly a rented one, on the cover of their 1988 album *Follow The Leader*.

But in opposition to the album's cover, Ultra went the opposite way with its words. Lyrically mixing concrete brags with Keith's outer-space and often cannibalistic imagery, Ultramagnetic could be considered "un-reality rap" – the diametric opposite of a group like their 1988 peers N.W.A., who glorified the hard knocks of inner city life. Keith says: "Me and Ced was from the projects, and we could have easily put our pain on that album and rapped about things that were fucked up. But we just had fun. It was definitely a kind of escape. I'd see bodies laying down every day, I'd see people putting sheets over other peoples' heads, crackheads, I'd hear gunshots all the time. So we was like: 'Fuck it, let's do some space shit.' We were definitely illusioning ourselves away from that for a minute. I didn't have to write about that shit because I lived through it. Most of the people who wrote about that kind of stuff lived in the suburbs. It would have been monotonous to talk about reality all the time. We were like authors of something else, even though we were living in that life."

"THERE ARE NO RULES AS LONG AS YOUR SHIT IS RIGHT"

Looking at the big picture, what Ultra brought to the table was an amazingly potent combination, ruled by a desire to create music and lyrics unlike anything that had come before them. Ced-Gee makes a very simple and crucial point about the group's mission: "Music is one of the few things where you can make a statement, so why would you want to be like everybody else?" Ced also reminds today's hip-hop fans about the doors that he and Keith broke down on the lyrical side: "At the time there was a certain way that you were supposed to rap – ABC, ABC. Rakim took people out of the screaming mode and showed people that you can *talk* and be fly. Ultra showed people that you didn't necessarily have to even rhyme, if your flow was on time. It broke all the rules. It said: 'There are no rules as long as your shit is right.'" He adds, addressing the group's lyrical complexity: "They may not follow you all the time, but if the beat is bad enough, they'll like it anyways."

The legendary DJ Red Alert, a longtime fan and crucial early supporter of the group on his Kiss 98 radio show, recalls: "In 1988, everyone was coming out with something different, and Ultra definitely fit right into that. They was really abstract, almost beyond reach. A lot of people were influenced by them." They were also amazingly innovative on production. Legendary producer Prince Paul, the mastermind behind such groups as De La Soul, Gravediggaz and, more recently, the Handsome Boy Modeling School, recalls: "'Ego Trippin" [Ultra's breakthrough single] freaked me out when I first heard it, because nobody had ever really looped a beat before. Crash Crew did it with 'Get Up And Dance' in 1980, but that was without a sampler. When I heard that first Ultra song I was like: 'Wow, you can *do* that??!' People take sampling for granted now, but back then it was crazy."

Gang Starr's DJ Premier, arguably the most influential producer of hip-hop's modern age, has this to say about the Ultra one-two punch: "They were saying shit that no MC was saying back then. Some far-out space shit. They was like the astronauts of hip-hop. And at the same time Ced-Gee's beats were amazing, they were so hard. The group just sounded like The Bronx, you know? Where hip-hop came from. And I'm definitely the aftermath of what they started. I bow to those cats."

Ultra took beat-making and lyricism to levels that had not yet been imagined, even as hip-hop music plowed head-first into its teens. Public Enemy and Eric B & Rakim broke new ground every time they went into the studio. By 1988, the year that they were both making their sophomore albums, they also had the press watching their every move, waiting for their next single, and – at times – their next controversy. Those groups had pressure, they had responsibilities, they had contracts with major labels to make good on. Ultramagnetic worked on a different plane, as they holed up in their Ultra Lab studio and at Queens' remote Studio 1212, mostly ignored by the commercial media, garnering a mention by *Billboard*'s esteemed columnist Nelson George in January of 1988 that called them "highly regarded" and little else.

When *Critical Beatdown* dropped in the early fall of 1988, even those who were already hipped to the group through a course of multiple singles were not ready for what the album held. And while it only sold around 65,000 copies – a fraction of the numbers racked up by its aforementioned peers – it was nonetheless one of the most important records of the year, because of their sound and the fact that people today still don't fully understand what lyrical genius/madman Kool Keith was talking about in his rhymes.

As longtime Ultra fan and frequent Keith collaborator Kutmasta Kurt explains: "Lyrically they didn't rap about things that people could easily understand. The lyrics were just very abstract. Any kind of pop music, even now, is about having hits, and those hits have words that people can remember and repeat. Ultra's lyrics and hooks weren't that way." He adds: "If you were a fan of rap, you loved Ultra and you knew that they were good. If you were just a music consumer who kind-of liked rap music, the kind of person that has to like your record if you're going to move a lot of units, then you'd hear the group and be like: 'What is *that*?!?'"

So much came out of the Ultra spaceship of 1988 – an Earthbound sci-fi movie that blasted off from a bedroom in the Bronx. These guys weren't going to get hands raised in the air. They were more about getting your finger up to scratch your head in wonder, or disbelief.

ULTRA'S EARLY YEARS

Ultramagnetic was far from an overnight sensation. The Ultra phenomenon had been years in the making, and they had always been ahead of their time.

It all started in 1984, with high school classmates Cedric Miller and Keith Thornton. "Me and Ced would read a lot of space and UFO books and astronaut magazines," Keith says, reminiscing about the group's beginnings. "And one day I just said: 'How would these words sound on some ill tracks?' We would experiment, and make them fit on those songs."

Ced recalls conversations with a young Keith before they first recorded: "Keith was pretty weird in high school and I always told Keith that he just had to be himself. He's just abstract, and even when he tries to be normal it comes off as being funny. It's just the way he is." Keith has his own recollections: "I'm just a different person, I'm not like a programmed robot. I'm into spaceships and the future. I was just a weird kid."

Ced-Gee and Keith dubbed themselves the Ultramagnetic MCs, and they set about injecting a radioactive catalyst into the shape of hip-hop to come. Ced says that the group had one unified mind when they were setting out on their quest to transfer energy onto wax: "We said we were gonna be on another metaphysical plane." The name came from Keith. DJ Moe Luv recalls the concept: "Ultra was the highest form, and magnetic was to get people to attach to us."

Taking shape under a loosely organized production umbrella called Mastermind Productions (which included Boogie Down Productions' Scott La Rock and KRS-One, among others), Ultramagnetic's initial form included several different MCs. Keith and Ced both started out with their own solo recording plans and intents, but after cutting a demo together on a Ced-produced song called "Make You Shake" in 1984, the duo liked their chemistry and decided to give it a go. Ced's cousin Moe Luv (aka Moe Love) was a club and party DJ in Brooklyn at the time, and was recruited to fill the space behind turntables 1 and 2. "Even from the start we were trying to be ahead of our time," recalls Ced today. "We thought that everybody was sounding the same, so we wanted to be different."

"At first we did solo demos and that didn't work out so we did some group stuff and we shopped it like crazy," Ced remembers. Unable to find the label interest they sought, Ultramagnetic took matters into their own hands in 1985, forming a short-lived label called Diamond International with DNA, a radio personality on WNWK out of Newark. They released "Make You Shake" with "To Give You Love" on the flipside. The record got a smattering of attention on New York's airwaves, enough to do a second pressing of what Ced says was 500 copies. This time around, though, they put what was to become their breakthrough on the b-side: a revolutionary song called "Ego Trippin'," featuring a clunky, uber-funky, chopped beat sourced from Melvin Bliss' "Synthetic Substitution," carefully-placed piano stabs and an undeniable amount of MC charisma. The song begins by dissing Peter Piper and his "childish rhyme" and rolls at a steady rate of ten mind-boggles per minute from there.

"AS THE RECORD JUST TURNS, YOU LEARN": EGO TRIPPIN'

As the record just turns
You learn, plus burn
By the flame of the lyrics
Which cooks the human brain
Providing overheating knowledge
By means, causing pain
-- Kool Keith, from "Ego Trippin'"

Moe recalls: "We put that second pressing out real quick and Red Alert was fascinated with 'Ego Trippin'.' He started playing it, then [other NYC hip-hop radio giants] Chuck Chillout, then Marley Marl and Mr. Magic. And at that time the record wasn't even in stores yet, we just had test pressings, but the DJs was loving it. Red Alert took us to Next Plateau and that's when we signed the deal."

Red Alert recalls hearing Ultra's first work of genius: "DNA brought me that record on a test pressing, and I had worked on a track [that never came out] with Keith and Ced years before that, so I already knew them, although Keith was known more as a dancer back then. I liked it, and I played it on my show on Kiss. That beat really grabbed my attention and the stuff they was saying on there was out of this world. I took them to Eddie O'Loughlin at Next Plateau, and the rest is history." O'Loughlin recalls: "They were the most unique performers I had ever heard at the time. 'Ego Trippin',' wow, that was something. Great beat and wild lyrics."

"Ego Trippin'" was unleashed onto the world at large in early 1986 on Next Plateau. The song's mix of rapid-fire, non-linear and abstract imagery had precedents in the work of Rammellzee, the Treacherous Three, T La Rock, Melle Mel and Spoonie Gee, but the combination of the muscular, minimal track itself with Keith's and Ced's aggressive, technical lyrics instantly took hip-hop to a new level. "With 'Ego Trippin'' we had the sales to get on radio but radio was saying to us that the vocabulary was too big," quips Ced. Moe says: "Ced and Keith was way ahead of their time, especially in '86. People didn't know what the hell they was saying [laughs], but it just sounded *good*."

The attention that got them to Next Plateau was no fluke. Ultra arrived at just the right time, a breath of fresh air in 1986, an important transitional year. The scene was easing out of the excess of an era which saw Melle Mel turn from a street poet into a leather-bound S&M comic book character. Run-DMC had been the new sheriff in town for three years, slapping partytime rap in the face with no-frills reality and fresh-faced everyday-isms. But there was still room for more innovation than anyone at the time could have imagined. Aside from moving minds on the lyrical tip, "Ego Trippin'" was an aural breakthrough, bolstered by Ced's recording expertise. Keith notes: "When we did 'Ego Trippin'' we were at the end of the DMX drums, the mechanical sound, and the beginning of sampling." The sampler would play a large role in both Ultramagnetic's sound and also their enduring legacy.

SILVER WALLS AND THE ULTRA LAB: SP-12 IN THE HOUSE

Ced-Gee's storied 16-Track "Ultra Lab" studio was actually his silver-wallpaper-lined bedroom, located at 169th Street and Washington Ave in the Bronx. It was where all Ultramagnetic activity started. And aside from being Ultra's liftoff pad, it was also an important incubation unit for the equally ground-breaking rap crew Boogie Down Productions. Ced, in fact, introduced DJ/producer Scott La Rock and KRS-One, who was then living in a homeless shelter. KRS remembers the Ultra Lab and Ced's warmth and ear for talent: "They were in Webster Houses, in the projects, and it was crazy to have all that stuff. In his room was his bed, and then all of his equipment. Not even a TV. Ced was an engineer/producer type. Every week his moms was buying him some new equipment. I'd go to his house and I'm very appreciative because I know I was stinkin', my clothes was dirty, I smelled like the shelter. Ced-Gee didn't look at all that. He looked at my talent and I will never forget that, to this day. There would be no KRS without Ced-Gee."

With help and inspiration from Ced's younger brother Patrick, the newly unveiled Emu SP-12 sampler [an updated version, the SP-1200, was introduced in 1987] became a compliant instrument in the hands of the highly musical and inventive Ced-Gee. Together with fellow SP-12 master and recording engineer Paul C (last name McKasty), whom the group used as an engineer and brainstormer for the recording of *Critical Beatdown*, Ced had an exciting new technology at his fingertips. KRS says: "At that time [1985-86] Ced-Gee was the only person in the Bronx with an SP-12, and he was just the absolute man when it came to that machine."

Ced and Paul C gleefully played mad scientist with the SP-12, tweaking it to maximum capacity, along the way giving technical advice to future rap legends like Scott La Rock as well as Eric B. "[Paul C] knew things about the SP-12 that I didn't know and I knew things he didn't know, so we started doing things together," Ced recalls. "That's when we went to the apex of what could be done with the SP. You had to have imagination to do some of the shit we were doing. We could do things that would bug people out 'cause they wasn't in the manual!" If Paul C hadn't been murdered in July of 1989, we can only guess what further heights the technology could have been taken to.

Ced's use of the SP-12 was important for more than the sonics it produced. He was also a pioneer in bedroom technology, especially in the Bronx. Ced says: "Marley Marl had [an SP-12] in his studio and they had one at Unique Studios, but I was the first person in the ghetto who had an SP-12. My brother Patrick used to read up on music stuff and he told me about the SP at the time. It cost $2,500. And when I bought it, Ultra was formed. We broke down the sampling door, because we said you don't have to sample loops, you can chop your samples up and rearrange things." Moe Luv adds, to clarify: "We was the first *group* to do sampling. Marley Marl was the first person to use one, with 'The Bridge' [from 1985] but we were the second, right after him."

ULTRA'S MAGNETIC POWER

Bobbito Garcia, noted journalist, footwear expert, DJ and label-head (Fondle 'Em Records and Fruitmeat), is an Ultramagnetic fan of the highest order. He explains why: "People might not understand them, but Ultramagnetic is one of the best hip-hop groups ever." He adds: "I think that some of Ultra's fans don't completely understand them, and I think that there are some Ultra records that even Ultra doesn't understand! That's the beauty of it, they appeal to a different emotion in people. When I heard their song 'Funky' for the first time I just lost my mind. No one had ever touched my surreal side like that. They just broke all the rules."

Prince Paul, who has worked with some of the greatest MCs on the planet in his years behind the boards, still remembers the impact of Keith's lyrics on "Ego Trippin'": "My nephew took a sheet of paper out and wrote that song down, lyric for lyric, and memorized it. Lots of people were doing that kind of thing, analyzing what Keith was saying. That's how amazed we all were by it." Paul's co-worker, Posdnuos of De La Soul, told journalist Angus Batey: "I think the only people that we looked to for a blueprint when we were making *3 Feet High and Rising* were the Ultramagnetic MCs. They were very different, how they rhymed..."

The Ultramagnetic group sound was a classic two-MC lineup at its core, and both rappers had distinct styles and duties on the mic. "Our style was Intelligent B-Boy," says Ced. "We took hip, intelligent vocabulary and made it street. And we broke down the door so you didn't have to rhyme every line, you can rhyme one word or a whole line. When you hear people today who rhyme one word for most of a track, that's something that Keith invented." Kutmasta Kurt, who was a college DJ on Stanford's KZSU when "Ego Trippin'" hit, recalls: "I remember the first time I heard 'Ego Trippin',' I was like: 'Hey, they're not even rhyming! This is funny.' But it definitely sounded amazing whether they were or not. So much so that a lot of people didn't even notice. I don't think anyone had ever done that before them, and no one has really done it since."

Keith says: "Sometimes we'd be like: 'Let's take this one way out, we don't want the crowd to even try and figure this one out.' We were getting off on making records that were so out-there that we didn't care if people understood what we were talking about. We'd just put 'em on funky beats and make some stories out of them. Everyone was trying to use words that were 30-feet-long back then, there was definitely a big-words craze in the Bronx at that time. All the '-ation' stuff. Approximation, assimilation. So I went into chemical formulas, and stuff that didn't rhyme."

Lord Finesse, a fellow Bronx-resident and one of the most respected lyricists of the '90s, discusses the Ced/Keith dichotomy that was central to the Ultra allure: "It was always about matching dope beats with Keith's wildness. I mean, in his rhymes Keith will take you to Central Park and then Germany and Japan, and you'll get lost trying to follow that nigga. But with Ced's beats everything just complemented everything, the music and the rhymes. If Keith was to rhyme a capella you'd really get thrown off. Keith was definitely in danger of being too complex, because all that scientist shit is just too much for the average consumer to digest. You need a chaser behind it."

1987 AND THE SPEED OF THOUGHT

For those that missed the spaceship that Ced and Keith were on when "Ego Trippin'" hit the world in '86, then 1987's "Travelin' At The Speed Of Thought" single (also on Next Plateau) gave sleepers another chance to catch up. Using a sample swiped from the Troggs' frat rock evergreen "Wild Thing," Ced and Keith were off again. By now attracting special attention from DJ Red Alert on Kiss 98, Ultra were equally aided by their association with burgeoning rap phenoms Boogie Down Productions (Ced, although not properly credited or paid, was a major force in the making of BDP's 1987 classic *Criminal Minded*). Ced recalls: "Me and Scott [La Rock], we grew up together on the West side [of the South Bronx]. He lived in the projects and we lived in the tenements. He'd come upstairs, we'd put the beat together in the Ultra Lab, and then we'd go and knock it out at the studio. *Criminal Minded* and *Critical Beatdown* were really all the same thing, in a way."

The album version of "Travelin'" was a much more together affair than the single – tighter on production and more bizarre than the looser, possibly Beastie Boys-influenced rock-rap of the single, with Kool Keith lines like:

As I take your mind off
To a new track
To tame ducks, how to act
Respect me, when I whip your brain
Skip your brain, and dip your brain
In a lotion
While I take your skull...

The single's b-side, "MCs Ultra (Part II)," brought more Ultra trademarks to the table, making it in reality a "double a-side." The beat was a frenetic, booming affair with guitar stabs and more amazing SP-12 chops. Keith yet again bends reality:

Perhaps on the mic
I continue, elevating
By a physical source
Through particles
Which burn the human ear
Into dust...

1988: SINGLED-OUT

1988's "Watch Me Now," their fourth single ("Mentally Mad," not included on the album, had preceded it), upped the ante again. Over a brutally funky beat punctuated by sampled piano stabs, Ced's and Keith's tag-team style moved from the present quickly into the future of rap lyricism:

Sometimes I rhyme off-beat
Awkward -
But different - with the rhythm
Back and forth, one, two, then I give 'em
A chance to see
The world's greatest MC
-- Ced-Gee

On the mic, innovating this patter-an
You fell off, your brain is on Satur-an
Take steps, and climb my ladder

And climb, climb, climb
Taste the rhythm, and clock the time
-- Kool Keith

Now that abstract groups like De La Soul, A Tribe Called Quest, Organized Konfusion, Freestyle Fellowship and the entire backpacker nation have followed in Ultra's wake, these lyrical notions don't seem so extreme. But back in 1988 it left fans scratching their heads. As Ced relates, it was their club and radio audio hangovers that were leading fans to the record stores, not the lyrics: "Some people understood it, but lots of people told us that they bought [our stuff mostly] because the beats were dope. They said: 'I didn't know what y'all was talking about, but I bought it anyways.' That's just always gonna be Ultra."

CJ Moore, an engineer at 1212 Studios, described this complexity to Dave Tompkins in *Big Daddy* magazine by saying: "The average rapper was not understanding that [Ultra] were touching down on actual philosophy on different things. They were hitting you with poetry in a different context. It didn't have to make sense because of the cadence of the music. The music makes you totally forget what's going on. It was very literate. It was like Ornette Coleman had stepped in. It didn't match anything. It was following nothing."

At times, misunderstandings about the group's lyrics went to extremes, as proven with reaction to the group's album track "Break North." Ced remembers: "One magazine that wrote us up back then said that we was demon worshippers, because of 'Break North.' I guess because of a lyric saying that I chopped rappers up and references to bones. And then about going to see the devil in a bus. All that voodoo type of stuff. We thought that was pretty funny." Keith adds: "I wrote a lot about brains in my lyrics. People thought we were Satanic or cannibalistic [laughs]. We thought people would just smoke a joint and sit up and listen to this shit. But a lot of people thought it was really crazy."

Bobbito Garcia views Keith's lyrical artistry from another angle: "Keith is definitely more bugged-out than he appears, but I think that a lot of people underestimate how truly insightful and intelligent he is. Behind a lot of the stuff he says there's [a lot of] meaning. Crazy metaphorical meaning that people will maybe never figure out."

After a string of single-based doses of genius, the world had been sufficiently primed for the group's magnum opus, *Critical Beatdown*. In fact, it was past time, as Keith relates: "We were singled-out before we even put out the album. The president of the record company [Eddie O'Loughlin] was like: 'You guys got about 20 singles out, why don't you do an album? We didn't even think about doing an album at the time."

STUDIO 1212 AND THE BEGINNINGS OF A BEATDOWN

With an assignment in hand, the group set about making new tracks, which traveled not only at the speed of thought, but quite literally across New York, via the mass transit system. Almost all initial work and brainstorming was done at the Ultra Lab, but the finished products were laid to rest in way-out Jamaica, Queens, at a tiny studio in an ominous-looking warehouse at the tentacle tips of the E and F subway lines. It was the soon-to-be-legendary Studio 1212, owned by Mick Carrey and helmed by production genius Paul C, who can rightfully be declared Ultramagnetic member #5.

"[Studio] 1212 was in a warehouse, definitely a low-key spot, like a Bat-Cave type of thing on the third floor [of 9232 Union Hall]," Keith recalls. "Definitely a stash-away spot. The building had a dark feel to it." Regardless of the "Escape from New York"-ness of the surroundings, working with Paul elevated Ultra's sound to higher levels than ever, and the communal vibe was always strong. Ced explains: "The vibe there at 1212 was always relaxed, just like at the Ultra Lab. When you're recording, no matter where you're at, it always just depends on your engineer. Paul was such a good engineer that you knew you'd get things done." Moe remembers: "It was a small place, but it was cool. Paul C had a lot of his records there, that's where he stored them. Lots of cool breakbeats that we didn't even have. It gave us a lot of flexibility to have all that stuff there at our fingertips."

"When we were full-on into making *Critical Beatdown*, we went to 1212 about every other day," Ced says. He adds: "It was a big pain to get there. We had to take the F train all the way to Parsons, so it was kind of out there. We'd be there all times of the day or night, lugging equipment. But it was worth it." Moe Luv proves how much they wanted to be there by how much they had to carry: "Since nobody had a car back then, we'd have to take the subway all the way. We'd have to bring Ced's Akai 12-Track [to "bounce" the initial tracks done at the Ultra Lab into equipment at 1212] and my turntables with us. It was crazy. One time we just stayed there for a whole weekend, Friday to Sunday. We slept right there in the studio, on the floor."

Because of a low recording budget, the group made the most of it by recording at off-peak hours, making their commute there even more surreal. Keith recalls: "Making the record was pretty tough, really. When we'd do the initial work at Ced's, we'd be up late and would come out of Webster projects at four in the morning. It was a strain." Nonetheless, he also looks back fondly on late nights at 1212: "We always had these graveyard sessions, like 9 pm to 9 am, because it was a cheaper rate. I don't think that a lot of groups could handle that kind of schedule. It was definitely a pain to get there, but back then it wasn't about cars. It was cool to ride the train, to look at chicks and all the different people. It was ill because we'd be leaving that fuckin' studio at dawn. You'd be getting on the train and you'd be all dirty from last night, seeing people going to work. People had no idea that you were just coming from finishing 'Ease Back' all night. You're just getting home and people are going to work with cologne on. We didn't mind, though. Because we loved making records back then. I loved going to the studio."

By the time the album was being recorded, Ultramagnetic were at the peak of their musical powers, and had a confidence that allowed them to tackle just about any task put in front of them. Even ideas that sounded great in the Ultra Lab could be trashed if an even stronger inspiration came along once they hit 1212. Keith explains: "We would sometimes stop in mid-air on a track and then trash the whole thing and just start again. Not many groups can do that. But we were very critical of ourselves. We'd all take a vote to see if we thought it was happening, and if it wasn't then we'd move on." Ced recalls similar occasions, as he explains in the liner notes for the Roadrunner *Critical Beatdown* CD reissue: "We would come into the studio with something in mind, start working, scrap the idea and then start from scratch and come up with something entirely new." He adds: "We did that with 'Ease Back.' We did one version of that at the Lab and then when we bounced it over [at Studio 1212] it wasn't sounding right. So we just re-did it. Moe had a record there and we sampled the drums off of it, and made that crazy beat. Paul had some Meters records, so we chopped those up and put them on there. We did it right there on the spot."

Keith recalls another example of the group's flexibility and ability to roll with whatever was thrown their way: "The warehouse that 1212 was in had a lot of rehearsal spaces [Metallica and Anthrax reportedly used the building at the time, along with dozens of other bands], and there was a rock band next door who used to rehearse all night long, when we were there. If you listen to 'Break North' at the end, some of that band's guitar bled onto the track. It was pretty funny and it sounded good.

Somehow it fit right in with the music, and how we were making music back then."

Whether ideas were started at the Ultra Lab or done on the spot at 1212, the track-making went amazingly smoothly over the two or three months that *Critical Beatdown* took to finish. The only problem, which has been remedied by the Roadrunner reissue, which gave another 30 minutes to the album's running time, was space. Ced says in the reissue liners: "If we had used all of the singles and single-like radio promos (like "Bait") [which is on the reissue], we wouldn't have had any room to create new songs." Choices had to be made to make the album what group members felt best represented them at the time.

Looking back on those recording months in 1988, Ced says: "There were really no roadblocks making that album, because we were a team working together, and everyone knew their role." Moe agrees: "The recording for that album went really quickly, because it was from the heart. We worked as a team on that record. Ced made the beats, me and T.R. had the records, and Keith had the lyrics."

Even though Next Plateau wasn't lavishing Ultramagnetic with advance money or any of the trappings they might have had if signed to a major label, the group did have complete creative control. Ced tells Angus Batey in the reissue liners: "I'm not sure that you could have had a record like *Critical Beatdown* on a major label, especially at that time, since so many hip-hop hits back then were happy. Being on Next Plateau had its ups and downs, but if we did a record like 'Funky' and brought it to Eddie [O'Loughlin], he'd say 'I like that.' He'd bring it to Red Alert and if Red got a good response on the air or at a club then Eddie would go ahead and press it up. That was beautiful, you know? Now, the game's changed."

NO FOLLOWING THE LEADER

Released in the fall of 1988 in the face of fierce competition (Public Enemy's *It Takes A Nation Of Millions To Hold Us Back*, Boogie Down Productions' *By All Means Necessary* and Eric B & Rakim's *Follow The Leader*), the album was an all-out triumph. "It had a big impact on the way that people produced when it came out, during 1988 and later with people like Large Professor and DJ Premier," beams Ced. "But also, groups were free to say: 'We can do any style that we want, we don't have to rap like everybody else." Ced notes groups like the Jungle Brothers, De La Soul and A Tribe Called Quest as inheritors of the Ultra freedom.

Keith says, "When we made *Critical Beatdown* I think a lot of rappers respected us because of the different cadences we adjusted to, and the diversity in what we were saying on different tracks. It made us dominant, and the diversity shocked people." Keith also points to the uniqueness of his voice, which is something not to be overlooked: "My voice and MC Shan's are the two voices that can't be duplicated. Everybody else has been copied. I felt sorry for Rakim."

In a way, the most important track on the album itself was "Ease Back," released as a single when the album hit stores. Keith says: "That song made it into rotation in New York. WBLS used to play it every morning, three or four times a day. That was the only record we had like that. 'Ego Trippin'' was big on the street with mixtapes and all that, but 'Ease Back' was actually rotated." The song's success was impressive indeed, considering that it was just as complex and groundbreaking as the rest of the group's work. Notable is Keith's trademark of rhyming words at the end of lines with themselves or even within a line, i.e. "Writing and biting and fighting" and: "I want it like that / I got it like that / I have it like that / I need it like that" in very rapid succession. Keith also continues his futuristic vision by claiming to have purchased a 1990 Saab Turbo in the song, a model that would not be available for at least a year.

On the blazingly-fast "Ain't It Good To You" (Ced calls it a "bicycle record" because of its pace, adding: "A lot of rappers back then could only rap on medium and slow beats"), Keith manages to cram these lines in the listener's ear in a matter of seconds:

I'm a scientist
Your satellites are weak
They get dimmer
Every time I speak
On my gyroscope
You hope to see the style
And cope
Aesthetically it bugs you out
On the mic - Kool Keith in a spaceship
Rising....

Even throwaway Ultra verses could have been hits for other MCs, even today. Imagination, complexity and dope beats have rarely combined for such a wild ride.

ULTRA'S CRITICAL SHELF LIFE

Even though the album was a huge hit in the streets and among fellow hip-hoppers, the reality of retail and radio was the only negative aspect in the *Critical Beatdown* saga for 1988 and 1989. Next Plateau label-mates, pop-rappers Salt 'N Pepa were platinum with their album *A Salt With a Deadly Pepa* and groups that Ultra stood shoulder-to-shoulder with artistically, like Public Enemy and Boogie Down Productions, were selling many times as many units as Ultra. "It definitely bothered me that people we knew were selling so many more albums than we were at the time," Ced says today. "If you start something and you see somebody else doing what you do, basically, and they're getting accolades and selling while you're struggling to let people know that the album's even out, it's not easy." Moe agrees: "It was definitely frustrating to see other guys at our level selling so much more than we did. That's why we ended up going with Mercury for the next album [1992's *Funk Your Head Up*]. There was money there."

One big reason was a lack of publicity and radio push from Next Plateau, according to all Ultramagnetic members. Ced recalls: "We realized right when the album came out that we weren't getting any support. Uptown [Management, helmed by Andre Harrell, worked with Ultra at the time] was pushing [Next Plateau] and they just wouldn't spend the money. We never had a publicist working on the album and the only radio promotion we had was from Jimmy Love at Uptown, who basically loved 'Ease Back' so much that he worked it for free."

Keith has his own philosophy about Next Plateau's lack of support: "We generated a lot of money for that label. Our street value was so big that Eddie didn't feel like he had to spend any money promoting us. He did a lot of things for Salt 'N Pepa that he didn't do for us. Because they *needed* promotion to sell records. We was just selling steadily because our music was good. Eddie even told us later on that he had fucked up. He said: 'You guys was big on the streets but I could have done more with you guys. I made a mistake.'"

Keith adds: "I think other groups during that time did better than us because they had videos [for the record, Next Plateau did put out a video for the song "Travelin' At The Speed Of Thought" after the album came out, and it did garner play on *Yo! MTV Raps*]. Public Enemy capitalized with a bigger label, doing the same shit that we was doing." Keith also says: "The record was just really a New York and Tri-State record. It wasn't broadly marketed. I don't think the rest of the United States knew about it, or cared."

Whether they were being promoted by their label or not, Ultra always looked out for themselves, setting up radio interviews and doing their own street promo. Moe says: "We wasn't promoted like other groups are today, but Keith and I handled the street promotions on all of our albums. We sniped everywhere. We'd be out early in the morning putting up posters all over the tri-state [area]. When *Critical Beatdown* came out we'd just be out in the streets, playing our music. We have a box and just blast Ultra shit real loud. We never said it was our music, we'd just watch people bob their heads to the music and we knew that they were feeling it." Keith says today, in hindsight: "The only roadblock we hit in 1988 with *Critical Beatdown* was the lack of promotion, and sales. Otherwise, it was perfect."

ULTRA ON STAGE

One of the reasons that Ultramagnetic didn't realize their lack of promotion right away was because they were doing so well in their hometown. "We didn't care about touring back then," Keith remembers. "We made a lot of money, like $4,000 or $5,000 each weekend, going to Philly and back to Jersey and New York. We were everywhere in New York. All those shows were booked by hustlers and drug dealers back then, and we were definitely treated like stars. We had limos pick us up and everyone treated us with luxury. All the promoters were competing with each other to have the best hospitality." Moe says: "We didn't really get any kind of advance money for making *Critical Beatdown*, so we was just making money from the shows we were doing. That's where we got our sneaker money, or maybe enough to get a gold chain. It wasn't huge money, but it was good enough back then."

"We had pretty incredible shows back then in New York and that area when *Critical Beatdown* came out," Ced says, even though he adds: "We never really worked too much on our live performances. I always believed in feeling out the crowd once we got there. We did start taking our shows more seriously once we saw Stetsasonic [the legendary first real "live hip-hop band," from Brooklyn]. They were incredible. Public Enemy was great, too. We learned from watching groups like that."

By all accounts, even from group members, Ultra wasn't known for an overwhelming live show, but they did always show their uniqueness, even if it was in the smaller details. "The shows definitely got better as we went along," Moe remembers. "We never really practiced the live show, we'd just do it, from the heart."

DJ Premier still vividly remembers a show at New York's The World in 1987: "I remember it was Busy Bee and Melle Mel and Ice Cream Tee on that bill, and Kool G Rap later that night. All of a sudden, Ultra walked in with mink coats on and mad jewelry, like all of them had four-finger rings. And all of them had walkie-talkies, and I was like: 'Yo, this is incredible!' They stood there with their walkie-talkies, like they were astronauts. And everything matched and made sense. It all worked, with the music and the album cover and all that. I was just blown away, that they really were *that* bugged out." Keith remembers the gig in question: "We bought those walkie-talkies at Radio Shack. But," he emphasizes, "We bought the *real nice* ones. One time on-stage we wore suits with those glasses that light up. We usually wore some regular shit, but we put other things around it, to make things more interesting."

Keith reminisces, perhaps with a bit of exaggeration: "Back then in '88 and '89, we were having fun, getting money, traveling to Europe, all that. I had five sets of rings for all ten fingers, walking around with $2,000 in my pocket all the time. We went to Paris and places like that before a lot of more commercial artists did back then. It was a big thing. When we went to Paris and got off the plane I thought I was one of the Beatles, with people running up to me on the street. London was the same, I felt like I was Paul McCartney. We were definitely more appreciated over there." Despite their East Coast and European gigs, the group would not head west for another 3-4 years.

THE ULTRA LEGACY

Whether it went gold or not or brought the group the worldwide fame they deserved, the real proof of how important *Critical Beatdown* is can be summed up with one fact: the record sounds as good today as it did back then. Kids who are sick of the artifice shown by shallow, copycat rappers like Chingy and Fabolos these days end up finding the album, maybe from their old-school uncle, maybe from their skater friend or older brother or cousin. And it still blows their mind. It still gets them dusted.

It can be argued that most of the groups coming out today still don't have the production skills and lyrical wizardry that Keith and Ced showed back then, even with almost two decades of hip-hop hindsight. Ultra's rep is burned into the minds and hearts of true hip-hop fans. It was never about how many records they sold or how much press they got anyways. It was about skills and it was about love for the rap artform.

As Next Plateau's Eddie O'Loughlin explains: "Nothing could hold their creativity back. They were definitely never the type to sit around trying to figure out what people might or might not buy when they made their music." DJ Premier preaches about his own Ultra respect: "The whole *Critical Beatdown* album is dope to me. I used to play it daily. Everything they dropped was amazing, they were always consistent and I was never disappointed. I always used Ultra's music as one of my guides, because they were one of the groups that influenced me to even want to make hip-hop music." As Chuck D told Angus Batey: "They changed the whole game. I thought the Ultramagnetic MCs were the future."

Looking back, Keith lays it down like so: "1988 was the Golden Era, it was the best year for rappers who were distinctive and had different voices. When we went in to do *Critical Beatdown*, we knew what we wanted stuff to sound like, and it worked. We're also a great match because we grew up knowing what we want, plus we're all musicians and we make our own stuff. Our lyrics are different, and they should be on top of some different shit. *Critical Beatdown* is a classic because we didn't copy anybody, we were ourselves, we were the originals. That record stuck out like a sore thumb. There was nothing else like it."

Ced glances behind him and beams: "It wouldn't have mattered where we made that album, because with our team it was meant to happen that way. Today you have groups coming out sounding exactly like another artist, and they say: 'I'm better than him,' but by copying that other artist. That's insane. Ultra was never going to sound like anyone else."

Moe says: "We were definitely ahead of our time. A lot of people are using our beats and our music right now, today. They didn't understand us all the time back then, but people are copying us now." DJ Red Alert chimes in: "So many groups, back then and even now, studied their sound and their style. People took what Ultra did, flipped it around and molded it into their style. They had a huge impact on the rappers and groups that came after them."

Being a futurist by temperament and of course by his Ultra association, Ced shoots past the present and into the future, with the final word: "Ultramagnetic is like one of those ancient, Shakespearean characters who were ahead of their time and will never be fully appreciated in their time. In the year 3000 people will pick up *Critical Beatdown* and say: 'Goddamn! Those motherfuckas were on some shit!'"

JUNGLE BROTHERS

Straight Out The Jungle

(Idlers / Warlock, 1988)

The Jungle Brothers were always different. While most groups in the mid-'80s were battling to claw their way to the top, the JBs were rapping about their genitalia, like fourth graders. While the advent of the SP-1200 sampler led technologically savvy producers towards layers of sound, the JBs – core members Afrika Baby Bam and Mike G, with DJ Sammy B – looped tracks manually, often recording two turntables and a mic live onto tape. They didn't do anything that the rules of rap said they should have. And that's why they were so dope.

The group met and began working together in 1985 at Manhattan's Murry Bergtraum High School for Business Careers. Mike was one year older and lived in Harlem (and was in Queens before that, up until the mid-'80s). Afrika was in Brooklyn. Early versions of the group, with names The Final Four and the Bugout Crew, included DJ Brooklyn B and the X-Clan's smooth-tongued Brother J. As Mike says: "I was the last guy to get in. We all got together and did a cypher and it was me and Afrika who lasted. It's been like that ever since."

After talent shows at Bergtraum in '85 and '86, Brother J and Brooklyn B dropped out (Brooklyn B in part because he had mild stage fright, according to Afrika) and Mike's Harlem neighbor Sammy B was brought in as DJ. Mike explains: "My uncle was going out with Sammy's cousin and we just started hanging out. He had makeshift turntables, but he was definitely getting the job done."

Afrika had also been learning to DJ at the time: "I was learning more about DJing back then, from Sammy B. Brooklyn B had taught me how to backspin and Sammy was showing me how to do scratches. They had a thing in Brooklyn, where my grandmother lived, called 'Albany Day' in the Albany Projects and the DJs at the time were playing all those breakbeats that we learned and used when we started. That's where I really picked up an interest for learning how to DJ. I had just got a pair of turntables in 10th grade, and a tape deck, drum machine and microphone. I also had a bunch of my father's old records in the closet. Brooklyn B would bring over some breakbeats that his uncle had lent him and we used those to practice." In addition to records, Afrika was seeing some of the greats live, including Afrika Bambaata and Soulsonic Force at Brooklyn's Empire Rollerskating Rink.

Mike had skills as an MC, but he hadn't taken hip-hop too seriously in his younger years. He says: "I never really thought too much about MCing, at least not until I got to high school. I was mostly into graffiti at the time. My main influences back in the early '80s were Cold Crush

Brothers and Soulsonic Force, with Mr. Biggs and Pow Wow. They had the best messages, with 'Unity' and everything. That's what it was all about to me. They encompassed the true spirit and meaning of hip-hop."

During the week the two budding MCs would work on routines at night over the phone, and on weekends Afrika would travel to Harlem to visit Mike, and hang out with Mike's famous and influential uncle, the legendary DJ Red Alert. Mike's insider hip-hop knowledge started as deep as you can get, and at a very young age: "Red would take me to the [Zulu Nation] jams at the Bronx River Houses when I was eight and nine years old."

Red was a mentor to the group from day one, helping them with musical knowledge and giving them a view of the rap world that very few young pups ever got to see. As Afrika explains: "Hanging out with Red you got to meet other 'quote' superstars and saw how it had went to their head already. How they were acting all silly, and wearing silly clothes. Red would look at them and laugh to himself. If I had met those stars by myself I probably would have been blown away. But through Red we were more grounded. Hanging out with him was definitely a huge influence. His demeanor, how he carried himself. One funny thing was that I didn't even know that Mike's uncle was Red Alert until maybe the second time I went up there and I met him. I used to tape Red's show all the time but I never even remembered the name, I guess."

Even though they weren't performing actively at the time, they were watching other groups and learning. They took notes when they watched Red DJ in clubs like Union Square and the Latin Quarter, as well. Mike says: "One of the other big things that Red gave us was knowledge of how to keep control of a crowd, how to keep the focus on the crowd when you're performing. Keep them entertained, use crowd participation. We tried to always give our show a lot of character, a lot of joking, no real dance steps or nothin'. Just like a DJ at a great party. The party perspective definitely helped us a lot when we started doing real shows."

Red Alert gave the JB's more than perspective. He also played a demo tape of theirs on his Kiss 98 show in 1986, a song called "Braggin' & Boastin'," which gave them instant five borough notoriety. Afrika says: "We recorded that track as a demo, with a recording mic and two turntables, straight to cassette, at Tony D's TTO Studios in Coney

Island. We found Tony through Red Alert, because they knew each other. We did the cuts and vocals at the same time, in one take." Mike adds: "The first song we actually worked on when we first got to Tony's studio, was called 'It's The Breaks.' But that song never really developed." Afrika finishes the story: "Someone had paid for the studio time and they said we could use their time, but we had to use the person's beat they had already made. It was a drum machine beat and it didn't match too well. Part of it was [Bob James' "Take Me to the"] 'Mardi Gras' and part of it was [Rufus Thomas'] 'Funky Penguin Pt. 2.'"

Afrika says: "Basically, every time we were writing a new routine back then, that was a song. We'd just go into the studio and record it, after a while. We'd do the break first, then the routine and make the song, just like that." Mike adds: "As we started to do more songs, it became more natural for us. And I think Red helped us a lot, too. He more or less saw the picture as a whole, and as we went along he also saw the album as it was developing."

Under Red Alert's umbrella the JBs were in great company. As Afrika explains: "Back then, in 1987, there were three groups that Red was running the same process on. Boogie Down Productions, Ultramagnetic MCs and the JBs. He was giving advice and feedback, getting acetates and carting them up for airplay, and playing them on the radio. Outside of [this trio of groups], people were just trying to get their records on the radio, like everyone else."

Tony D wasn't just the studio owner, he was also a knowledgeable producer and, like Red, played a mentoring role to the group as they began to put beats and rhymes to tape. "At first I was shouting and what-not," says Afrika. "I thought I was Run from Run-DMC. Tony said: 'No, you don't have to do it like that.' He toned my style down, and that worked. He also taught us a lot about putting songs together." Tony also owned Idlers Records, which was distributed through Warlock, and with a great group that was guaranteed play on Red Alert's show, he was more than happy to put their songs out. "There wasn't no contracts or no studio budget or anything," says Afrika, "But he was a good guy, and he got our stuff out there."

After releasing the singles "Braggin' & Boastin'," "Jimbrowski," and "On The Run/I'll House You" in 1987 and the first part of 1988, they dropped their first LP, *Straight Out The Jungle*, by the spring. "When we started doing all those songs, the demand for the album just came," says Mike. "BDP, Public Enemy, Stetsasonic and Ultramagnetic all had albums by 1987 and 1988, so it was our turn." Overseen by Red Alert every step of the way, it was destined to succeed.

And although they've released several albums since, *Straight Out The Jungle* still stands (arguably tied with their second LP, *Done By The Forces Of Nature*, on Warner Bros from 1989) as their most important record – if not simply for the fact that they went against the grain and it paid off. Their rhymes were loose, fun and intelligent, and the sound was natural and infectious. Mike says: "We didn't have the knowledge of Ced-Gee [from Ultramagnetic] and Scott La Rock when it came to production and using the SP-1200 [sampler]. Our sound was more home-grown than those other groups. Plus the way we carried ourselves made the appeal even more flavorful."

TRACKS

Straight Out The Jungle

Afrika: I had that beat first, I made a pause tape of it at my father's house. That Bill Withers beat was out of my father's collection and the Mandrill horns were, too. We eventually looped it in the studio. The rhymes were written off of the Withers and Mandrill parts alone, then we used the Melle Mel sample to reinforce our own message. That's one of my favorite tracks.

What's Going On

Afrika: That originated in Tony D's studio. The beat for that was originally done by Mike from one of Red Alert's *Ultimate Breaks & Beats* records. I remember it had a pink label. Then we worked the rhymes over that, and used the Marvin Gaye stuff over top. That was one of the only songs that we ever used a drum machine on. We worked on that one really late at night. Tony D taught us about arranging songs, then we added some hi-hats off the drum machine to it.

Black Is Black

Afrika: That song came from a track that Q-Tip had put together with Ali [Shaheed Muhammad, also from A Tribe Called Quest] on Ali's Uncle's 4-track. That was the first demo that Q-Tip [a fellow Murry Bergtraum student] had presented to me with music *and* rhymes. The final lyrics were almost identical to the way we had it on that demo. We were consciously trying to show a more serious side on this and "What's Going On." They were songs that meant a lot to us.

Jimbrowski

Afrika: The idea for that came at the end of a studio session, with Mike, me, Red Alert and a woman Red was dating at the time. Red was flirting with her and kept saying "Jimbrowski" the whole night. Mike and I wrote the rhymes on the way back from the subway.

I'm Gonna Do You

Afrika: We made that track about halfway through the full album. It was off a Meters 45 that Tony pulled out. The bassline was on the flip side. I sped up the bassline, sampled it and played it up high for that keyboard part. With the lyrics, I was just sitting on the couch in my living room and I started to sing the chorus. I don't know where it came from. That song took us a couple weeks to finish.

I'll House You

Mike: That was produced by Todd Terry and us. It was another Todd Terry song, initially. They left us with the track and we wrote the lyrics to it, and did our mix version to it. At the time, we were getting into house music, and hitting all the house clubs.

Afrika: They were laughing at it at first, but it became our biggest hit of that time! We were just having fun with it. There used to be a house show on Kiss after Red, so he'd always play that as his last song.

On The Run

Mike: We didn't mix that song right and then Red [Alert] played it on the radio one night. Man, that was so disappointing. It didn't really come off as strong as we had anticipated.

Afrika: That was complicated to make. Sugar Shaft from X-Clan used to cut up that break all the time. "Push Up," by some rock band, I think. I looped it up like a machine gun beat. The bassline was from "The Mexican" [by Babe Ruth]. Mike kicked the lyrics to me at first over the phone, when he was in Lefrak. He said: "I'm a Scooby Doo so I don't be late" and I was like: 'Wow!"

Behind The Bush

Afrika: That was recorded on Valentine's Day, but we didn't even realize it until after we finished it. We triggered the beat up, and spent the whole night trying to match up Grover Washington's version of "Inner City Blues" with the beat.

Because I Got It Like That

Mike: That was our biggest hit off the album when it first came out. I think "Jimbrowski" was cool and it got everybody off, but "Because" was the one that really rocked in the clubs.

Afrika: That Sly beat is just ridiculous! I got that out of Red's collection. Mike wasn't sure about that track at first, but I messed with it and got something nice. That was a track that was almost ready, we didn't have to do much to it. Q-Tip turned me onto Prince's *Sign 'o' the Times* and that beginning singing part was written for Prince. I even fooled Mike at first into thinking that it was Prince's new song. I had the most fun on the album doing that song, and maybe "I'll House You."

Braggin' and Boastin'

Mike: We were still doing demos at Afrika's house and Red Alert took that one and played it on Kiss 98.

Afrika: The routines on that were already written and we were working them out over the phone, then we rehearsed them at my house. Sammy B used to love to cut up that Headhunters beat. That was the one routine that was done in the studio *exactly* like we had done it at the house. We recorded it live onto tape. It took three times until we got it all right together.

Sounds of the Safari

Afrika: That was the last jam we did for the album. I put that together using the "Sing Sing" beat and I used some jungle sound effects that I got from Sugar Shaft. I just put together a jungle instrumental thing.

Jimmy's Bonus Beat

Afrika: That was me cutting on that. I also cut on "Because I Got It Like

That" and "On The Run." We had just gotten the "Jimbrowski" single pressed up and I just said: "Instead of some jungle sounds, I'll get some Jungle Brothers records and make a bonus beat." So that song went on the b-side.

The Album

MANTRONIX
MANTRONIX
MANTRONIX

MANTRONIX
The Album
(Sleeping Bag, 1985)

In the mid-‘80s, hip-hop was making an important transition from early party- and live-based forms into the oncoming rule of the master producer. One crucial bridge between Afrika Bambaata, Run-DMC and the advent of Public Enemy, Marley Marl's Juice Crew and dozens of others to follow was Mantronix. Influenced and informed by electro and the spirit of the garage disco scene popularized by Larry Levan, but even more firmly rooted in the boom-bap of a Roland 808 kick-drum smack, producer/DJ Kurtis Mantronik (Kurtis Khaleel) and rapper MC Tee (for the record, not the same person as Tricky Tee of "Johnny The Fox" fame, with whom Mantronik also worked) dropped a sonic bomb on the hip-hop world with their debut, *The Album*.

Although the title was simple, the music was anything but. Intricate, ever-changing drum programs, the crackle of high-volume handclaps, thick basslines and walls of sampled and cut-in keyboard stabs ruled the Mantronix sound scheme, buoyed by edits from production whizzes the Latin Rascals (Albert Cabrera and Tony Moran) and always iced by Tee's glib, matter-of-fact, party-moving rhymes. "I was a nerd and really into technology so I was definitely into the production side from the start," says Mantronik. He adds: "I always used the latest technology, just like I do today. I used the [Roland TR-] 808 drum machine a lot back then because I just loved the bass that it gave." He says that he never played musical instruments as a child, but nonetheless taught himself how to program the 808 like a drum master.

Mantronik was born in Jamaica and raised in Canada. He moved to New York in 1980 in his mid-teens. "I listened to a lot of rock music when I was growing up," he says. "I loved Kiss' 'Beth' for instance." But his tastes changed soon enough, and he got his club music jones filled working at famed Downtown Records (not to be confused with Downstairs Records, the breakbeat mecca), where every DJ in New York and the world shopped both for disco/R&B club hits and breaks for hip-hop beat fodder. It was the ultimate job for a producer-to-be. And while he did DJ when he was in New York, production is where he started. He says: "I wasn't a DJ first, before I became a producer. That came later."

Saving up $80 for studio time, Kurtis cut the demo for the song "Fresh Is The Word," with Tee, in one quick day. Mantronik says: "I can't remember where I actually met Tee. He performed with me a lot back then, at places like the Roxy. That's where I used an 808 live on stage for the first time, and it blew peoples' minds." The group didn't perform much at the time, though, as Mantronik says: "Mostly studio, back then."

The tape caught the attention of Sleeping Bag Records' Will Socolov (a frequent Downtown Records customer), who released it as a single in 1985. Kurtis recalls: "Will liked what he heard and just put it out. 'Fresh' and the other singles sold very well, I think easily 40,000 units each. Sleeping Bag was a cool label, they let me do my thing." Socolov and Sleeping Bag were certainly aware of Mantronix's appeal and talent, and with single sales to match they signed the duo up for a full album. Consisting of only seven songs, it was still a beefy platter, because the songs were longer than most at the time. Some of them pushed seven minutes in length, with Mantronik's musical assaults filling in the spaces where Tee wasn't rapping. "The songs weren't supposed to be long on purpose, they just came out that way. 'Rappers Delight' [by the Sugarhill Gang] was long and so were other club tracks back then. It wasn't out of the ordinary, at least outside of the hip-hop world."

For the historical record, Mantronix continued to play crucial behind-the-scenes roles later in the '80s, doing A&R work for Sleeping Bag, where he helped sign the legendary EPMD, among other groups. Mantronix eventually moved to Capitol Records, and Kurtis along the way worked with some of the most important MCs of the mid-'80s, including T La Rock and Just-Ice. Still active today as a DJ and recording artist (*I Sing The Body Electro* was released on Oxygen Music Works in 1998), Mantronik finds the music world of today a very different place than it was when he first impacted, two decades ago. "It's great to be back [after a lack of recording in the '90s], but I have found that the music scene is so fragmented now. In the old days there were distinct types of music, so you could make a record just for one target market. You can't do that anymore."

He also laments the lack of respect and credit he gets these days. The pinnacle may have been musical LCD-peddler Beck's mid-'90s sampling of Mantronix's "Needle To The Groove" (uncredited) on his hit "Where It's At." But there have been others. Mantronik says: "I do get some credit for what I did, but with the other stuff I just want to be properly acknowledged. It's not about being egotistical, I just think people should know how things really happened and that the music they hear today usually came from somewhere else."

Kurtis muses about how important he thought *The Album* was back then and if he was shocked at its impact, replying, simply: "I guess I was surprised. I just made music because it was cool and fun. As long as you got a sound to move the crowd, nothing else mattered."

TRACKS

Bassline *[edited by the Latin Rascals]*

I played that bass-line on a Juno, I think. The track itself came together pretty quickly. I think it took us only a day to record the whole thing. It was Will's [Socolov] idea to get the Latin Rascals to do the edits, and I had no problem with that. They had a name on the street from their [W]KTU radio show. They did edits only. I still work with Albert because my manager has a thing about edits and Albert always rocks my shit. I think that doing hip-hop edits is a lost art these days, which is a shame, because you can really do some cool stuff with editing. Things that you can't get from regular productions. Aside from the Latin Rascals, Omar Santana and Chep Nunez were the most popular guys doing them back in the '80s.

Needle To The Groove

That's Tee on the Vocoder. I changed up the beat and the drum programming on that because it just felt better to keep it moving. Beck took that for one of his hits ["Where It's At"] and never gave me credit or money for that. It bothers me when I'm not even acknowledged, but it's even worse when they sample your shit and you don't get any credit, like Beck and Snap. Some people give props. DJ Shadow and the Chemical Brothers have both said nice things about my music.

Mega-Mix
[edited by The Diamond Two: J. "Chep" Nunez and Charlie Dee]

That was done at the end of the record. I've always had mega-mixes on my records because it's so much a part of where I come from. It's that cool hip-hop cut-up thing that good DJs do to hype the crowd. I don't think The Diamond Two did too much together other than this track, maybe a couple other things. Charlie did a bunch of other solo edit stuff in the '80s. And Chep died in a fire in the mid-'80s.

Hardcore Hip-Hop

That's about the roots of hip-hop. A lot of the sounds and change-ups on there were really just done because they sounded cool and we were all experimenting to top each other with new shit. Not only in clubs but also on records. I never had any musical training, I always just like learning things for myself, so experimentation came very naturally from that.

Ladies

That song was written with a special lady in mind. That's why I've always had a soft spot for it. It's definitely my favorite track on the album, still today. Our music back then, and my music now, is all about being different, not like today where people are too busy trying to be like this or like that. Back in the day it was better when you *didn't* sound like anyone else. Otherwise you were considered a biter.

Get Stupid "Fresh" Part 1

That one was done on the spot, but I usually don't like taking a day to do a track either way. I usually think about what I want to do beforehand based on the technology available. We always goofed around a lot in the studio, but we always got things done.

Fresh Is The Word

That was the first song I ever had on wax. I saved some money and just did the track on my own. Will from Sleeping Bag heard it and offered me a deal. The demo and the album version are the same. I used the [Roland] 808 [drum machine] a lot back then because I loved the bass. When I used it in a show at the Roxy with Tee – the first time anyone used an 808 on stage – the crowd freaked when I hit that first kick. I had a good amount of cutting on there too. It was all about capturing the hip-hop vibe you heard in clubs, but making it *bigger*.

ICE - T

Power

(Sire, 1988)

Although Ice-T (Tracy Marrow, sometimes incorrectly listed as Morrow) wasn't born in LA, he certainly came to embody the flashy West Coast lifestyle to the fullest – first in his real life and later in his rhymes. Throughout the early '80s he built wealth on the down-low while he built his rap reputation across Southern California, and by the close of the decade he approached platinum every time he hit the studio, with no radio play. An intelligent, frequently humorous and almost-always controversial figure, he became one of hip-hop's most important and thought-provoking voices as the '90s hit, after his albums *Rhyme Pays* and *Power* established his national prominence.

Born in Newark, Ice grew up in Summit, New Jersey (about 15 miles outside of New York City), where he attended Summit Junior High School. His earliest years were normal ones in a nice suburban town, but drama hit before he entered his teens. "My mother died of a heart attack, when I was in the third grade. And my father died when I was in the seventh grade," Ice says today. Contrary to facts listed in some bios and reference books, a car accident didn't claim his parents' lives. "When my father passed, I moved to Los Angeles to live with his sister. And I never went back. I had no family, no connections, no friends. It was gone."

He lived in the View Park section of LA when he arrived at his aunt's in the early '70s. "It was a nice upper-middle-class area," he recalls. For school, he was bused to Palms Junior High, a mostly white school in Culver City. "At that point in time my life hadn't gotten traumatic," he says, despite the fact he had, of course, lost both of his parents. He continues: "The drama started in high school."

"When I got to high school age, I decided that I didn't want to be bused anymore," Ice says. "I wanted to go to Crenshaw, which was one of the roughest high schools in LA. I went there just because I didn't want to take the bus. I wanted to walk, to go to a local school. But in my neighborhood not that many people went to Crenshaw, so I was basically going to school by myself. That's when I got introduced to the gangs, mostly for survival." He continues: "When I got to Crenshaw, the kids in my grade were already cliqued up. So I got in with these kids from the Avenues, the flatter area of LA, the more dangerous area. I had to connect with them and roll with whatever was rolling, because I was a one-man team coming into school, with no back-up. This was right when the Crips was jumping off, the beginning of the era when the LA gangs were *really* getting going."

Ice doesn't glorify or seem to exaggerate his gang activities back at that time. As he says: "To put actual work in for a gang, that meant you had to kill for them, but I never went out and did that. I was more what I considered a 'gang affiliate,' I wore my colors. Most motherfuckers ain't never killed for a gang, even though they act like they did. My main allegiance came with some kids in the 40s [Avenue numbers], who really didn't gang bang. They were more hustlers than anything."

When Ice graduated high school in 1976, he went down a decidedly non-hustler-like path: joining the Army as a Ranger (an elite combat-trained force within the armed services). Why? He answers, with no hint of humor: "I did it because I wanted a black beret." He adds: "When I got out of high school I had a kid, so going into the military was my attempt to try and get some stability in my life." He was in the service for four years: "I got jump status and I went to the 25th Infantry. Schofield Barracks in Hawaii." Was it a good experience? "Nah, it wasn't a good experience. The military is crazy! It was interesting, I guess. Maybe it made me structure my life a little bit."

In 1980 he was a civilian once again, and he started figuring that DJing parties would be a good way to make cash. He explains his next move: "Back then, I wanted to do parties, I had bought all this equipment and everything. But my friends picked me up at the airport, and by then they were doing a lot of heavy crime. So we started making moves on jewelry stores and doing all kinds of robberies. In a little while I was able to obtain a lot of wealth. Within a year I think I had close to a million dollars. That's when I built my street reputation, being a flashy character in LA."

Even though he was doing well on the crime side, he did give the party circuit a shot. He remembers: "I started giving parties, but I didn't like carrying all the equipment. This is around when 'Rapper's Delight' was out and rap was starting to break out all over the place. So I tried my luck on the mic. And even though I was wack, I was still better than everybody else [laughs]. I found that I could make more money and enjoy myself more by going from party to party, just rapping." And thus a side career was born, which he undertook each weekend on the party scene, in clubs and at house-parties.

Oftentimes he was aided by another upstart rapper from LA: Kid Frost. "Once me and Frost started to get known, our names would just start popping up on flyers, whether we had said we'd be there or not," Ice says. "So we'd just bumrush parties that had our names on flyers, anywhere we could. When we'd show up, the promoters' eyes would open up, 'cause we was actually there, and that meant they'd have to pay us. We were jacking promoters like that. On any given Friday or Saturday night we could run from party to party and make $1,000 or $1,500. That was a lot of money in the rap game back then."

After a couple years on the scene, Ice put out his first single, "The Coldest Rap," on the Saturn label in 1983. "I didn't make any money from that, or from any of those early singles I did [including his second single, "Killers," from 1984 on Electro Beat]." Either way, even though he was making decent money on the party scene, his hustling ways continued. He says: "My illegal hustle didn't really stop until I got my first record deal, for *Rhyme Pays* [in 1987]. All throughout all those independent records there was no money. I was living a certain lifestyle back then and a rap record wasn't going to change my life. I never thought I'd make a career of rap, it was totally just for fun. I mean, how could I think about it as a career? Nobody had even bought a car from rap money back then."

Rap also served another purpose for Ice: "I looked at rap as a way of covering my [illegal] game. Hip-hop was a front for me. It was my way of having the things and telling people that I got this Porsche from rapping. But that stuff I had on my album covers, I never could have bought that jewelry and that stuff from rap. So I had to use it as a cover up."

Even up through the mid-'80s, the hip-hop scene in Southern California had taken its time building a real foundation. Ice had a couple records out, and so did local legends like Frost, Egyptian Lover and Uncle Jamm's Army, World Class Wreckin Cru, Bobby Jimmy & the Critters and the LA Dream Team. But much of the LA scene was localized before 24-7 rap radio stalwart KDAY started to rev up in 1983 and 1984. The New York explosion crept up on the area slower than you might think, even after the success of "Rapper's Delight" in 1979. "There just wasn't any real New York influence in LA back in the late '70s," Ice explains. "LA cats didn't really even know that New York existed. The first time we noticed was when the New York City Breakers were on [the TV show] 'That's Incredible.' That was the first time we ever saw breakdancing. And breakdancing preceded any music coming out of New York. They were locking in LA for a long time before they were rapping."

One place that Ice cites as a major influence on him in the hip-hop world was a hipster club in downtown LA called Radio [later known as Radio Tron]. "It was an underground, European hip-hop club, run by a guy named Alex Jordanov and this guy KK. It was all white kids, because it was a Russian club, and because there were really no hip-hoppers in LA back in '82 and '83. Alex was a Russian motherfucker by way of France, by way of New York. They were graffiti artists and brought [Afrika] Bambaata in, Grandmixer D.ST, Rocksteady Crew. That place was way ahead of the curve."

Ice tells of his first experience at Radio: "Back in '83, I had [one of] the only record[s] out in LA at the time ["The Coldest Rap"], and they were playing it every night at that club. They booked me for a show, so I went down there. There wasn't a black face in the joint, it was a totally different crowd than I had ever been in before. I walked on stage and everybody in the audience knew every word of that record. And it was the first time I had even heard of this place! I hung out there a lot after that, and heard them play a lot of music in there that I had never heard before. Cold Crush Brothers, Crash Crew. Chris "The Glove" Taylor was the DJ at the club, but Alex [under the name AJ] would DJ there, too."

Ice, in fact, went on to be, as he calls it "the stage manager" of Radio in 1984 and 1985. "I went back to that club every weekend at first, and I'd bring more and more friends, all my hustler buddies. Eventually, anybody who wanted to perform at Radio would have to come to me first." Among those he put on stage there were a not-yet-famous Madonna ("I take credit for telling Madonna to show more cleavage," he beams). More importantly, though, he met one of his crucial future collaborators there: DJ and producer Afrika Islam, who was the touring DJ for the Rocksteady Crew back at the time. Ice and Afrika hit it off and agreed to stay in touch, and when Ice's 1986 single "Dog'N The Wax" came out on Techno Hop, he sent a box of the singles to New York, asking Islam to spread them around.

Instead of just handing the singles out, Islam convinced Ice to take a trip to New York City, to meet the city's hip-hop cognoscenti himself and to do performances at shows like Union Square and Latin Quarter. Ice recalls: "I got a cheap ticket and flew to the South Bronx. I was staying with Afrika on 156th. And because Islam is the man [he was closely allied with Afrika Bambaata, the Soulsonic Force and the Zulu Nation] he introduced me to New York City hip-hop from the top down. Scott La Rock, Chuck Chillout, Red Alert. All the top people."

Although he was from LA, Ice admits that the new single's b-side, "6 In

The Mornin," was of particular interest to New Yorkers. "Sound-wise, that song is more of an East Coast style record, definitely. Less music, more beat, different cadence. And it was loosely based off of [Schoolly D's huge proto-gangsta single from 1985] 'P.S.K..'" Ice impressed locals not only with his rhymes and beats, but also with his style and panache: "New York loved me, and I looked the part. They could see I had paper. I was a half-assed rapper, but I had a Porsche turbo," he smiles. "And they were trying to figure that out. They wanted to know how to get the money, and I wanted to know how to be a rapper. The only resistance I got was from Kool Herc. He didn't like the fact that I cursed [laughs]. He still doesn't. I respect that, but that's all I know how to do!"

Ice returned to New York frequently and continued to build his rep on both coasts in 1986 and early 1987. Then an opportunity came that changed his life and his hustle. Afrika Islam's friend Ralph Cooper knew Sire Records president Seymour Stein though Cooper's father, who managed the famed Apollo Theater. Ice explains: "This has actually never been written about before, but Ralph presented a compilation album concept to Seymour Stein. The compilation was me, Melle Mel, Grandmaster Caz, Donald D and a guy called Bronx Style Bob, who was down with Afrika Islam. Seymour was ready to do the record, but all the other guys had contractual issues, so nobody was able to get released. I was the only guy who had a record out and who was free. So Seymour said: 'Why don't we just do a record with Ice-T?' By him just saying 'Fuck it!' it got me in the door. He didn't even know much at all about hip-hop. He told me it sounded like Bob Dylan to him."

Signing the edgy Ice-T wasn't as far out as it might seem, as Ice explains: "Sire had the Talking Heads and Madonna, who were avant-garde in their time. So hip-hop was right up his line. Mine was the first rap record on Sire, the first on Warner Bros, and one of the first on a major label." He continues: "I got $40,000 for the record budget, with no video. And that's when we did *Rhyme Pays*."

By "we," Ice means he and his new close friend and producer Afrika Islam, who was fully on-board by that time. They recorded the album in about 30 days in New York (contrary to the listing on the back of the album). He says: "The album took one month and we mixed it in one night, at Secret Sound, all in New York. We got $40,000, bought an SP-12 [EMU SP-1200 sampler/drum machine] and fucked off some of the money. The record probably cost about $25,000 total to make. We made that whole album with one drum machine, the SP-1200, using the sounds that were in the machine. We didn't even know how to make the fuckin' machine sample!"

Even though they were learning certain techniques as they went along, both men knew the gravity of the situation: "An album was serious shit, and I knew it had to be good. You always want to get to the second album. I came out with the best I could do at the time. I also knew that I had to rap a lot of different ways if I was going to do a full album. I couldn't rap the same way each time, because I hated when other rappers did that. I knew I had to have different cadences and different topics. Street shit, some politics, some sex shit." He adds: "Public Enemy's album came out at that time and it was dope, but it was one thing. I knew that if I went that route, I'd never be able to tell a joke or to have fun with the audience."

In addition to the single "Somebody's Gotta Do It (Pimpin' Ain't Easy)," the album was solid top-to-bottom, with Ice's array of approaches: Sex ("I Love Ladies" and "Sex"), politics ("Pain"), reality ("Squeeze The Trigger") and good old fashioned partying ("409"). Of course Ice, the savvy, flashy LA player, knew that the album cover would be important. For that, he enlisted one of hip-hop's most important photographers: Glen E. Friedman. "Glen gave me that album cover for *Rhyme Pays* that made me stand alongside the big cats," Ice says, of the image: Ice scowling from behind the wheel of his purple Porsche, with a fine female standing tall in the passenger seat, DJ Evil E in the back, and a palm tree hovering strategically above their heads. "He made sure that we got the girl, the Porsche and the palm tree in it. He said: 'The palm tree is the most important thing in this shot.' LA was very important to the image I was getting across. And images were very important back then for an album cover. At that time there was only like 10 or 15 albums out in total, so people were definitely going to see your cover."

On the strength of all the items and angles discussed above, *Rhyme Pays*, released in 1987, went gold [Ice says that sales were around 800,000] with no video and very little national radio airplay. An impressive feat to be sure, and one that made Sire very happy. Ice explains, about the sales: "At that time you could literally go out and buy every rap record in one place. It was easier to sell records then, because there weren't as many people in the game. Also, I honestly believe that most hip-hop fans back then just bought everybody's record." And with a great record, as Ice had, you would also be converting non-hip-hop fans along the way.

It should be noted that Ice's DJ for most of the '80s was Evil E, the brother of fellow New York Spinmaster [their DJ group, which was very popular in LA at the time] Hen-Gee. "Those guys came into the fold way back in the Kid Frost days, really," Ice says. "When I started doing clubs, they was in the party scene already. They was from New York, so they called themselves the New York City Spinmasters. When I first broke, Chris 'The Glove' was gonna be my DJ, but he didn't want to do it. I needed someone who was willing to go to all those parties with me. And Evil and Hen were already at all those parties! Henry [Hen] started becoming more of a manger and Evil and I just started doing routines. E was so eager to make money that I could call him up for any party and he'd always be glad to show up." Even though Afrika Islam was a talented DJ in his own right, as Ice says, "Me and Evil was always a team." So Afrika stuck to producing, and Evil was behind the decks.

1988 rolled around and things couldn't have been better for Ice. Aside from a gold record with *Rhyme Pays*, he was also featured on the soundtrack to the film *Colors* (Ice says the soundtrack went platinum) and convinced Warner Bros to release the Rhyme Syndicate album *Comin' Through* in early 1988. With all this swirling about, he and Afrika Islam were on a big-time roll, and they walked directly into their next major work: the *Power* album. "By the time I got to *Power*, I was aware that people were listening," Ice says. "With *Rhyme Pays* I didn't even know if people were going to listen or buy it. But with 800,000 fans it's a whole different thing. I knew *Power* had to be more serious, and that I had to get some points across."

Once again, the album's cover was important, and Friedman was tapped for it. The front featured three people: Ice, his gorgeous and scantily-clad girlfriend Darlene and DJ Evil E. Since she's wearing very little, it's easy to see Darlene's shotgun, which she displays at her side. Ice and Evil aren't giving away any secrets until you look on the back cover, where their hidden shotguns can be seen. "I thought up that concept," Ice explains. "We had three powers on there: Weapons, the power of sex, and the power of deception. To me, deception is one of the biggest powers. I mean, the government uses it all the time." But, as he astutely adds: "Once you got past the cover and into the album there was just another bunch of crazy records in there."

The recording of *Power* was different from *Rhyme Pays* in many ways, except for the amount of time it took. "The recording was fast. I pretty much record every record in a matter of a month, maybe two at the most. It's better because you can stay in one mental set." Thanks to strong first-time-around sales, the budget was also bumped up. "We had more money for the next one," says Ice, "And we did that one in LA. We recorded it on a 14-track Akai machine in Evil E's back house. That was Syndicate Studios West. The board was connected to the biggest system we could build that resembled a car stereo system, so we could check how it sounded when real people who would buy our tapes listened to that shit. Big woofers and all that. We had a little bitty closet where we did the vocals."

The album's 11 main tracks are another tour de force for Ice, and they yet again explore a wide range of topics, moods and approaches. As with *Rhyme Pays*, Ice's most important approach may have been the one that he was most misunderstood about: his descriptions of and subsequent condemnation of the gang-banging lifestyle. Tracks like "Drama" and even "I'm Your Pusher" are morality tales, that start posh and end badly for those that choose that way of life. Ice discusses this style, inherited from his late father: "My dad, when he would teach me lessons, he would never just say: 'Don't do it.' He would tell me stories and he would get me into it. It would be like: 'He was about to get a million dollars, but that night he ODed.' So I always used that technique. Bring the audience in and then catch 'em. Because I do really, truly come from the game, I can't write a story about the hustle that doesn't end up in prison or dead. Because all the real stories do. If I'm rhyming and I shoot somebody, I'm on the run in the next verse."

Despite Ice's upbringing in LA, he never got involved in any battles with New York, even despite the Big Apple's frequent resistance to West Coast rap in the late '80s and early '90s. "Back then I had a Syndicate meeting and said: 'Look, New York is always going to have a resistance to West Coast stuff.' So I took a pen and I circled New York, Philly and New Jersey on a map. And I said: 'OK, they can have those. But the West Coast starts *right here* and I was pointing to everything outside of the circle. Because a motherfucker from Detroit doesn't give a fuck if you're from New York or LA, because he's from neither. I knew we could sell a million records with or without New York. We could just take the rest of the country."

Ice never got involved on the political side either: "I never really played the East/West game. My thing is that I'm from Earth and I'm playing the whole map, and I go anywhere. I rep LA, but I gotta be down with New York. For me to rep the West and dis the East would make me a fake, because I was born in the East. Plus Islam put me on, so I could never dis New York."

Now that Ice was making money legally, his illegal hustle was a thing of the past, and 1988 was his best year yet. "It was really nice to be the hot shit back then. My star definitely banged from *Power* right until around

OG [his 1991 Sire album]. I was on the covers of all the magazines. When I look at the magazines now and I see all the new guys, I'm like: 'Yo, they deserve that, because we had it.' There was a time when motherfuckers had to look at us every day and they probably got sick of it, too [laughs]."

Power neared platinum back in 1988 and 1989 and, as Ice claims, has passed that mark by now. The album cemented Ice's rep as a top-draw and also as one of rap's most creative and important provocateurs. "There are a lot of laughs and a lot of good lyrics on there," Ice says, looking back. "I mean, I predicted on that album that rap would be outlawed, and look what happened to 2 Live Crew and to me [referring to his "Cop Killer" situation] a couple years after that."

TRACKS

Colors *(not on* Power *album)*

That song never appeared on any of my albums, it was only a single and on the Colors movie soundtrack. The soundtrack itself went platinum. I don't know why I didn't include "Colors" on the *Power* album, it was probably just timing. I never really thought about it, to be honest. I love that song, that's the one that I close my show with, even to this day. We close with "Colors" and encore with "6 In The Mornin'." "Colors" was never actually intended to be a record. They were gonna use my song "Squeeze The Trigger" on the soundtrack to that movie and I saw a screening of the film and knew I could do the title song to it. The Rick James song ["Everywhere I Go"] was supposed to be the main song, but I was like: "Rick, I can handle this." We went in and took the beat from King Sun's "Mythological" [Ice rhymes part of King Sun's song, to prove it]. We took the beat, turned it around, played a bassline over it and I used pretty much the same cadence that Sun had. I turned it in to the Warners people and they loved it. It had a video and it was huge. Dennis Hopper and them was looking for gang-based records, so I was perfect for it. That song was just me hustling. I saw the movie and we knocked out the song over the weekend. I mean, c'mon, ain't nobody can write a record about gangs if they haven't been in a gang. And so I let them know how it goes. The Ice-T style is to put myself in whatever person's place I'm writing a song about. I did that with "Cop Killer" and got myself in some trouble [laughs loudly]. That's what I talk about at the beginning of the song "Power." That's the way I write records. It's more powerful to say "I" than "You are" when you're writing.

Drama

That's the same bass machine on there we used to use for a lot of shit back then, like with "Colors" and "Squeeze The Trigger" [a Roland TB-303]. I don't see how anyone can think that I'm glorifying hustling in that song, 'cause the guy's dying in the electric chair [laughs]. It's a crime record, but at the same time it's supposed to be an educational record. I was explaining: "This is what happens." I know I can't tell a street story and have it come out good. Like I said on *OG*: "That invincible shit don't work." I didn't really care that I was misunderstood in my lyrics, really. And by the time I got to the *OG* album I was done explainin'. If you guys ain't figured it out yet, there was nothing I could do.

The Syndicate

That one's got Donald D and Hen-Gee on it. The Syndicate kind of became a gang of cats in LA who wasn't down with the N.W.A. scene. I would collect tapes from people and it just started to become an organization. To me a syndicate was a group with a common goal. We had guys like Def Jef, Everlast and [DJ] Muggs was around when he was in 7A3. I was the kind of guy who was like: "Yo, if I get my shit off, I'm gonna help you guys." And that's how the Rhyme Syndicate album [*Comin' Through*] came out. When I got my power at Warner Bros after the first album, I did that. That Syndicate album did decent, it sold a couple hundred thousand. Not bad for a compilation with no single. I was able to get an Everlast and a Donald D album out of it. All the guys who were on that track were actually originally from New York, but it wasn't planned that way, of course. It might seem ironic [New York-bred rappers repping LA] but that's just who was in the studio at that time. The beat came up, we was feeling it and we just wrote that song.

Radio Suckers

Yeah, with Chuck D on the hook! The first time I saw Public Enemy I didn't actually meet Chuck. I saw them at the LA Sports Arena on some tour. I saw Griff and all these mo'fuckas with guns and I was like: 'Oh, this shit is *dope*.' I knew of them also through Glen Friedman, since he took pictures for both of us. Me and PE clicked on intensity, we clicked on battle scars and we also understood each others' position. Chuck was a Nationalist position. He was trying to get all black people to understand the problems of the world. I was a 'hood politician. I wanted people to understand what was going on in the city. He rapped about the president, I rapped about the police. My politics never reached past city limits. I rapped in a smaller room. I was rapping about the guy who says he's gonna kill you tomorrow.

That song was basically just saying "Fuck radio," and I still say it to this day. Fuck 'em. Basically, I was able to sell platinum records without ever being on the radio. Public Enemy even got more radio play than me. I haven't gotten radio play since KDAY [Los Angeles' first hip-hop station, which went off the air in the early '90s] shut down. And I'm still bitter! I'm like: "You can't tell me that my records aren't as good as some of the *bullshit* that y'all are playing. I'm selling the records, so people want to hear it. So what is your issue?" I would never go to radio and kiss their ass. Radio likes to be stroked. But I'm not going to kiss your ass and the next day you're fired and I have to go back and kiss somebody else's ass. If you're playing my records, I'll come in and kiss your ass. One time I asked somebody at a station why I never got play and they told me: "Well, Ice, it's because you're too *real*." Some radio station in Texas. They'll listen to another rapper say they'll shoot somebody and I guess it seems corny. But with the tone of my voice I guess it sounded too real? So if I made myself corny, they would play my records? But I still don't give a fuck about radio. I've never gotten radio play and they can all eat a bowl of dicks. You'll never find an Ice-T clean album. N.W.A. did entire clean albums, but I thought that was selling out. C'mon, they can bleep that shit. N.W.A. made more money because of it, but I had my integrity. You can bleep it out, but I'm not going to change any of the words.

I'm Your Pusher

That was the first single and the first video we ever did for one of my albums. We didn't have one for the first album. That song is one of the first rap records to ever have a singing hook on it. Prior to that no-one really ever sang on hooks. And it hit, and I was like 'Wow, this is too easy.' Pimpin' Rex sang the chorus of that song. He was one of my buddies, a real live pimp [laughs]. I always loved the old blaxploitation films, so I wanted to do it like Curtis Mayfield in "Super Fly." Pimpin' Rex sang it perfect, we flipped the words, put a dope beat on it, and it worked. Rex was just a pimp, so he just knows that type of flavor [laughs]! The video for that song was just following the lyrics, basically. A drug kid walks up and wants some dope, then I'm on the corner handing out CDs like we're doing drug deals.

I dissed LL [Cool J] again on that track. You see, LL at that time was on his “I’m the greatest rapper in the world” thing. Me being from LA, I was trying to rep our entire city alone, so I had to step to him. It was no personal shit with him or anything. He was basically telling the world: “You gotta kiss my ass, I’m the greatest rapper of all time.” And LA was like: “Ice, he ain’t all that.” So it was me saying: “Fuck LL.” I was just shooting at the number one cat at the time. I didn’t have any fear of LL, and I thought I could beat him rapping anyways. Eventually it would have gotten worse. He dissed me in a record called “To The Break of Dawn,” I think he called me a little rat raccoon or some shit [laughs]. And he was dissing my *Power* album cover. It was about to escalate because we had written a record called “Open Contract.” But LL got with Afrika Bambaata and Bam asked us to squash it. So we did, before it got crazy.

Girls L.G.B.N.A.F.

That song was kind of another LL [Cool J] thing. We were making fun of the fact that these niggas was making love records. Because we come from the school of if your girl likes the record then it’s no good. This is some real male rap shit. Locker room rapping. If your girl was into it then you fucked up [laughs]! We were supposed to be offending them [women]. I came up with the concept and [Audio Two’s] “Top Billin’” was a big record at the time, so Afrika was like: “We need to do a beat something like that.” So we did that beat and I used a similar rhyme flow. That’s Evil E talking behind my words on there. That song is always a crowd pleaser when we perform it. It’s definitely in the “La Di Da Di” [by Doug E Fresh & Slick Rick] tradition.

High Rollers

That was the second single and video for the album. We were all up at this house in the video, just hustlin’, high rollin’, with guns, girls in bathing suits and all that. Videos for us were funny back then because we had to use all our own props. There was no car rentals and all that. Nowadays you see a guy in a video and all that shit isn’t even his. But we had to bring out the shit ourselves. As I said in one of my rhymes: “The guns in my promo shots ain’t props.” When we was shooting the “High Rollers” video there was so much heat and so much shit on the set that the crew was getting nervous. We had coke on the set and they was freaking out. My boys were bringing out knots of money. It was the real deal back then, it was fun.

Soul On Ice

That was my tribute to [author] Iceberg Slim. I took my name from him, back when I started out. I started reading him in high school. My buddy Michael Carter, who was a young player, gave me the books and that shit was just fascinating. It had a huge influence on me. I was fucking around with gangs at the time but that shit made me wanna be a pimp. It totally introduced me to a fly lifestyle. I started quoting [Slim] in high school. I was a 14-year-old kid quoting 40-year-old man shit. I read a lot of his books before I ever heard his tape [Iceberg Slim's spoken word/jazz album *Reflections*, from 1976], and also the *Hustler's Convention* album [by Lightnin' Rod aka Jalal Nuruddin of the Last Poets]. I met Iceberg Slim [who died in 1992] on the phone once, through Fab Five Freddy. And I met his daughter in person.

BIG DADDY KANE
Long Live The Kane

(Cold Chillin' / Warner Bros., 1988)

Believe it or not, Brooklyn's supreme loverman and king of the brag rap, Big Daddy Kane (Antonio Hardy), started out as a behind-the-scenes kind of guy. "Make sure you mention that I grew up in Bed Stuy," he says adamantly, at the start of our chat. He continues his history lesson: "When I first started messin' with hip-hop I tried to DJ, but I wasn't all that good. I was writin' rhymes for my cousin Nicole, and I was writing them for myself, too. I also had a cousin named Murdoch who started rhyming back then. He was much older and I was a young shorty. I always looked up to him and I'd do whatever he did, so I started rhyming really just to hang out with him. This is like 1982. I basically patterned my style after Grandmaster Caz [of the Cold Crush Brothers], at least when I first started writing."

Introduced into the real rap game by the diabolical Biz Markie, Kane ghost-wrote lyrics for Biz's earliest classics: "Nobody Beats The Biz," "Biz Is Goin' Off," "Pickin' Boogers," "Albee Square Mall" and "Vapors." "I really started taking rap seriously when I met Biz," Kane explains. "He started telling me: 'Yo, you're *nice* on the mic!' I met Biz at the Albee Square Mall [in Brooklyn] in 1984. We had a mutual friend, a dude from Central Islip [Long Island]. I also went to Sarah J Hale High School, which wasn't too far from Albee Square. Biz used to come around a lot, and he'd take me to a lot of parties, like Mike & Dave used to throw back in the day. We'd go on stage and rhyme. Biz would get in lots of spots for free, and lots of them would let us get on the mic. Like Latin Quarter, all the Mike & Dave parties, and spots on Long Island."

Kane's stage name came together in two parts. He says: "At first it was just MC Kane. The Big Daddy part came from something that happened on a class trip. It was actually a joke that cats was teasing me about. Then they were like: 'Actually, that's kinda hot, you should use that.' The Kane part was from cats teasing me about being so infatuated with the TV series Kung Fu [in the series, David Carradine's name is Caine]. I was that cat at 3 o'clock on Saturdays in front of the TV, for Kung Fu Theater. The name didn't always mean 'King Asiatic Nobody's Equal,' not back then. That came later on, when I used it in a song."

Through Biz, Kane met another Juice Crew luminary, Roxanne Shante. "Fly Ty [manager and owner of Cold Chillin' Records] asked me to write some stuff for Shante, and I had a lot of respect for her, so I was like 'No doubt!'" Kane wrote several hits for her, including "Have A Nice Day." Although he downplays them, Kane did indeed have skills on turntables back then, and was even Shante's DJ for the Def Jam Tour of 1986. "After the writing stuff I did, Shante asked me to go on the road and DJ for her. Cool V [Biz's DJ] knew I could DJ and Mister Cee [who would become Kane's DJ] knew, but nobody else. I'd be in rehearsal, battling with Marley and this other brother named Backspin. I got on and showed 'em my thing and Shante thought I was pretty good, so she asked me. I only did one tour. She was paying me a nice amount of money for it, so I had no problem with it."

Kane breaks down his different ghostwriting situations and challenges like this: "Writing for Biz was in a whole different style, so that could be a challenge. But Fly Ty wanted Shante to have my style, so I wrote for her in that way, and it wasn't a problem, of course. Biz had invented this whole different style and wanted to flow like that, he just couldn't always work the words out. So I wrote in that style for him. Because it was different, the way I wrote for him, it didn't sound like nothin' that would come from me, so it was harder to tell. Shante would always tell people that I wrote rhymes for her, it wasn't a big deal. The Biz thing was something that we kept on the hush. Anybody that was really into the artwork and reading all the credits on albums could put one and one together and figure it out, but it wasn't something we mentioned back then."

After all his backstage success, it was eventually very clear that Kane wasn't meant to be hidden away. The spotlight demanded to shine upon him, with his dashing good looks, calm, strong demeanor, and his inimitable way with words. Juice Crew kingpin Marley Marl knew there was something there. "When Marley found out that I was writin' stuff for Biz, he started wanting to have me record, to see what I sounded like," Kane recalls. Marley definitely liked what he heard, and by later in 1986 the two were working together. Their first output on wax was Kane's debut single "Get Into It," released on Prism in early 1987. The intro to the A-side featured the already-known Biz Markie, and the B-side was Kane's goofier "Just Rhymin' With Biz" (in addition to the track "Somethin' Funky"). "'Get Into It' was getting played," Kane explains, "But everyone thought it was Biz's song, so I wasn't getting no shows." The answer: "I went back into the studio and did 'Raw,' so I could get some shows of my own."

When it came to live shows at the time, Kane traveled with a whole crew, who also joined him on stage. He says: "Me and Murph grew up together, went to school together. He was my sidekick, kind of Jerome to my Morris Day. He decided to become a family man, so he left it alone, eventually. And Scoob and Scrap [Lover], they got involved from the Latin Quarter days. I met Mister Cee, my DJ, around 1984. I got down with his crew, the Magnum Force. They were some cats out of LG

[Lafayette Gardens, in Brooklyn]. I started rhymin' with them. One of the members got killed and another one had a bad accident and another one went away to the service. But me and Cee stayed together."

The "Raw" single, released on Prism in late 1987, was Kane's first real calling card: five intense minutes of pure, unadulterated braggadocio, with an incredible Marley-freaked James Brown loop and Kane's unmistakable, testosterone-charged voice. The single took off, convincing the powers-that-be at Warner Bros. (who were partnered with Cold Chillin', where most of the Marley Marl / Juice Crew output was placed) that Kane deserved an album.

The *Long Live The Kane* album was recorded at Marley Marl's home studio in Queens in early 1988, with all cuts done by Mister Cee. "Recording the album went real quick," Kane recalls. "Me and Marley worked together on things. Sometimes I wrote to the beat, sometimes I already had lyrics that fit a beat Marley did. Marley had a gritty feel for music. Regardless of how clean or brand-new the record was that he was sampling, or how light the production may have been, he always gave it a really gritty feel when he sampled it. He always put the 808 to it and gave it a heavy bottom and warm feel." Kane notes that two songs were supposed to be on the full-length but never made it: "Somethin' Funky" (on the b-side of his first single), and a newly-recorded song called "This Is For Your Own Concern."

Despite the respect he had for his producer, Kane recalls that the two talented artists butted heads often: "Honestly, me and Marley always disagreed in the studio. But then at the end of the day when the song was done and everyone else liked it, everything would be cool. It wasn't beef between us. Two creative minds in the studio are just gonna clash. I think they clashed in a good way." Kane also notes that back at that time the seemingly tight-knit Juice Crew weren't spending every minute together, as fans might have assumed: "We became a solid unit at shows, but we all lived our separate lives. Even so, we'd always do shows together, ride in the same limo and all that."

From the minimal Meters loop of the opening brag-workout "Long Live The Kane," to the more politically-charged final shot "Word To The Mother (Land)," the album is a perfect snapshot of New York hip-hop in 1988. It was getting smoother, but rough edges still abounded. Marley's unbeatable production and Kane's god-like lyricism makes it one of the most quotable and complete hip-hop albums of all time. "It was my debut and there's a lot of classic songs on there that I still perform today," Kane says. "A lot of people still remember it."

TRACKS

Wrath of Kane

Warner Bros. wanted to go with "I'll Take You There" for a single, and I didn't want that. I wanted "Set It Off." But they was calling the shots. I wanted a fast-paced song and they said I could do "Set It Off" as the next single, so I didn't want to waste it as a b-side, so I just recorded "Wrath of Kane" for that. I wanted to have something that was street.

Raw *(Remix)*

When it came to battle rhymes like that, I wrote that kind of stuff all the time. Like my man Murph would say: 'Yo, there's this kid in Bushwick that was talking shit about you and wants to battle.' So I'd start writing rhymes like that. We put the original "Raw" out in the fall of '87, on Prism, because Cold Chilln' was then part of Warner Bros. and Warner Bros. was only interested in Biz, Shante and Shan at the time. They didn't really want me at first. After [Warner] saw that it was doing good they picked it up for the *Colors* soundtrack, and that's when they signed me. Greg Mack in LA was bumping it hard on KDAY and we was finally getting a lot of shows, and having the record played in a lot of places. Marley did that remix after mastering, I had nothing to do with it. I wanted the original version on the album, but Marley made a smart call. It turned out for the best. The same day I did "Raw" back in '87 I had [Kool G] Rap with me, and after we finished the song we brought the track back up and just rhymed back & forth for a while until the beat ended. So, Marley took some of the rhymes I did on that take and mixed it in on the remix, so there was a few extra lyrics on there. I think Mister Cee must have done the cuts on there [instead of Marley].

Set It Off

That's my favorite song from the album. That's my favorite song of all the songs I've ever made, actually. I just like the adrenaline of it. I wanted it as a single, but Warners was excited about "I'll Take You There." I understand where they were coming from. They were older cats and they saw the relationship between the message and the Staples Singers thing. I still perform "Set It Off" all the time.

The Day You're Mine

Andre Booth co-wrote that. He was a keyboard player that Marley used, a real talented dude. He did that "Left Me Lonely" joint for Shan. He also did the "All of Me" joint I did with Barry White. I wanted to do a "Left Me Lonely" of my own. It wasn't written about any specific woman.

On The Bugged Tip *[with Scoob Lover]*

We were definitely going after the Cold Crush Brothers old-school style on that one. That was the style that Scoob rhymed in anyways. We used the old beat from *Wild Style* [the movie] to try and capture that feeling. That's what I grew up listening to, so I wanted to pay homage. I think I even got those [*Wild Style*] records from Tony Tone from Cold Crush [who was in the film and on the soundtrack]. He let me borrow them, the instrumentals. We went over to Marley's crib, Mister Cee cut it up and me and Scoob just went for it.

Ain't No Half Steppin'

That's the song that I'm most known for to this day, definitely. That was the first single they put out off the album, and we did a video for it. When I look at it now it's funny because that was the suit from my graduation. It was tight, way too small, but I was still tryin' to do it [laughs]. My man Lionel Martin blessed me with a lot of fine women for that video. It was cool, the whole boxing ring thing, it was pretty unique. That was the only video we made for that album, believe it or not.

I'll Take You There

That was actually the first song I ever did with Marley, before "Get Into It" and all that, the first time that he ever heard me rhyme. Marley had the Staple Singers ["I'll Take You There"] 45 and I remembered it from my man Understanding, when I used to be with this crew The Debonair Three. When we heard the part where it says "Big Daddy" I knew we had to use it. We wrote the rhymes and made the track but apparently Prince owned the rights to all the Staple Singers songs and wasn't tryin' to let no rappers use them. So we put it on the back burner. When I signed with Warner Bros, that was the same label that Prince was on, so then Prince was cool about it. I was trying to paint a picture about Paradise, not about religion. It's about being happy and living comfortably. Enjoying life without any drama or any problems.

Just Rhymin' With Biz

I really did the beat for that over at my man Shim Shom's house. He helped me put it together, with his little sampler, but it was too cheap to actually use for real production, so we had to re-do the whole thing over at Marley's place.

Marley Marl (from *In Control* interview): Frick & Frack was actually on that one, originally. It was just a two-track I lifted off the DAT tape. That track just happened, when the beat was playing. Kane just started out with "Check it out, y'all..." and it went from there. The levels are fucked up on the track, but it is what it is. Frick & Frack weren't signed to Cold Chillin' so I had to cut their verses off.

Word To The Mother (Land)

Those are words from Farrakhan tapes at the end of that track. I felt that he was dropping some serious jewels that a lot of young cats weren't really paying attention to, so I thought that they'd pay attention to a piece of what he was sayin' and would wanna go and get a Farrakhan tape, to hear it. People always asked me what that stuff was there at the end and I was glad to tell them.

PUBLIC ENEMY

It Takes A Nation Of Millions To Hold Us Back

(Def Jam, 1988)

"Mine and Hank's goal, originally, was to destroy music," says Public Enemy's Chuck D, about how he and "anti-musician" Hank Shocklee approached hip-hop. Provocative words, but in reality what Public Enemy destroyed was the hip-hop status quo, changing everything that came after them. Public Enemy hit the rap scene of the mid-'80s like a black nationalist Noah's ark, preserving the essence of artists like Run-DMC, Melle Mel and Schoolly D and leaving the rest in their wake – repercussions and shockwaves felt not only in hip-hop, but all music, making people reconsider the power of music and lyrics in a way that arguably hadn't been done since Bob Dylan brought real issues to real music, two decades earlier.

The extended Public Enemy family that the world came to know – William "Flavor Flav" Drayton; DJ Norman "Terminator X" Rogers; Richard "Professor Griff" Griffin; musical patriarch Hank Shocklee; Hank's brother Keith Shocklee; producer/musician Eric "Vietnam" Sadler; and conceptual and musical overseer Bill Stephney – came together in Hempstead and Roosevelt, Long Island long before Public Enemy began their musical assault on wax. Shocklee (at the time using his given last name, Boxley) started his Spectrum City mobile DJ crew in 1975, and brother Keith was helping by 1978 or so. Says Chuck: "Hank was always a legend in Roosevelt, and he always had Spectrum City."

Chuck joined the crew in 1979, after enrolling at Garden City's Adelphi University (he studied graphic design, graduating in 1984). "I rapped back in 1978 and '79 and I was vicious," Chuck brags. "I had a Satchel Paige story by the time I got to records. I had the strongest voice of anybody around me and that was key, because most sound systems were cheap. You had to be able to cut across a cheap system. Guys like DJ Hollywood and Melle Mel had no problems with something like that. Back at that time Hank heard me on the mic and I spanked everyone else, so he figured I would be the final component to what he had going. Me and Flavor was blessed with having voices on two different ends of the spectrum, and they could both cut through any live situation very easily. Flavor has bass in his treble and I have treble in my bass."

In 1982 the Spectrum City crew made it to Adelphi's radio station, WBAU, encouraged and guided by program director Bill Stephney. Flavor Flav also had a show on the station. Chuck remembers: "Flav was the greatest of all time on the air. He was just the same as he was on our records. Sometimes he would play like six tracks of his own stuff a night. He was the Uncle Floyd of hip-hop radio!" He adds: "Flav's early ad-libs would come from him mimicking this guy who lived around his way named Youngster or something like that. It was weird, but the better he mimicked that guy, the more he found an identity for himself."

The 90-minute "Super Spectrum City Mix Show" was a popular attraction on the station, and Hank and Chuck quickly realized and embraced the power of radio. The two made pre-show tapes at their homebase/clubhouse/studio: 510 South Franklin Street in Hempstead. The studio, in use by Spectrum City since 1981, became an important breeding ground for local Strong Island rap talent. "We would host 10 or 20 local rap groups from the area," Chuck recalls. "We'd record 'em up at our spot and put 'em out on the radio."

At 510 South Franklin they also met an important future component to the PE sound: Eric "Vietnam" Sadler, a local musician who had a studio in the same building. Vietnam soon became part of the Spectrum City mix. Chuck remembers: "We called him Vietnam because he'd always wear these old army jackets and these shades that made him look like he was a paratrooper [laughs]. He had a studio downstairs at 510 and we went down there and asked him to come up and start making music. He was a good guy and he worked well in our mix."

"Initially, Spectrum City never put out anything on wax," Chuck notes. "We just made tapes and put 'em straight on the radio. People always thought we had stuff on wax, but we only made songs to promote the radio station. I would do a song every once in a while to fill the void of not having enough records for our air-time. We was only interested in being radio jocks back then, we even tried to get a syndicated radio deal back in the day. Records just didn't hold much interest for us. I had interviewed so many nightmares in the record business by doing the radio show that I just wasn't interested in being involved with that."

Hank and Chuck grew ever better at recording, eventually acquiescing to record a single (as Spectrum City) on the Vanguard label in 1984 called "Lies." Chuck notes that the b-side of the single won: "We recorded the song 'Check Out The Radio' with the extra time we had on the session. It was a *severe* b-side [laughs] and was damn near fallin' off the record. The only reason we did that cut was to have more people know us as DJs and radio jocks. But that whole [recording] situation wasn't good, and it kept me from recording for a while." But, he adds: "'Check Out The Radio' was a very influential cut, for artists like Run-DMC and the Beastie Boys, who listened to the radio station religiously. It was a slower track, and it definitely influenced DMC and Run to write 'Slow and Low' for the Beastie Boys."

Despite the single, in the end it was a 1984 radio-only cut, "Public Enemy #1," that gave Spectrum City its eventual new name and its future record label as well. Def Jam co-founder Rick Rubin pursued Chuck for two years after he heard it on WBAU, until the deal was signed. "I put that song together on two tape decks and a Roland 8000 drum machine," Chuck laughs. "I pause-buttoned it together, did a vocal and overdubbed it on another tape deck. Flavor just happened to be in the other room, so that's how he got on it. 'Blow Your Head' [by the JBs, the main sample on the track] was a favorite of mine at the rink, but you could never find anyone who could DJ it and put it together quick enough, so that's why I had to use the tape decks."

Chuck and Hank left WBAU in 1986 (Stephney had bailed two years previous). Chuck says: "Hank and I left to run a club full-time and, at Bill's insistence, to move into recording." And move they did. After Rick Rubin's championing of the group, a deal was set and the group was making a record for his quickly-growing Def Jam empire (with partner Russell Simmons).

Public Enemy's 1987 debut *Yo! Bum Rush The Show* was one of the more powerful albums of the era, consisting of intense battle rhymes like "Miuzi Weighs A Ton" and "Public Enemy #1," and pointed social/political fare seen on the anti-crack manifesto "Megablast" and the talkin-loud/sayin'-nothing update "Rightstarter (Message To A Black Man)." Most of the album's pre-production work was done at 510 South Franklin. Chuck recalls: "Everything on that album was pre-recorded and then we would enhance upon it at regular studios like INS in New York. Basically we knew exactly what we was gonna do before we even went into the real studios. We wanted to execute quickly because we didn't want to pay somebody else's bills."

Musically the album was complicated and dark, with highly musical 808 drum programs, righteous funk samples, funky live wah-wah guitar (by Vernon Reid and co-producer Bill Stephney). And, of course, there was Chuck's booming voice, which grabbed you by the lapels and spit knowledge at you. In the background, edgy court jester Flavor Flav did the honors, getting his own solo shot on "Too Much Posse." It pushed forward, but it also stood on the shoulders of giants. Chuck explains: "The first album was something presented off the heels of *Raising Hell* [by Run- DMC], which I would call my favorite record of all time. We came at things differently than other people back then. The fact that I rapped about a car ["You're Gonna Get Yours"] on the first album was different than most rappers. I was older and had a different point of view. I was 26 years old in 1986, so of course I wouldn't rap about no high school shit. I was rapping from a grown man's viewpoint."

Despite the greatness of the album, they didn't enjoy its growing popularity for long. Chuck says: "On the day that *Yo! Bum Rush The Show* was released [in the spring of 1987], we was already in the trenches recording *Nation of Millions*." Hank and Eric didn't tour with Public Enemy – they stayed behind to work on cuts in the lab, so that the vocalists could hit the ground running whenever the group returned. Chuck adds: "The first record should have come out October of '86. When it actually came out it was past the timely point. [CBS labelmate Bruce] Springsteen pushed back the Beastie Boys, which pushed back our shit. *Yo!* to us was outdated. By the time it came out Eric B & Rakim and BDP had come out and changed the terrain of how you can rap. Our records were all recorded at the same time, but those guys came out first, so they were thought of as more innovative. Either way, they changed the phrasing of rap, which allowed you to be able to rhyme on a faster tempo, a faster groove."

The Bomb Squad, as PE's production team was now calling itself, had an intense work ethic, and they knew all too well that they were onto something big. The duties shared by the trio of Shocklee, Sadler and Chuck himself (credited in the album's liners as Carl Ryder, a pseudonym dating back to sports reporting he did on WBAU) had become much clearer as they began their epic sophomore album, *It Takes A Nation Of Millions To Hold Us Back*. Chuck explains: "Eric was the musician. Hank was the anti-musician. Eric did a lot of the [drum] programming, [Hank's brother] Keith was the guy who would bring in the feel. And me, I would scour for vocal samples all over the Earth. I would name it, title it, tag it and get the vocal samples. The friction between Hank and Eric worked very well. Hank would put a twist on Eric's musicianship and Eric's musicianship would put a twist on Hank."

Chuck adds: "Hank would come up with the final mix because he was the sound master. I wouldn't even fuck with the mix. Hank is the Phil Spector of hip-hop. He was way ahead of his time, because he dared to challenge the odds in sound. Once hip-hop became corporate they took the daredevil out of the artistry. But being a daredevil was what Hank brought to the table."

Crucial cuts "Rebel Without A Pause," "Bring The Noise," and "Don't Believe The Hype," were recorded at various times in-between tours in '87, but the bulk of the record was laid down during eight intense weeks in early 1988, for a modest $52,000 (*Yo! Bum Rush The Show* cost $17,000). Chuck says: "From January to the end of February, we just *rapped*." Originally with the working title *Countdown To Armageddon*, the group decided to call it *It Takes A Nation Of Millions To Hold Us Back* in the end, which was a line from *Yo! Bum Rush The Show*'s "Raise The Roof."

"We made [*Nation of Millions*] like it was just for cassettes," Chuck says. "We wanted to have an album that was equal on the first side and the second side. We didn't want to have any room at the end of a side, so there would be no dead time. We worked really hard to equal those sides, through the interludes and also the timing of different songs. Because of the interludes, the album was also the first rap record that didn't go cut to cut, it had stuff in-between songs, to make it all stick together, like glue." Some of the interstitial items used were live crowd noise from a show in London, recorded on November 3, 1987. "We used that live stuff for two reasons," Chuck explains. "First, to build on our importance overseas, since we were having lots of success over in Europe, and no rap group had ever done that. But we also wanted to show people in America that we had it goin' on, with 'em or without 'em [laughs]."

A little-known fact: the album's two sides were originally the other way around, having the album start with the song "Show Em Whatcha Got," going into "She Watch Channel Zero?!" (which is side two, the "Black Side"). Shocklee decided to flip them at the last second, just before mastering. "Of course the change worked!," Chuck laughs.

Bolstered by *Yo! Bum Rush The Show*'s acclaim, no small part of which was seen overseas, Chuck, Shocklee and Sadler knew that the work they were doing for *Nation of Millions* was going to be big. "*Nation* was just pure confidence," Chuck says. "We were like '*Nobody's* doing this shit here.' We wanted to build on the concept of faster tempos. We wanted to take a lot of shit over 107, 109 beats per minute. We knew our music would be faster-paced than anything out there. We knew that we could handle the speed and do it strong. Nobody out there could perform live on our level. That record was so intense that these young cats couldn't even keep up with us. We were all jocks and into martial arts, so we could go for an hour in a frenzy. It was like Mike Tyson at his peak. Because the material was so strong and because we could kill on the stage, we knew for a fact that the album would be a big hit. We made our records to tour, and we toured to make our records."

From the provocative cover by Glen E. Friedman – "We shot that in the city jail at 32nd Street, between 6th and 7th. We definitely wanted to get the idea across, that we were standing on the fuckin' American flag, too." – to every last one of the dozens of samples buried in the mix, the legend of *It Takes A Nation Of Millions To Hold Us Back* is one of the most storied in hip-hop. The album still stands to this day as, in this writer's opinion, the most important and influential rap platter ever made.

"Sometimes on the outside looking in I say: 'Damn, did I really have anything to do with that record?'," Chuck muses. But he most certainly did, and hip-hop is a better place because of it. Chuck offers one final thought, about influence and continuity: "*Nation of Millions* made [N.W.A.'s] *Straight Outta Compton* possible, later that year. The first two copies that I had of *Nation* actually went to Dr. Dre and Eazy-E. We were in Vegas and they were on tour with us and I had just got the vinyl in. That's what this is all about. Because Run-DMC and LL Cool J gave me energy. And if our energy happened to be transferred to N.W.A., then that's what this whole thing is for. Schoolly D influenced me on the first album as much as Run-DMC and I found out later that Ice Cube was influenced by how I broke shit down. Schoolly told me that he was influenced by Melle Mel. And that's just how the cycle goes."

TRACKS

Bring The Noise

That came out first on the "Less Than Zero" soundtrack, before our album. We recorded that in late September of 1987, after we did "Don't Believe The Hype." The original name of that was "Countdown To Armageddon." I got the music to it while I was on the Def Jam tour with LL and I tried to tackle it all summer long in '87. I wrote three different verses for it and it just didn't pan out for me. I just could not nail it. Then Hank came at me with the suggestion that I attack the song with three different verse styles. We were doing a show in Atlanta and Harry Allen came down, and he had a mix of it, from Hank. I listened to it on headphones and got so mad at it that I threw it across the room and damn near out the window. I was like: "We fucking failed!" I came back from tour in September (of 87) to record that at Sabella Studios here in Long Island and I still could not totally nail it. All of us plus

Terminator were there at the time. Eric and Hank did all the drum programs. I brought in the top stuff, those samples. We were 75% of the way through it and I hit a creative wall, but then I pulled through in the end. At 5:30 in the morning Terminator came over to scratch, and we all thought what he did was kinda wack until we took the bass out during the mix. I love that scratch to this day, now! We learned that you can pull the bass out during the mix and there can still be some great topping. We went overseas the second week in November (of '87) and me and Griff told Terminator to put the track on, because we had an acetate. We did it and the crowd went berzerk. So it was meant to be. Flavor's comments on there, and on all tracks, were always ad-libbed. I don't think he ever wrote anything down. We would guide him on which ad-lib to use, but that was about it.

Don't Believe The Hype

When I was coming off a tour in '87 I was given some crazy terrain by Hank and Eric, like "Bring The Noise" and "Don't Believe The Hype." "Hype" came up before the tour and we recorded it right after "Rebel Without A Pause," although it didn't come out until '88, as the first single off *Nation of Millions*. We recorded that in September of '87. It didn't have a video. We said: "Why the fuck should we? We ain't gonna see it nowhere." A video was actually put together over in London because of our massive following over there. We refused to do one in the U.S. because there was no guaranteed national exposure. When "Yo! MTV Raps" came about, PE did the pilot show, in the summer of '88. That was the green light to say: "Hey, our second single should have a video." We actually originally were going to use "Don't Believe The Hype" for the *Less Than Zero* soundtrack, but we wanted the jam to be turbulent, not funky. "Don't Believe" was more regular than something like "Bring The Noise" so we just put it in the can and forgot about it. It got the eventual nod of approval because Hank went to this spot on the Lower East Side and heard DMC play the shit in his car, and it renewed his interest. The comments about writers were pointed at guys like John Leland [from *Spin* and the *Voice*] who just didn't get it. When it says "It's a sequel" we meant that it was the sequel to "Rebel Without a Pause." That song was a really big hit in Atlanta first, thanks to Ray Boyd at B103. I got him tickets for a show and the next week it was added. To this day "Don't Believe" is played as one of the classics in the ATL.

Cold Lampin' With Flavor

Initially we wanted to bring Flavor through into the recording contract and Rick [Rubin] and Russell [Simmons] pretty much detested the idea. They were like: "You gotta sign a vocalist, and what the fuck does he do?" And me and Hank said: "Well, we can't really explain what he does, but he brings flavor to the situation. You'll see." I said I wouldn't sign with Def Jam unless they signed Flavor. We knew he was an integral part. We were big fans of James Brown and Bobby Byrd, and that was the kind of stage relationship it was, in a weird way. "Cold Lampin'" was bringing more Flavor flavor to the equation. On the third album he really came forward because "911" was our first single.

Terminator X To The Edge Of Panic

The music to that is "Rebel Without A Pause" backwards [laughs]. We was rockin' that freestyle out, around '87. We had the track backwards, and we wanted Terminator's name to shine more. We put some Farrakhan speeches on it and we had something out of nothing. It was one of those things that was put together at the last minute. Griff gave me that album with the Farrakhan quote at the end. It was the Minister from the 1980 Jack The Rapper convention, telling black radio that they had a responsibility to inform the people.

Louder Than A Bomb

With that Kool & The Gang "Who's Gonna Take The Weight" sample we just found the sound that fit the ideal. I don't remember who brought that one into the mix. Spectrum City [the studio at 510 South Franklin] was just two rooms full of records. That song was simply about the fact that the FBI was tapping my phone. My phone would go dead between 1 and 2 o'clock every night, even when I got the phone people to fix it. I was saying: "I'm not keeping any secrets because everything I'm saying, I'm saying it on record." It was one of our favorite records, but we never performed it in concert. We designed our show around peaks and valleys. That song would start on any other team but not on this bench.

Caught, Can We Get A Witness?

That record was dead and damn near out the window. It was a good topic, talkin' about samplin' beats, but we couldn't build upon that groove until the last minute. The topic made it come through in the end, we put some Bar Kays on it. We got sued religiously, a lot after the fact, but not at that time [when we made the song]. The song itself was just challenging the purpose of it.

She Watch Channel Zero ?!

That's a Slayer loop there ["Angel of Death"]. We already had that Slayer record. We had Rick Rubin's [who produced Slayer] blessing but he didn't spend any time in the studio with us, except some of the mixes on the rock songs that we'd bring him in on. We were the group that Rick gave total confidence and total blessing to do our thing. People said that it was an anti-female song, but my answer to that is that you're not looking at the self-criticism in other songs on the album. We attacked everything. I didn't think it was misogynist. I said: "Hey, fuck those soap operas." And I say it to this day. Jerry Springer and all of that. I'd say the same to a guy if he's just sittin' in front of the football game with a beer, talking shit. I mean, you couldn't say: "He/She Watch Channel Zero." You make a song and you make a statement.

Night of the Living Baseheads

That's a Khalid Muhammad speech at the beginning. A lot of those speeches came from Griff and the S1W's and I would figure out where they would fit. Most of them were off of tapes. "Baseheads" was the second single off the album and the first video that we made, which we did by committee. We knew we had to make it as cutting edge as our music, because we were coming out late in the [video-making] game. We filmed it outside of the Audubon Ballroom [where Malcolm X was murdered] and other locations. I think we did that video for about $40,000. It got played ridiculously, because "Yo! MTV Raps" had come out, which forced BET to come out with their own show, "Rap City." For the track itself I wanted to write a song about how much crack was affecting us. It was all the way around us, 360 degrees.

Black Steel In The Hour Of Chaos

Back when I was seven years old I saw my uncle come to my grandmother's house to get his draft papers for Vietnam. Of course as a kid you're trying to see what's going on. I saw their faces drop. I thought about the whole draft policy, it just stuck with me. I was like: "If I have to go to jail for not fighting in a war, then breaking out is righteous."

Rebel Without A Pause

By the time we actually came out with *Yo! Bum Rush The Show* Hank and I began putting together "Rebel Without A Pause." It came out first on the b-side of "You're Gonna Get Yours" [from *Yo!*]. Hank and I came up with the track and then I locked myself in the house for two days, trying to nail it. There was so much aggression in it because we were trying to prove a point – that we knew what the fuck we were doing. Hank got a partial writing credit on the lyrics – it was a Lennon/McCartney thing. It took about two weeks to get that right. I did it the first day and wasn't happy with it and I went home mad. Then I came back three or four days later and nailed it. I can't recall ever nailing anything on the first take, at least not anything that I was satisfied with. I remember when me and [Ice] Cube and [Big Daddy] Kane were recording "Burn Hollywood Burn" [which came out on *Fear Of A Black Planet*] and I was amazed how they could actually nail a cut in one or two takes. But they had different vocal delivery styles. I could never rely on just sittin' back, relaxing and letting the studio make me sound good.

Prophets of Rage

That was a last addition cut. I was going through a whole bunch of old tapes that happened to be sitting in the studio, that Eric and Hank had concocted. I was sittin' in traffic and I was so impressed by it that I actually wrote to it right there. To this day I still love it, it's one of my favorites. That was a big live song, especially with Griff. When he left we stopped doing it, when he rejoined a couple of years later we brought it back into the set. You have to be really physically fit to handle that song [laughs]. It's breakneck speed. The title came from an article I saw in *Life* magazine that had that caption about Malcolm X. It said: "What ever happened to the prophets of rage?" I like to make the title to a song first because it helps me write the rest of the song. I operate from the title on down. That track was done later in the recording process. I think vocally I stretched the limits on that one. I was just never satisfied with my takes. I was known as the "Hundred-Take Man" [laughs].

Party For Your Right To Fight

With flipping the Beasties like that it was like: "Together we're on Def Jam, but we're not them" [laughs]. It wasn't a dis, it was just saying we were the opposite of what you think the Beastie Boys are. The Black Panthers were the party we were talking about, of course. The track itself was so quirky that it definitely fit inside the concept of the album, and we knew that we had enough muscle bangers on the album that we could afford to do something that was totally left field. It became a performance cut because of the difference. It was a contrast that set a stronger record up.

THE D.O.C.

No One Can Do It Better

(Ruthless / Atlantic, 1989)

This much is indisputable: no one could fuck with N.W.A. by the time 1988 rolled around, not once *Straight Outta Compton* took the nation by storm. But N.W.A. wouldn't have been the same or blown up in the same way without the input of one of its lesser-known co-conspirators: The D.O.C.

Hailing from West Dallas, Texas, D.O.C. was first known as Doc T. "I was born and raised in the projects," he says, "And my first experiences in hip-hop were just hanging out and playing the dozens on the street corner. Rappin' against guys, but we didn't know we was even rappin' back then. We was just horsing around." Eventually he became involved with the four man (finally whittled down to three) Fila Fresh Crew (with Dr. Rock, Fresh K and a rapper named Curtis), one of the only local rap groups at the time. They released the self-produced cut "I Hate To Go To Work" in 1986. As Doc says of the record's style, with a chuckle: "That was D.O.C. in my Fresh Prince days."

The group's DJ, Dr. Rock, was tight with a then up-and-coming DJ and producer named Dr. Dre, from Los Angeles. Dre at the time was a member of the popular World Class Wreckin Cru, more of a dance-oriented unit than a hardcore hip-hop mob. "Dr. Rock had a local radio show and knew Dre," Doc says, "So Dre came to town and went on his show. Dre heard us bustin' rhymes and actually did a couple tracks for us on the spot. Dre and I just clicked and we was working together from there."

The Dre and Doc chemistry was so good, in fact, that Doc decided to move from the Lone Star State to a very different place: Los Angeles. "I moved to LA in late 1987 and all the other N.W.A. guys were coming together," D.O.C. recalls. "Dre and Yella was in World Class Wreckin' Cru. Eazy wasn't in a group, he was the neighborhood dope man, and Ren was Eazy's man, who could rap. When I got there, N.W.A. started happening. They had already taken pictures together. Arabian Prince was down with them. And they were trying to make music together but they hadn't found that direction yet. They was still makin' Wreckin Cru type of music." Doc even changed his name upon arrival: "When I first came to Cali I was Doc T, but since my new crew was N.W.A., I put the periods in my name as my connection to the group. Like: 'I'm with you, but I'm over here.'"

"I knew that something was going to happen when I moved out to LA," he continues, "Because I was pretty damn good and Dre was, too. When you mix good dope with good dope you get great dope [laughs]." D.O.C.

was part of the crew, but wasn't part of N.W.A. officially, and that was fine with him. "When you look at all the old N.W.A. videos, you won't see me in any of them. I'm not on the cover of *Straight Outta Compton*, that's Arabian Prince, he's the sixth guy on there. But it wasn't on purpose that I was left out, I just wasn't around sometimes. I didn't ever want to be in N.W.A., I just wanted to play my role and help everybody out. I was really confident in my own skills, so I was just waiting for my turn."

Aside from appearing with the Fila Fresh Crew (who had four tracks out of 11) on the album that started it all, *N.W.A. And The Posse* from 1987 (He says: "That album was just something they took off of all our independent singles and records and threw 'em all together"), Doc also says that he played crucial behind-the-scenes roles in the N.W.A. organization. The first was writing many of Eazy-E's rhymes, starting with the hit single "We Want Eazy" in early 1988. Doc talks about his style from West Dallas through his early days in LA: "My style changed from when I left Texas and got to Cali in 1987. Maybe it was something in the water [laughs]. It developed and grew, it went from raps to conversations. When I got there, something like 'We Want Eazy' was literally the way I used to rap. Happy and silly. But by the time I got to my album they were conversations."

Writing for Eazy wasn't always an easy task, but it was certainly a challenge that Doc was up for. "Eazy wasn't the greatest rapper in the world, so you had to make him sound as good as Ice Cube, especially if they were on the same track. Technically it was tough. He just couldn't rap very well, he was not an MC. Eazy was just a guy having fun. All he wanted to talk about was bitches. That was his whole focus. He was a character and he just had *it*, whatever that was, and you just let him have fun. And he did a good job at it." Ren and Ice Cube also wrote rhymes for Eazy at the time, including "Eight Ball" and "Boyz-N-The Hood," respectively.

By late 1987 into early 1988, it was all about Eazy's record, which hit first and paved the way for *Straight Outta Compton*. Doc recalls: "What we did was focus on Eazy's record. I wrote songs for him that weren't so frightening to the white man, so we could get it on radio. Because radio hadn't even really accepted rap, period, much less a track like 'Boyz-N-The Hood.'" He cites the first single, "We Want Eazy," as a perfect example, explaining: "Fresh Prince could have rhymed 'We Want Eazy.' That was the design – to make 'em laugh with Eazy and not be afraid of him. That's how we did Eric's record. That was my job, to help him get to the radio. Because 'Suck my dick, fuck the bitch in the ass' wasn't going to cut it. We'd tell funny little stories that would make the ol' white man laugh at him."

He adds: "Once Eazy got mainstream radio play back in 1988 you couldn't hold us back, it was all over with. We did a song that had no cuss words, but it was hard and it kept its integrity. So we got little kids in suburbia who would never have a chance to hear this shit and they're being introduced to Eazy-E. And when they go and buy the album, it's of course a totally different story."

Doc's second role was, as he explains: "Serving as another set of ears, ears that were open to what radio wanted to hear. I was a big part of *Straight Outta Compton*, for sure. I spent my time concentrating on how everyone else was doing. I was so confident in my skills that I wanted to make sure everybody else was confident in theirs, too [laughs]. I was really an Executive Producer, but I didn't even know it back then, and I definitely didn't get credit for it." He also claims to have written "a considerable amount" of Eazy's rhymes on *Compton*.

After *Straight Outta Compton* was released and proceeded to blow up (much like Eazy's debut), the next crew album was readied: D.O.C.'s debut, *No One Can Do It Better*. "Everybody was just in line to put out albums in those early days," he says. "It was Eazy, N.W.A. and then they was going to do Miche'le's and then mine. But once Eazy's and N.W.A.'s records jumped off so big and so fast, they decided to do my record next." D.O.C. had been on tour with N.W.A. and Eazy throughout the year, so he was already well-known to fans of the group.

No One Can Do It Better was recorded in one month in mid-1988 at Audio Achievements in Torrance, CA, with Dr. Dre behind the boards. It was undeniably the first album where Dre showed his greatness as a solo producer, and D.O.C. lived up to the challenge of the tracks by bringing his A-Game on the mic. "That album took us about a month of solid work, maybe," Doc says. "We were just doing songs when we had a minute, while everybody else was doing shows. I had already been working on stuff and when N.W.A. would perform I'd open up for them, when they was at skating rinks and shit. The crowds were really into it, so we knew we had shit that was working. We had also worked the songs out already, so my album really didn't take much time to make."

The album hit stores in May of 1989, according to Doc. "When my record came out we were still on the *Straight Outta Compton* tour and

I wasn't paying attention to my record deal. I was just having fun. I didn't think anything about the business. In the early days when Ren and Cube and them got paid, I didn't even get any. My record was my chance for that. It was my time to shine."

Skillfully rhyming over both fast and slow beats, D.O.C. showed on his debut that he was one of the West Coast's most talented MCs. He also showed that although he was an important part of the N.W.A. family, he wasn't coming out with guns blazing: "There was no way I was going to be confused with N.W.A., especially when my record came out. My style was a total departure from their stuff. And here is the one point I'd like to make that really means something to me: the phenomenon was N.W.A., and when N.W.A. hit it changed the face of rap records, and everyone wanted to do the N.W.A. thing. My record came out the following year and was just as hard as *Straight Outta Compton* but with almost no cussing and none of the violence. To me, you was a real MC if you could do that. The kids wanted you to cuss, but if I could make something just as hard as N.W.A. without doing that, then to me that was the shit."

He adds: "So many rappers today, even ones that people claim are the greatest of all time, you can hear in their flows what I did on *No One Can Do It Better*. You didn't know how I was going to flow from one song to the next. I did it all."

The album was catching fire on the heels of Doc's N.W.A. touring involvement and on the strength of the lead single "It's Funky Enough," when tragedy struck. On November 11, 1989 at 4:30 in the morning, D.O.C. was involved in a car crash that put him in a coma for two days and severely damaged his voice, turning his strong, smooth flow into a rasp. "After the accident, everything shut down, I couldn't do anything," he says. "I couldn't even talk for six months. I had to perform to a tape, because I just couldn't get any of that shit out. I didn't get a chance to perform my own stuff very much before the accident, and unfortunately I never even got the opportunity to fully grow into that album."

After years of downward spiraling, fueled by drugs, drinking and depression, Doc says: "Things started to get better in 1998. I started to see things more clearly." His advice to those who are heading down the wrong road: "The most important thing I can tell people is that with drugs you can't win. For me the crash came early. For other motherfuckers it'll take 15 years. But the crash *will* come."

Thankfully for the hip-hop world, the D.O.C. wasn't lost on that fateful day in 1989, even if it did dramatically damage his vocals and his career. But he continues on to this day, and if anyone wants proof that he was the shit, all they have to do is pop in *No One Can Do It Better*. Case closed.

TRACKS

It's Funky Enough

That was the first single, it came out in May of 1989, when the album hit. That one is also my favorite video. We were on tour when it came out and I hadn't seen the video we had made and all that. But when we got to the East Coast, kids in the audience was singing my songs and it was freaking me out, although of course I loved it. So I think it touched down on the East Coast first. I think that video was the last one with all the N.W.A. guys in it together. I had to beg Dre to make the music that way for that track. See, the track it's based on, "Misdemeanor," [by Foster Sylvers] had no room to loop it where it was just instrumental. So we replayed the whole thing. The music is all live instruments. I asked Dre a couple times and he kept saying "There's no room." After the third time he gave in. Andre Bolton, Stan Jones and Yella were the band who replayed the track. Sometimes I had a Jamaican flow on there because I had been drinking that day and when I heard the track in the booth it sounded kind of Jamaican to me. I didn't write the rap like that, it just came out like that.

Mind Blowin'

You can definitely hear the humble beginnings of Bone Thugs 'N' Harmony in that record. Dre did the cuts on there, not Yella. Dre was actually gonna be my DJ way back, when things was forming there in 1987. He wasn't even going to be in N.W.A. at all, although I think that lasted about two days [laughs]. With my lyrics on there and my style, no one was rapping fast like that on the West Coast. I was East Coast-influenced, so no one was fuckin' with things like that back then.

Lend Me An Ear

That was a faster track. I did it that fast because I could do anything. I rapped to whatever beats Dre had. He knew there wasn't too much that I couldn't hold onto.

Comm. Blues

That was just us drinkin' and smokin', that's what we'd do. That's Michel'le on the vocals there. She didn't really know how to sing the blues, so I had to sing that for her first, to show her.

Let The Bass Go

That was one of the first tracks I ever made. I did that track and "Whirlwind Pyramid" in early 1987 in Eazy-E's momma's garage. It ended up on the album untouched, even two years later. Those tracks were really just straight samples, musically. People were more into deep bass in Dallas than in LA, I think. They didn't really give a fuck if it sounded good. In LA it had to sound good *and* be loud and deep. I shout out DJ Speed on there, he ended up being my DJ. He was just one of Eazy's homeboys.

Beautiful But Deadly

Dre *had* to do "Cosmic Slop" for [the music on] that one! He was the biggest P-Funk fan ever. That song wasn't about a woman, it was about cocaine. Nobody knew that at the time, and I didn't either, really, because I started doing that shit later on. I didn't write that song for myself, I wrote it just talking about drugs in general. Cocaine is definitely beautiful but deadly. Maybe it was a precognition, that that bitch was gonna run my way. I didn't think I'd ever do it at the time when I did that song, though.

The D.O.C. & The Doctor

That was my Run impression. I was Run on that one and nobody could tell me different. He was my hero coming up. If you listen to "Together Forever" [by Run-DMC] it's damn near the same thing. That was a single off the album, too.

No One Can Do It Better

That sample at the beginning was Rudy Ray Moore. We did that song later in the album sessions, and at that time N.W.A. had all but stopped coming down to the studio. It was just me and Dre there most of the time.

Whirlwind Pyramid

That was a way to take a lot of the shit that I had been reading at the time and put it in a song. I'm a spiritual dude and back then I was taking notes on people that were talking about the Masons and I was reading about how those groups go so far back in world history. A whirlwind pyramid was some sign that they had, like with the eye on the dollar bill.

The Formula

One night Dre came back home and he had been to the movies with Michel'le. He said: "I had a daydream that you wrote a song called 'The Formula' to Marvin Gaye's 'Inner City Blues.'" I wrote that song that night and we recorded it the next day. It's my favorite track on the record. I've always felt a kind of connection to Marvin Gaye, somehow. My parents loved his music. There may have been a lot of arrogance in my writing but I also wore my heart on my sleeve and said whatever was on my mind. I was just a cool dude who could rap real good. Without Dre's daydream we would have never made that track, though. I stayed up all night and wrote that song. The first verse of the actual song is the formula, as if you were a chemist with little beakers and liquid in 'em. You had high energy, wisdom, sense of a rich man, knowledge, and rhythm. You stir it all up and that's what the formula is.

The Grand Finale

I wrote Eazy's rhymes on that, of course. That's the last time we all rapped together, right before Ice Cube left. Dre wasn't on there, really, except to direct the rhymes. He wasn't a rapper, really. The rappers were me, Cube and Ren. And Eazy was just the man. If Dre didn't have to rap, he wouldn't. He didn't force it. I think that Cube has the best verse on that track, even better than mine. He says "Stutter steppin'" on there, that was the rhythm I used to rap a lot. You stick a whole bunch of words in a little space, but if you're rhythm is right it'll sound like you're tap dancing, almost. When Cube said that in his rhyme, it made me feel so good.

MARLEY MARL

In Control Volume 1

(Cold Chillin' / Warner Bros., 1988)

Long before the Wu-Tang Clan began to spread their tentacles; when P. Diddy was still using the name on his birth certificate; and while the heads of the Cash Money and Roc-A-Fella families were likely trying to get a date to the 7th grade dance, Marley Marl and the Juice Crew ruled hip-hop. They were the first rap dynasty, with a distinct ruler and amazingly talented field generals. In the late '80s there was no one making music like producer and DJ Marley Marl. And 1988 was the year it all broke out.

To cap off a year that saw debut smashes by Big Daddy Kane, MC Shan, Biz Markie and Roxanne Shante, Marley Marl's *In Control Volume 1* dropped. It was important not only because it contained dope tracks by Juice Crew members young and old. It was also a record that pointed to the producer as much more than a behind-the-scenes puppet master. "It was definitely an important thing to have a producer thought of as an artist, especially back then," Marley says today. "Up to that point, the vocalist or MC was the person that an album was about. Positioning me like that on the album was something different for the whole game. I had never even thought of doing my own album, but with *In Control* I was one of the first producers to actually step up as an artist."

The labels involved, Cold Chillin' and their parent company Warner Bros., were gung-ho about *In Control* as well. Marley says: "Warner and Cold Chillin' were definitely into the album because I was building seed for them, since they had me as a producer. When we hit them with the idea of me as an artist, Benny Medina at Warners was all over it."

The album itself, rather than a fully-planned effort that took years to conceive, was brought about by a fruitful problem: Marley still had great tracks from Juice Crew members that didn't fit on their albums. He recalls: "At that point, we had made a lot of records, and I had a lot of heat in the crib that hadn't even made it on an album, for different artists. Because so much of that stuff was already done, it didn't take long at all to put together."

A close perusal of the artist listings on the platter shows that Marley was more concerned with bringing up newcomers who hadn't hit hard yet, like Tragedy [aka Percy], Craig G and the newly-signed Master Ace. Marley confirms this: "Kane and G Rap had gold chains by '88. I was trying to bring the young cats up. At that point I was mostly concerned with Craig and Tragedy. That's why they had solo records on there. Ace, too. Everybody else was already stars, so I wasn't worried as much about them."

Named after his long-running "Marley Marl In Control" radio show on WBLS in New York, the platter did exactly what Marley intended. And aside from introducing the world to the next wave of Juice Crew talent (sadly, none of the three he was pushing ever had the success of their predecessors), the album spawned one of the greatest posse cuts in hip-hop history: "The Symphony," featuring Ace, Craig G, Kool G Rap and Big Daddy Kane. It was the only track done exclusively for *In Control*.

The album's cover was a true classic of the late '80s era as well, with Marley poised in the cockpit of a private jet, with a crew group photo on the back. "That cover shot was my ex-wife's idea," Marley laughs. "I told the people at the label about it and the next thing I know we're at an airport, in front of a private jet, with a pilot suit for me. That suit was just a prop, of course. And the gold chains I was wearing were a prop, too. I never owned any big gold chains like that, believe it or not. They were probably Kool G's or Kane's."

"It was good for me that *In Control* came out after everybody else's album in 1988, no doubt," Marley says. "My album was much more anticipated because of the success of all the other Juice Crew hits." As for sales, Marley claims that he never paid too much attention, which would be a first for a producer with points. "I'm not sure if that album went gold," he muses, "But the first week it was out it probably sold about 50,000. That was a nice buzz record, definitely." He adds: "That was my approach to that whole era. I wasn't even doing it for the money. I was really loving just doing it. It just so happened that I made money, so I wasn't arguing with that. What I didn't know is how much history we was making."
"I like to revisit my older stuff, like that album, sometimes. It puts me in that state of mind again. I go through those tracks and they give me a sense of how they played a part in forming the hip-hop and R&B that's around today. Like 'We Write The Songs' and 'The Symphony.' They still sound phenomenal to me."

He ends our chat by dropping a newsflash that will make Juice Crew fiends froth: "I've got an album called *Juice Crew Unreleased Gems* that I want to put out. I have a Tragedy song on that motherfucker called 'Son of the Block' that I made the same week that I produced 'Make The Music' for Biz [Markie], 'Eric B Is President' [for Eric B & Rakim] and also [MC Shan and Marley's] 'The Bridge.' So you can go figure what that must sound like. Back then I would have a sound of the week. Whatever drum sound was in the sampler, that's what I went with, for whoever I was producing."

TRACKS

Droppin' Science *[with Craig G]*

Wooooooooooo [Makes high-pitched exclamation when song title is mentioned]! That version on the album was the original one. The one that a lot of people know is the single version, which had a different beat to it [using Lou Donaldson's version of "Who's Making Love"]. I think that remix, the single version, is one of my favorite beats of all time, and it was only on the single, it never came out on any album. Craig didn't even like it at first, either, he liked the first version. That track and "The Symphony" were the singles from the album. Craig was only 17 or 18 when that came out. He was too young to even sign to Cold Chillin', like Tragedy. Craig had a lot of mic technique and a lot of presence, even at a young age. He got that from watchin' us out in the park.

We Write The Songs *[with Heavy D and Biz Markie]*

Aww, yeah! I loved working with Biz, his spontaneity. He was so quick, you had to record him all the time, or you'd miss something. A lot of the time when he was around I'd have a 120-minute DAT recording, rolling just in case. I think Biz must have come up with the idea for that track, since he sang the hook. And Heavy D and I go way back. I helped produce "Mr. Big Stuff" for him and I did some stuff on his first two albums. Heavy D was a big, fun guy. He brought some fun to the game, most definitely.

The Rebel *[with Percy / Tragedy]*

Tragedy recorded his two tracks for *In Control* way before I even thought about doing the album. They were just demos. And when the album came out in 1988 he was only 15 or 16 and in jail, still just a kid. So we set up a fund for him, so that he came out to some money. He got out the week we did the video for "The Symphony." The first time I worked with him was on the Super Kids "The Tragedy" single [Nia Records, 1986]. That was him and Hot Day Dante. He was only 12 or 13 when that record came out, and in jail already.

Keep Your Eye On The Prize *[with Master Ace and Action]*

Everybody always said Ace & Action, but Master Ace had two DJs – the other one was Steady Pace. Ace was from Brooklyn, but he got hooked up with me because he won a rap contest at United Skates of America in Queens. The grand prize was to go into the studio with Marley Marl. I liked his style, so I kept him with me after the demo. That was Steady Pace cutting up at the end of that, not me.

The Symphony *[with Master Ace, Craig G, Kool G Rap and Big Daddy Kane]*

That track was the only one made specifically for the *In Control* album. We did the photo shoot for the back cover of the album [with most of the Juice Crew present], at an airport on Long Island somewhere, and went to my studio in Astoria right from there. Everybody was together and was freestylin', and I was like: "Yo! We need to go make a record right now." Shan is in that photo shoot, but he didn't come to the studio. He was supposed to meet us later, but he never showed up, so he's not on the record. As soon as the record company heard that collaboration, we all knew right away that it was the lead single for the album. We knew it would be huge. I don't know if I could choose who has the illest verse on there [laughs]. Maybe mine was [laughs loudly]! Kool G Rap actually rapped from where his verse started to the end of the whole song. I have that version somewhere. I had to cut his part off, when Kane's verse comes in.

Duck Alert *[with Craig G]*

That's definitely my favorite song on the album. Definitely don't forget about "Duck Alert"! That was a promo for my radio show and it was directed at Red Alert and Chuck Chillout, both of them. They were both on Kiss FM, the opposing station, and hip-hop was all about dissing. We used to call Chuck, "Duck Illout." Craig G only did one verse on the original radio promo of that, and after we decided to use it on the album he went in and we added a couple extra verses. To be honest, I never saw Red Alert as competition on the radio, but it was just the thing to do, to make a dis track. Red and I both work for Power 105 in New York now [in 2003] and we chuckle about how much radio history we made back then. And how we didn't even know how much history we were making.

Freedom *[with MC Shan]*

That was just a different mix of a track on Shan's album from earlier that year ["Give Me My Freedom"]. Shan and I were going to go on stage with Nas for the Hot 97 Summer Jam this year [in 2003], to perform “The Bridge” in the middle of Nas’ show, and then do a quick battle with KRS-One. But it fell through. That would have been something!

Wack Itt *[with Roxanne Shante]*

That song was on Shante’s album, I just took a different version of it for mine. I had the track done and she just got on the mic and started dissing. All you had to do was give her an idea and she’d run with it, she never even wrote her lyrics down. That song was kind of like a joke, more like a skit. I don’t think she cared that much about Salt ‘N’ Pepa or JJ Fad either way.

TOO $HORT

Life Is... Too $hort

(Dangerous / Jive, 1989)

Oakland rap legend Too $hort may be a pimp, but he's always been a relatively low-key one. "From day one I told everyone around me that I didn't want to be famous," he says today. "In Oakland everybody knew the voice and the name, but in my early years nobody had a face to put with it." Anonymity may have been easier in his pre-platinum days – he released four albums before 1989's classic *Life Is... Too $hort* and has released more than a dozen since – but he soon had to give up his dream of living the non-famous life.

Born in Los Angeles in 1966, Todd Shaw moved to East Oakland in 1979, to live with his mother. Shortly thereafter he began the dream of being a rapper, influenced by the music of course, but as much by pimps he saw in his neighborhood. He took drum, guitar and horn lessons in high school. $hort's first experience in the rap world was with his friend Freddy B. In the early '80s they made their first tape, which was a tribute to a local pimp named Hot Lips who they knew from around the way. He paid them $20 for it, and they were off, making many more home-made tapes on a regular basis, with general names like "Game 1" and Game 2." These sold well locally.

While his tape-selling days were going strong, $hort noticed other local artists who put their music out on vinyl, with professional-looking packaging. "I had always figured that you had to be on a label from New York to have a real record out back then [in the early and mid-'80s]," $hort recalls. "But before MC Hammer started doing his thing in the Bay, there was a guy named Motorcycle Mike who put out a record called 'Super Rat' on a label called Ho Disk. The label was owned by a drug kingpin named Mickey Moe. The song was on the radio, it was good. The rat was talking shit, basically. And there was another record by a guy named Steve Walker that was real inspirational to me. His record was called 'Tally Ho' and he pressed his own record up and took it to the store himself. He was from Oakland, too."

$hort's and Freddy's partnership putting out local tapes was going along at a steady clip, regularly selling thousands of copies of each release around the Bay. But they hit a big snag in 1983: Freddy got locked up. "We were 100% a group, and there was no possibility of us going solo up to that point," $hort explains, "But Freddy went to prison, not jail. It wasn't just county jail for a few months. He was gone for a while. By the time he got out he wanted to do something but then he went right back to jail." $hort didn't want to stop the momentum that they had started, so he reluctantly embarked on a solo career. According to $hort, Freddy himself did the same thing years later, releasing solo albums once he was out of the big house for extended periods of time.

$hort's solo career, then, began in 1985 on the 75 Girls label, owned by local entrepreneur, manager and producer Dean Hodges. He made three records – which were more like long EPs than full albums... the most tracks on any album was seven cuts – for 75 Girls from 1985 through 1987 (some sources say that these albums started in 1983, but $hort himself says 1985) – *Don't Stop Rappin'*; *Raw, Uncut & X-Rated*; and *Players*. Each release sold more and more copies, mostly on cassette and almost exclusively in Northern California. "Those were as popular as you can be, in that area," he says. "It was the hottest shit around there, but it was only local." The tracks themselves were basic, with replayed funk riffs swiped from popular '70s and '80s tunes. They were also far from brief. "Playboy Short" from *Don't Stop Rappin'* was more than nine minutes long. *Don't Stop Rappin'* wasn't just the title of his first album, it was also his songwriting motto.

$hort admits to making very little money with his 75 Girls career, but on the plus side, he didn't have any contractual entanglements. "Believe it or not, we never had any paperwork with that label," $hort says. "It was just like: 'Make an album, here's some money.' At first I had wanted a contract, but in hindsight it was the best thing that ever coulda happened to me. When I started my own company there was no conflict, no paperwork to resolve." $hort says that the label actually dropped him, instead of the other way around. But as always, Todd bounced back, as he had when Freddy hit the slammer.

$hort started his own label and production company in 1987 with his manager Randy Austin: Dangerous Music. The first release, that same year, was *Born To Mack*, which featured the hit "Freaky Tales," the song for which $hort may be best known to this day.

Around this time, $hort started working with musician Al Eaton out of Eaton's spare bedroom in El Cerrito, dubbed One Little Indian Music. $hort continued to use live playing, even though sampling had started to creep into hip-hop production at the time. He recalls: "I always kept two or three guys in the studio with me who knew how to work drum machines, knew how to play keyboards. A lot of those songs were me – the drums, the beat. But I never like to do it all myself. I always like to have a bit of extra expertise with me in the studio." He continues: "We were there, just fascinated by the procedure of recording a whole album. Back then I didn't even know you could stop and punch your vocals in. Every rap I did before *Life Is...Too $hort* was one take. I think a lot of rappers were doing that in the mid-'80s. I still do it today, sometimes."

Aside from being a prolific vocalist, $hort also was a savvy rap recycler: "I've made every one of my albums in 30 days or less," he states. "Between 1980 to 1985 I had released so many underground tapes, hundreds and hundreds of tapes with Freddy B. So between 1988 and 1996 I was rapping the same rhymes that I rapped before 1985. All the same words! I was writin' new stuff, too, but I was also re-writin' most of the old stuff. I recycled every rhyme I ever wrote that was on those underground tapes. That's why I was puttin' out albums so fast – I already had all the raps! I was doing an album every 9 to 11 months."

Born To Mack sold 50,000 copies in the Bay alone, in 1987. Jive Records president Barry Wise got wind of $hort's raunchy and record-selling rep and signed him to the label in February of 1988, re-releasing the album nationwide and selling another 200,000 without any promotion. "No advertising, no single, no video, no radio," $hort says. "Not even a poster. They just put that shit on the shelf and they sold 200,000, with the extra sales mostly in the South and Midwest. That was my first real introduction to America." $hort claims that the album is far past gold by now.

Always a hands-on kind of guy, $hort never got caught up in any major label politics. In actuality, he side-stepped them altogether. "I never even knew that they [Jive] *could* be saying something if they wanted to. I was always under the impression that it was the artist that was in control. I basically would make the album, we'd mix it and we'd send Jive the complete product, all sequenced. They'd master it at Sterling Sound and then manufacture it. That's all they'd ever have to do with me. I never really even knew any of the staff members at Jive. I would basically just talk to Barry and that was it."

As 1988 went on, it was clear that $hort was on a roll. And this time around, with a major label behind him, things looked better than ever. Recorded in less than 30 days at Al Eaton's, *Life Is... Too $hort*, released in January of 1989, was another huge step forward. "That album just felt good from the start," $hort says, adding: "The only difference between *Born To Mack* and *Life Is...Too $hort* was that there was going to be an official single and it was going to be played on the radio. It was the first time I ever got a poster, too. I always like to think that that's where the real Too $hort career started."

After selling 300,000 copies in three months with no promotion, Jive got behind it and released the title track as a single. "The only reason I remember that it was 300,000 copies at the time was because that was their whole ad campaign: '300,000 copies in three months.' RCA (Jive's parent company) had Elvis, *Dirty Dancing* [the soundtrack] and Country & Western shit and here's this rap guy that nobody ever heard of selling 300,000. They was like: 'Damn, what happens if we actually promote this shit?'"

A 1989 tour with N.W.A. bolstered his national rep and cemented his left coast immortality. "That tour was the biggest thing that ever happened to me in my life. We were playing 10,000 and 15,000 seat arenas every night and I had never even toured before. N.W.A. became commercial about the same time as me," $hort says. "When I put out 'Freaky Tales' they had 'Boyz-N-The Hood.' And when I dropped *Life Is...* they dropped *Straight Outta Compton*. I was just on some pimp/ player shit, though, you know? I wasn't trying to throw the controversy up in your face like they were. While we were on that tour sales of my album went from 300,000 to 800,000."

And a bizarre rumor pushed the album into rap history: "There were always a lot of stories about me back during 1988 and 1989. 'He's got light skin and long hair,' all kinds of rumors. There was even a fake Too $hort going around as me. Some little dude named Anthony. To this day Too $hort is bigger than I am. Oakland always had the rumor around that I was a crackhead. But after the N.W.A. tour somebody started the rumor that Too $hort got shot at a crackhouse. It started in Oakland and went everywhere. The biggest place that the crackhouse rumor hit was in Texas, where they were having memorial services for me and shit. Moments of silence on the radio. It was serious. But I wasn't mad at all. I was lovin' every minute of it. I've always been with whatever goes down."

He was also loving the fact that the rumors of his demise had driven up demand even more, to find out what this late (and, of course, falsely accused) crackhead was all about. "Those rumors made the album go even more crazy with sales," $hort grins. "It went from 800,000 to 1.3 million and eventually went double platinum. To this day it's my only double platinum record."

"*Life Is...* is definitely my favorite album. It's the purest work I've ever done," he reminisces. "That's what you get when it's for free. There's nothin' on the line, you don't have to follow-up on a platinum album, you've never been on tour. Nothing. Just: 'What can you do?' I was a broke mo-fucker when I made it and it came from the heart."

TRACKS

Life Is...Too Short

When we finished the album there was no doubt that "Life Is... Too Short" was the hottest track on there, so that was the first single, my first official single through Jive. The song definitely took off at radio. Then after selling 300,000 copies with no promotion, Jive said: "You got to shoot a video." For the video we didn't have a treatment or anything, we just turned on the cameras, pulled out the Cadillac and drove around Oakland and did shit. We showed up on a Saturday night at the Sideshow, where everybody brings out their fancy ghetto cars and guys are burnin' rubber and shootin' dice and whatever.

Rhymes

That was definitely Run-DMC influenced. Like where they'd just have a drum machine and you grab a record with horns and the DJ just scratches [imitates sound of DJ scratching a horn stab]. My DJ was from New York, DJ Universe. He always kept breakin' out these records that had East Coast drums. And we liked that shit. I might sound more New York style with my rhymes on that because Universe was in the studio, messin' with different stuff.

I Ain't Trippin'

That was the second single off the album, it's like a down South anthem, to this day. It did well, we shot a video, it got a lot of video play. But it didn't get as much radio play. I still to this day listen to a beat and have a different rap style for every beat, a different tone of voice. It's the musician in me. I took music lessons all my life and marched in a band and all that shit. So the musician in me said: "Don't rap the same way every time. Listen to the track and tune your voice to the track." That track was pretty laid back, and it took me a long time to come up with that style I used on there. I don't think I rapped like that ever again on record. It was a one-time style.

Nobody Does It Better

There were a lot of positive things said on that song, which went along with the rest of the album plan. Side A was supposed to be me, Todd Shaw, and Side B was supposed to be Too $hort. That was just the difference in me. I was always a good, positive guy. But I was always a smart guy, too, and I always saw that people wanted the dirty stuff. So I gave it to them as dirty as I could because it was like a joke to me. I'm famous for being a dirty rapper, but the biggest records I ever made, like "Life Is...Too Short," "The Ghetto" and "Gettin It" were positive songs. I could have made all positive songs if I wanted, but I knew that people wanted dirty stuff. Nobody seems to know that fact. Nobody ever dwells on that. I made one clean side and one dirty side for that album. I wasn't trying to clean anything up to make a video or anything. I was like: "This one is clean, this one is dirty."

Cusswords

That's my favorite track on the album, because it just comes on and I'm rappin', and it goes off and I'm rappin'. It's no hook, no nothin'. That was how I came up rapping. Everyone wanted hooks but I was like: "I just rap, fuck a hook!" On there I was trying to say the most explicit, extreme things I could say. I'm like: "How far can you take it?" Well, dammit, the president's wife gave me head. It was a big thing for the president to get a blow job himself [referring to President Clinton], and that was the late '90s. I was ahead of my time.

Don't Fight The Feelin'

That was kind of a posse track, with Rappin 4-Tay and my girls N'Tyce and Barbie on there. Those two were some little homegirls of mine, they were in high school back then and they're both doing good right now. That is definitely one of the most classic Too $hort records ever. To this day teenage kids are discovering that record for the first time and loving it. And old hip-hop heads have that record memorized in their minds for life.

City Of Dope

That song to me was painting a picture of where we lived, like: "This is us." It was like a Friday night on the first of the month, with people selling dope, crackheads out on the street. That was my version of [Grandmaster Flash and Melle Mel's] "The Message." I did the drum program on that and Al Eaton is playing guitar.

Alias Crazy Rak

That's a DJ track. I think I met DJ Universe through Chris Wayne, who was very important because he owned an 808 drum machine. That's like saying: "I got a million dollars in the bank." Chris was from San Francisco and Crazy Rak was, too. Universe's name was Enrique but his homies called him Rak. That track was just his thang, from what he grew up on. So I gave him a song. That was a one-time thing. I heard that he got burnt up in a motel or something. I had no DJ when I went out on the road with N.W.A. – I went off of a best-I-could-find super hi-fi reel-to-reel. Put the quarter inch reel on that shit and it was like CD quality. Just push play and I do a show. Records don't sound as good, plus they can skip.

Pimp The Ho

That's the whole Al Eaton flavor there. He wanted to re-do that Cameo song for that. I loved that. But when Al started acting like an asshole, I immediately went out and got me another guitar player, Shorty B. Hammer came out and he was so phony. I come back in the studio after Hammer had sold like 15 or 20 million and Al was like: "You gotta do what Hammer does. Hammer makes records for white people. You need to do that, because white people are gonna make you rich. Pop music is *it*." Al said he wouldn't play on an album that used the word "Nigger" either. He just went the fuck off. Al boycotted before we made *Shorty The Pimp* and that's when I started working with Ant Banks and Shorty B.

EPMD

Strictly Business

(Fresh / Sleeping Bag, 1988)

A little-known fact: if things hadn't worked out on the rap side, Erick Sermon might have been a landscaper and Parrish Smith could have been on his way to the NFL. Luckily for music fans, a higher power intervened. Says Parrish: "*Strictly Business* was God's way of taking two average kids and letting them express their hearts through music and rhyming."

In 1987, both talented young men were just out of high school in Brentwood, Long Island, (a "big, crazy, multi-cultural community" as Parrish says) about one hour to the east of New York City. Although Erick and Parrish (aka PMD) knew each other in junior high (Parrish says they first met in 8th grade), they became much tighter in high school, bonded by the hip-hop music and related activities resounding through their school hallways. "I was always into sports," Parrish recalls, "But after school everybody would meet in the foyer and that's where the rhyming sessions and the breaking would go down. I was a DJ from a young age, but I really started MCing in high school, when me and Erick started colliding in the hallway. The more I started getting into rapping, the less I DJed."

As Erick recalls: "Parrish didn't start rapping until I had already been rapping." The two bounced rhymes and ideas off each other, enjoying and building upon the collaborations. Erick continues: "We never wrote rhymes for each other, but our rhymes were always related. PMD would write something dope, and I would want to write something better than him. That's what made us dope, because we had a friendly battle between us. It made us better."

Parrish, an Eagle Scout, graduated high school in 1986, and started college that fall, studying communications and business and landing a scholarship spot as punter and receiver for Southern Connecticut State's football squad. Even while he suited up, he stayed with the music, working on rhymes and staying in touch with his rhyme partner E on the phone. Erick, starting his senior year in the fall of 1986, continued working on his style. "I had to rhyme slow because I had a lisp," he says today. "One day I got to school and these kids said 'Erick, some kid named Rock Wind has a record out and he sounds just like you.' People who knew me knew I rhymed slow like that."

Rock Wind was actually fellow Long Islander Rakim (from Wyandanch), who with Eric B had released the radical hip-hop juggernaut "Eric B Is President" and "My Melody" in 1986. The confusion told Erick and Parrish that even if they weren't on wax yet, they were on the right track. "Rakim had melody and EPMD had melody," Erick explains. "That's why we shocked the world." Parrish also notes both the artistic camaraderie and the influence of Rakim on their sound: "Rakim was the first to record a rhyme slow, but we brought the smoothness, too."

But let's go back to the early days for a second, because although EPMD was new to the world in '87, Erick and Parrish weren't exactly greenhorns. Back in the early and mid-'80s, Parrish's older brother (Parrish is the fourth of seven siblings), Smitty D, was a promoter who rolled with Afrika Bambaata and the Zulu Nation and even released a Tommy Boy single in 1985: "Facts Of Life." Parrish, aka DJ Easy P, was his DJ. Parrish remembers: "When I was like 13 my brother Smitty was bringing Bambaata to town for block parties, so I was already around real hip-hop from a young age." Smitty eventually became a member the Brentwood police force, around 1987.

Back in the day, Sermon didn't have to go into New York City to get his dose of the real thing, he just had to step outside. "It was real hip-hop where I grew up, in Regis Park. If I didn't know better I would have thought that hip-hop was started in Brentwood," Sermon says today. "It was real heavy." PMD remembers Regis Park as well: "I used to go over there. It was a little hectic in Regis, though, so my father bought me turntables for Christmas when I was 14, so I didn't have to go all the way to that part of town."

Around 1985, Erick moved over to another part of Brentwood to live with his grandmother. Her house was one street over from Parrish's, so at that point they knew each other from the neighborhood, and also from high school. Parrish was one year older. P's side of town wasn't quite like Regis Park, as Erick explains: "It wasn't like where I came from. It was just Parrish doing hip-hop on that side of town." Erick also says that although the Smitty D record was on wax, it didn't have much impact. The big stars from town were an up-and-comer from Noble Street, Biz Markie, and also Disco Richie from the Brooklyn-based group Divine Sounds.

Flash forward again, to 1987, and Parrish lacing up at practice for Southern Connecticut State's varsity squad. He began doing the math, looked into his heart and computed the following: "I started looking at the football game and I thought: 'What would be easier: to get on stage and rip a show or practice five days a week, with film on Sunday?' So I was like: 'Yo, I'll grip the mic.'" And a rap dynasty was born.

"When I came back from college in the spring that first year [1987], Erick was still in high school," PMD adds. "I'd go into the high school and sign E out like he had a dentist appointment and then we'd drive to New York in my '68 Camaro and start shopping our demo. We already knew what was out there and we was like: 'We can do better than this. If we get a chance we're gonna make it happen.'"

That spring, the two had recorded the demo in question, which included the song "It's My Thing." Shopping wasn't a very scientific matter, as Parrish recalls: "I wrote down all the record labels for stuff in my crate, and Sleeping Bag was one of them, because 'Latoya' by Just-Ice was hot at the time. We went to four labels with our demo and Sleeping Bag ended up saying yes." They were signed to the label for a single deal (with their other demo song, "You're A Customer" on the flip). "It's My Thing" was re-recorded with important help from Teddy Tedd and Special K, aka the Awesome 2 [see below for extended details], released in the late summer and proceeded to blow up on New York's ultra-competitive airwaves.

Parrish remembers: "When we got that first single deal with Sleeping Bag we got $1,500 total. When we got the first check we split it 50-50. Erick took his and went shopping but I had to take my half and put it back into my school money, since I had used that money to do our demo. I got it right in time, so I could go back to school. Once the single sold 80,000 copies, they called us in to do an album." As Erick says, they worked quickly and had a treasure-chest of freshness built up: "Everything we did in those days ended up going on *Strictly Business*. When we was in the studio back then we didn't have much money, so whatever we made, we kept!"

Recorded in less than a month at Charlie Marotta's North Shore Soundworks studio, *Strictly Business* blew up airwaves and video screens from Brentwood to Burbank, with singles like "You Gots To Chill" and "It's My Thing." The sound was deep and the samples (from artists like Eric Clapton, Zapp, ZZ Top and Steve Miller) were both recognizable and massively funky. Erick says: "The samples we used are well-known now, but back then they was more foreign to hip-hop. And people thought we was from LA, because we was so bassline-driven."

Using easily identifiable samples was also a double-edged sword, since the artists whose riffs and grooves formed the basis for EPMD's throwdowns knew just who to go to. Erick remembers: "We never cleared any samples on the first album. People would just come after us after they knew we had sampled them. Eric Clapton wanted $10,000, Roger Troutman wanted $5,000. They didn't even sue us back then, we just paid them and that was that."

Erick and Parrish were of course very hands-on in regard to the music on the album, unlike some peers who stayed on one side of the producer/MC wall. "When we came in the game we just thought that every MC produced and wrote their own music," Parrish explains. "So that's the way we came." Erick seconds this: "We thought everyone who had records out did that, we didn't know that some people were just producers. We didn't even know what a producer was. So I guess we became producers."

One provocative item, which goes against hip-hop's unwritten history, is Parrish's contention that Erick – now rightfully respected as one of the top producers in the game – wasn't the main producer for the group's first two or three albums [which credit the production to the group, not specific members]. P says: "Everybody now is using the music I produced, and the whole hip-hop industry is under the impression that E produced it. With the first three EPMD albums, I did most of the production and Erick just wrote his rhymes. He did one track on *Unfinished Business* [the group's second album]. I was already connected to the turntables, so it was natural for me." He continues: "I'm not bitter about people thinking Erick did most of it, not at all. It wasn't even about who's gonna do what back then. It was about 'Let's just get the job done.'"

Erick rebuts this contention, adding that neither of them *produced* their earliest work as much as their important and invisible third group member, engineer Charlie Marotta: "In the beginning, everything was both of us [Erick and Parrish]. PMD brought the 'More Bounce To The Ounce' sample for 'You Gots To Chill' because his father played Zapp records at parties. My dad was a big musical influence, too, just like Parrish's. He played records all the time, tons and tons of albums, so I just knew what good music felt like. The rest of the songs were just taken off breakbeats [records like the *Ultimate Breaks & Beats* compilations, which contained famous and often-used breaks of the day, compiled in multiple volumes]. We both put our minds together and it was a collaboration. We collaborated a lot on the first three records."

"And either way," E continues, "Neither of us knew how to make records back then. Charlie Marotta knew. Neither of us did anything technical on the first couple of records. We just got the records and gave them to Charlie. Charlie spliced all those samples in, because none of us knew of any machines that sampled for that long back then. But it wasn't as time-consuming as you might think. We'd take a loop and we'd splice it on 1/4 inch tape and then record it back to 1/2 inch." PMD remembers Charlie's manual-editing prowess as well: "We used to call Charlie 'MacGyver' because he did it all, no matter what the situation. We had no idea how that stuff worked. All those loops were spliced. We had 1/4 inch tape looped around pencils and chairs in the studio!"

In the end, it was the down-to-Earth quality of EPMD, aside from their witty brags and occasional tough talk that endeared them to fans. Parrish remembers: "When we toured and came through states a lot of people were pissed off at the artists who were there before us. They had their noses in the air and were disrespecting the audience. We were no different than the dudes next door, we just made dope music and rhymed. We had no aura or façade. We came straight out of our house, grabbed a mic and wrecked it."

"It was just two kids who heard wack stuff on the radio and wanted to do better," adds E. "We wanted to make records and we just happened to make Classic Material."

TRACKS

Strictly Business

Parrish: I brought that Eric Clapton sample. And that's me cutting on that track, too [makes noises imitating scratches]!

Erick: Yeah, Parrish did the cuts on that. He was nice! That was a one-bar sample, real short, and it was just dope. The concept was just dope. EPMD was making *music*, but we didn't even know that we were making actual music. While the world was sampling James Brown we was over here venturing out on something that was *other*. We sampled some other type of shit.

Because I'm Housin'

Erick: I think PMD got that Aretha Franklin record from his mom's house.

You Gots To Chill

Parrish: That was the first video we did for the album, and definitely my favorite video from back then. We never did a video for the first single. The "You Gots To Chill" video was done at an ice factory in Brooklyn, somebody at Sleeping Bag found it. I remember we had to stay out there because we did a show for Patrick Moxy. We had a beat-up limo that took us to the video shoot, but it got us there. That's K La Boss cutting on that track, not me. He was one of the dopest DJs from Brentwood. Diamond J was with us before that. Then after K La Boss, Jam Master Jay introduced us to DJ Scratch.

Erick: That's probably my favorite verse on the album [raps the first 8 lines, a capella]. It was like taboo to say your name in a rhyme back then, you just didn't do that in rap! But that's how real we were. I'm like: "Yo, I'm saying my name, Erick Sermon." The echo was heavy on that track. We brought that from the street. If you went to any type of house party or block party, the Echo Chamber was the main attraction [imitates effect]. It was Run-DMC, or Nice & Smooth. It was the essence of hip-hop. It was important.

Parrish: My father used to hang with this guy Mr. Roy, and he was a DJ. They'd go on a break and let me on the tables and that Zapp ["More Bounce To The Ounce"] was my favorite song to cut. We use a ton of Echo Chamber effects on that track, because that was always big. You gotta write about the Echo Chamber, please, for hip-hop. There's a lot of essentials missing in the game right now. I had two Echo Chambers myself. After we finished the song in the studio, Charlie [Marotta] showed us the button where the echo was and we could put it where we wanted. We were ODing on it, using it all over the place.

It's My Thing

Erick: The sound that we had back then was amazing. "It's My Thing" was like the groove of life! Red Alert was the first person to play that track on the radio. We was over at Parrish's father's apartment and it was like 11:45 and all of a sudden we heard helicopters [which are heard at the beginning of the song], then it started. It was just pandemonium in the house after that.

Parrish: We did that track when I came home after my freshman year in college, in May of 1987, when I had a break from football. When we first did the song, on our demo, I took the main sample off a scratchy breakbeat record. It was dope, but the loop was scratched. So Will Socolov from Sleeping Bag got in touch with the Awesome 2 (DJs, radio personalities and producers Teddy Tedd and Special K) and they got us the clean copy we needed. They added some accents, too, like extra drum rolls. Stuff we didn't know to put in there. They didn't know how to get out to us in Long Island so we had to pick them up in front of the Latin Quarter and bring them back to Charlie Marotta's studio. I knew "7 Minutes Of Funk" [by The Whole Darn Family, sampled in the song] from my brother's Jazzy Jay tapes that he'd bring back from the T-Connection and from Bronx River parties in the city. That was always the #1 song on a tape to get the party jumpin'. So I didn't just get that out of the blue. My family was around it.

Erick: We didn't know how to invent and write a chorus, so we owe that to the Awesome 2. After that record, we knew how to make choruses. They added that drum stutter, too. The original demo was just the beat playing all the way through, with no horns or drum roll.

Parrish: I had to go back to school for football camp in the summer and I was there when "It's My Thing" first started getting played on the radio, in August. We could barely get the station in, 98.7 Kiss, but we heard the helicopters and it was *on*. I'm pretty sure Red Alert was the first guy to play it. I knew Red from way back, through my brother.

You're a Customer

Parrish: That was the other song, besides "It's My Thing" on our demo, so that's why those two tracks were on the first single. That song took about four hours to record, and it was actually a mistake. I got that sample from ZZ Top's "Cheap Sunglasses" and I was playing around in the studio and muted out the ZZ Top to where just the bassline and drums were left. So I left it like that. Sleeping Bag didn't even listen to that song at first, but I made Virgil Simms check it out by asking him to describe how it sounded to me. When I called back later they said: "Yo, come in." Diamond J was our DJ then, but he didn't have any cuts on that song. We just shouted him out. He started touring with Prince after he left us.

Erick: Even though it was on the b-side of the "It's My Thing" single, which was big, that song was the one that really banged them out on the streets when the single hit. It took off even bigger than "It's My Thing," even though they were both strong. There was just something about that record! That Steve Miller song, the real full version, is a *serious* record.

Parrish: I went to Southeastern State University in Connecticut and it was a melting pot. You had white and black in the dorms and a lot of mornings I'd wake up and they'd be playing "Cheap Sunglasses" by ZZ Top. That Steve Miller ["Fly Like An Eagle"] was like, when I was in the Boy Scouts, on camp-outs dudes would be drinking Southern Comfort and listening to Steve Miller and Phil Collins.

The Steve Martin

Parrish: That was based on the Stezo dance that our man was rocking in the "You Gots To Chill" video. Even to this day, anyone who brings up that video has to bring up Stezo. We were just out there trying to take it a little further, and show Stezo some love. We didn't have a name for the actual dance, so it just became the Steve Martin.

Erick: That was a record we made for our dancer, Stezo, and it was the last song we made for the album, something that we did last minute. It was weird, because people *loved* that record. EPMD could do no wrong, the Steve Martin was big! And no, I never did that dance.

Get Off The Bandwagon

Parrish: That's another hot one [imitates bassline]! We didn't do that at Charlie Marotta's, but at the place where we took the cover photo, Island Sound in West Islip. Back then we weren't talking about albums when we were talking about people biting our shit, we were talking about our demo tapes. One time my roommate took one of my tapes and tried to bring it back home with him and I chased him down on I-95 to get my tape back, for real. Our music wasn't out yet and we didn't want to take any chances. We was tight with our music, because we knew we had something that was cutting edge. I played that music, on keyboard. I don't know how to play keyboard even to this day, but I know how to play what I want to hear. I did the bassline for "You're A Customer," too.

Erick: With the lyrics on that we were talking more about people around our way, not the industry. I mean, we was too brand new to have a problem with the industry at that point.

DJ K La Boss

Erick: K lived around the corner from Biz Markie, near Noble Street [in Brentwood].

Parrish: K was from Brentwood, we all went to the same high schools. I went to Sonderling and he and Erick went to Ross. We were overseas on a tour and something happened and La Boss had to fly back to the states, so we had to finish up like seven dates by ourselves, and we never used him again. We're still cool with him, though. He DJs for Puffy sometimes, and does mix-tapes.

Jane

Erick: That was based on a story that I kicked to Parrish when I first met him. I had "Jane" and a song about Bernhard Goetz and I had them both memorized. I never recorded the Goetz one. When I first made it up, it wasn't called "Jane," it didn't have any name at all.

Parrish: We definitely never thought we'd do a "Jane" on every album, no way. But as life goes on and as you get older, you start writing about the girl you don't know, the girl that doesn't exist. After all that shit, though, now there's a real Jane. I ran right into her. Her name isn't Jane, though [laughs]. That was the last track we did on the album, it usually is. That's how we know we're done, when we do a "Jane" song.

DANA DANE

Dana Dane with Fame

(Profile, 1987)

"All my songs are written like a short story," says Fort Greene, Brooklyn's old-school legend Dana Dane. "Once I have a conclusion, the rest is easy to write. The hardest thing is always building those stories into songs." As one of the greatest storyteller rappers in the history of the game, his tales had crowds moving and fans laughing in the mid-'80s, with a string of hit singles and a fast-selling debut.

Born in East Elmhurst, Queens, Dana was planted in Fort Greene around age five, and stayed put through his teens. "That's where I was raised for the most part, that's where I started to get my first little hip-hop thing going on," he says. Dane's first introduction into the hip-hop world was as a graffiti writer, working up pieces in his black book under the tag Kid Vicious. But as high school hit in the early '80s, things changed, in no small part because of the company he kept. As part of the informal but popular five-man Kango Crew ("We didn't use the 'L'," he explains, "Because we were a crew, not a hat") social clique at Manhattan's High School of Music & Art, Dane became fast friends with another soon-to-be storytelling legend: Ricky Walters aka Slick Rick.

Dane recalls: "I met Rick in our first year of high school. He was already rapping and that's when I started. Before that I was just tagging and working on visual arts stuff. I remember the first time I met Rick, it was in history class, and we had a substitute teacher. He told me he rapped and I was like: 'Word! Let me hear something.' So he did a rap about Polka music, set to the song 'The Gambler' [by Kenny Rogers]. I was blown away. I was intrigued by Rick because he was from the Bronx and he was intrigued by me because I was from Brooklyn. Bronx was the home of hip-hop and Brooklyn was where all the thugs was at. Before you knew it we was dressing alike." He continues: "There were five of us that were in a group that first year. Just friends, hanging out at first. I didn't even have my rap name yet. We all just hung out every day and wrote rhymes and routines. I was just listening and joining in sometimes. They would actually write my rhymes, in the beginning, back around 1979 and 1980."

He continues: "The Kango Crew came together at first more on the fashion tip than on a performance tip. We only performed in the lunchroom auditorium [laughs]. The only thing we ever recorded was at graduation in 1983. One of the family members taped us doing a two-minute thing on the stairs."

Rick influenced Dane greatly, and he started writing rhymes with elaborate stories himself. He even adopted a fake English accent, but not to steal Rick's style. He explains: "Rick, Lance Brown and Omega The Heartbreaker [other Kango members] all had West Indian backgrounds and accents. Rick always wanted to sound more American, and I was always like: 'You're buggin', I want to sound more like *you guys.*' What I ended up using was more like all of our sound, not just one person's. Rick couldn't escape using it, but I just ran with it. And once it caught on with 'Nightmares' it just kept going. Eventually I wanted to get out of it, but I had started something that was tough to get out of, because people loved it so much." He adds, with relief in his voice: "I'm a lot more myself when I rap now."

After graduating in 1983, Dane was enrolled at Bronx Community College, taking accounting classes. "After high school, me and Rick were planning on going to college together at Bronx Community, since I was always up there in the Bronx anyways. I went and Rick never showed up. Next thing I know there's a live tape going around called 'La Di Da Di' [by Doug E Fresh, featuring Slick Rick] and I *knew* it was him. So I called him up and he laughed when I asked him why he never enrolled. He was out on the battle circuit and I was going to become an accountant. After high school, everybody in the crew just went and did their own thing."

Despite his pocket calculator and class schedule, Dana didn't stay out of the rap game for long. After some convincing from a non-Kango classmate, Sam Jacobs, Jr. [later known as MC Holiday "The Gucci Man"], Dane agreed that he had skills and stories to tell, so he started working on his first single with Jacobs and his father (Sam Sr.). It was called "Nightmares" and it came out in 1985 on Profile. [For extended background on "Nightmares" see below]. The song, which Dana says hit streets on September 9 or October 12 in 1985, was a gargantuan hit, with catchy, Munsters-copped music and Dane's long-winded and constantly captivating tales, broken up into three different sections. Dana remembers: "By the time December 31 rolled around at the end of '85, it was big. Mr. Magic, Red Alert and Chuck Chillout were all playing it."

Things didn't go so well with Dana and the Jacobs father and son team (who were also managing him for a short time), so he broke ties with them. "We had a falling out," he says, "For the most part it fell apart when I started learning more about the business, and what they were taking and what I was getting." Dana didn't waste any time moving forward, and while he was still trying to void his contractual obligations to the Jacobses, he managed to pump out another great single on Profile in mid-1986: "Delancey Street." He says that the beat for "Delancey Street" was actually done when he was still recording at the Jacobs household, which made things a bit tricky. He adds: "And that's when Sam Jacobs, Jr. decided he would steal my story, to a certain extent. That's when he came out as MC Holiday, with 'The Gucci Man' [laughs]. It was actually pretty funny to me that he did that."

The "Delancey Street" single was, in the end, helmed by budding super-producer Hurby "Luv Bug" Azor, who was gaining fame producing Salt 'N Pepa and Kid 'N Play at the time. Dana's relationship with Hurby continued for several years, until, as Dana claims: "He was making more money off his other groups so he didn't deal as much with me any more." Dana recalls their first meeting: "I first ran into Hurby at the Apollo, at a show I was doing with Dr. Jeckyl & Mr. Hyde and Salt 'N Pepa. We were having turntable problems and so we used Spinderella's, and the rest is history. When I met Hurby he taught me a lot. He knew things about making songs, like counting bars and things like that. He had a structure that I could work with, because I had never had that before." Around the same time, Dana also lined up a DJ: Clark Kent. He states: "At that time in rap you had to have a hot DJ to be a hot rapper. Clark Kent was one of the hottest DJs anywhere at the time, so it worked out perfectly."

Profile tapped Dana for a full album in late 1986 after his promising single sales, and he and Hurby went to work after a brief pause: "Maybe four months or so after 'Delancey Street' came out. It was an in-between time when I didn't have much going on and Hurby was working on the first Salt 'N Pepa album." Most of the album was recorded at Bayside Studios in Queens, and it was a learning process for Dana, even though he had worked in studio situations before. He says: "At that time, in early '87, I was finding stuff for new songs and working on older ones. I never wrote to music. I always had the lyrics first, and then fit them to whatever music sounded best. Sometimes that was hard, but we got through it well enough."

In August of 1987, two years after the success of "Nightmares," *Dana Dane with Fame* hit record shelves, and proceeded to fly off of them just as quickly. The single "Cinderfella Dana Dane" had been released in July, to set things up. Dana recalls: "Once the album hit it took off immediately. It was on the radio everywhere, selling about 40,000 units a week. Three months after the album dropped, it was gold. That was unprecedented at the time." Dana also says that it was the first hip-hop album to go gold at such a rapid pace.

He sums up the appeal of the record with this: "Slick Rick had rhymes and stories, but nobody ever matched me with the hooks on my songs. That changed the way that hip-hop was heard. They were really in-depth songs, not just a rhyme thrown together over a beat. And with me as a public figure, people were influenced by the way I was dressing, and my style in general. The whole thought on that first album was 'Rags to Riches.' I was a star before I was a star, you know? I was Dana all along, and Dane was the famous dude that I had always wanted to be. And with that album, I had what I wanted."

People who didn't know about the close bond that Dana and Slick Rick shared in their earlier years may have thought that Dane was a knock-off of Rick's style. But that obviously wasn't the case. There was a push and pull there, and Dana always had his own unique panache. He says: "I never had anything against Rick and I don't know if he ever had any beef with me back then. I know he was perturbed because I was down with Hurby and Salt 'N Pepa had done the song 'Show Stopper' [a single on Pop Art, back when they were called Super Nature], which was a dis of Doug E Fresh and Rick. He thought I was betraying him, but if it wasn't for Rick I probably wouldn't have done this rap thing at all. So I owe him a lot."

TRACKS

Dedication

On that song I'm speaking in my real voice, not with the English accent. I made that song right at the very end but we put it first on the album.

Cinderfella Dana Dane

I had that whole song written, all the lyrics, and I knew it was one of my hottest songs, but I couldn't find any music that worked. Then Hurby had that Brick "Dazz" song one day and I heard it and knew that it was it. That was the last track we needed to finish the album, and we just put all the pieces together. That music was just a match made in heaven. There were actually too many lyrics for it, so I had to cut some of them down. That was the third single, and came out in early July of 1987, before the album dropped. I knew that one would be a hit. I came up with the idea for that song walking down the street, when I saw a Cinderella comic book in a store. Dean Martin & Jerry Lewis were my favorites back then and I loved the "Cinderfella" joint that Jerry Lewis did. I bought the comic book I saw in the store, took it home and just started writing the song. I was in college at the time, and every day when I was supposed to be in accounting class I was writing "Cinderfella." It probably took me six months to write the whole thing, in 1984. By the time I got into the studio with Hurby it was a done deal.

Dana Dane With Fame

That's the first hook I ever wrote, and it ended up being used for that song. That was like my theme music in high school. I walked down the hall singing that chorus all the time. I wanted to put out that song as a single instead of "This Be The Def Beat" but Profile said no. That's when my relationship with Profile started going downhill. That Japanese stuff at the end was just some bugged out shit. It was funny. I used to do that song second to last, before my closing song, "Cinderfella." The crowd went crazy every time. People know that song even today. Jimmy Young, who did some of the vocals on the chorus, worked at Bayside Studio. He was the Boy Friday for the place. He could sing but he had a high-pitched voice so we matched him up with the females on the chorus.

Delancey Street

That was my second single, it came out in 1986. We did [the demo] up in Hurby's attic and did the final version at INS. I came in there with the sample for that song. Hurby wanted to use it just like the original was but I convinced them to replay it instead. The single did well, but not as well as "Nightmares." It was Top 40 maybe, but not Top 20 or Top 10. It became a lot bigger once the album came out. Delancey Street [in Manhattan] is where I bought all my clothes. I never got jacked on Delancey [as he did in the song], but I almost got jacked on Simpson Street in the Bronx once, kind of like those lyrics. Except without the females. It was way back in high school, with me, Rick, Lance Brown and another guy. I got away that one time so I used it as an anecdote. And stories are always funnier when you use females in 'em.

We Wanna Party

My sister actually made up that hook on that song. We was in the crib, probably in 1979, and she sang that [he sings chorus]. I told Hurby I wanted to use that Staples Singers ["I'll Take You There"] on a go-go type of track, and there you go, he hooked it up. Hurby always took the ideas I had and brought them to life, and even added a lot of great stuff.

Originally I was going to do that song by myself [Hurby raps on half of it], but Hurby wrote me a verse, the first part, so I wrote the rest and then put Hurby on the track. We used to perform that song together all the time. That one could have even been a single.

Nightmares

I wrote my first rhyme in 1980, and it took me almost a whole year to write it. And that rhyme appeared years later as the third verse of "Nightmares." The one about Anita The Beast. Every day I would go home and write just two lines that rhymed and come back to school the next day. Halfway through the year I had eight lines and I was so proud. The guy who produced that song, Sam Jacobs, Jr., was a high school classmate of ours. He kept calling me after "La Di Da Di" came out and was telling me I should make a record, since I was down with [Slick] Rick and the Kango Crew. His father, Sam Jacobs, Sr., was a jazz musician and he helped with some of the music on that track. I would go to work in the daytime, go to college at night in the Bronx, and then I'd jump on a train and go and record that song. I had the lyrics and the hook for the song but we needed his dad to come in and play that Herman Munster-sounding music. We went to the studio and did a demo on it, then Sam Sr. sent out the tape to all the independent labels that might be interested. About a month later we heard back from one place: Profile Records. They wanted it and 15 days after that I was signed for a single. Once I knew we were going to do the song I wrote the rest of it. I had the "late to class" and "Anita the Beast" parts and I just wrote rhymes to connect the stories, and added the hook. That song actually came from Whodini's "Haunted House of Rock." They're like my favorite group of all time. Back then when that [Whodini] song came out I was working at McDonald's and every morning when I came in I'd hear Whodini on the radio. I wanted to make a funny song about nightmares. I didn't want the song to be disrespectful to girls, so I figured if it was a dream then it wouldn't be so bad.

Love At First Sight

You know, I don't even know why I wrote that song. At the time I guess it was trying to do something like [LL Cool J's hit] "I Need Love." I needed a song like that. That was before Slick Rick had "Teenage Love." The problem I was having at the time was that people were giving out my number, and I was getting calls from everywhere. Girls never wanted to talk to me until they found out that I was Dana Dane. So that's all part of what that song is about. I never really performed that song live, even though people wanted me to. There was never a place to put it in my set, it was too slow.

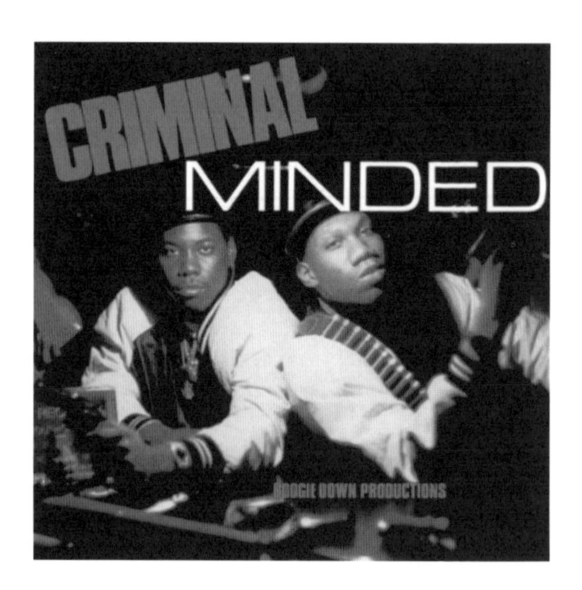

BOOGIE DOWN PRODUCTIONS

Criminal Minded

(B-Boy Records, 1987)

As you'll notice, this is in a different format than most of the chapters in the book. Essentially, it's a selective oral history of KRS-One's life from age 8 to about 22, culled from a three-hour-long interview I did with him on March 25, 2002. These are all his words.

As you'll also notice, not all of this is in linear/chronological order since Kris skipped around while telling his story. For the sake of order, I've tried to break things up into subject headings where applicable. And when he's talking about a specific song, I've bolded it.

EARLY YEARS

I had three starts in hip-hop and all of them were significant. Take it back to 1973. My mother moved from Manhattan to Harlem, a place called Lenox Terrace. I was attending the Charles B Rushworm School. It's still there, directly across the street from Lenox Terrace. Then my mother left an abusive husband, my stepfather, and moved to the Bronx, to 1600 Sedgewick Avenue, Cedar Park. It was across from 1520 Sedgewick, where Kool Herc lived with his sister Cindy. I started to experience these block parties, or better yet, jams. I didn't know that it was Kool Herc at the time. Nobody knew it was even hip-hop. It was just a fun time. That was my first experience with it.

Skip ahead some years to 1977 and I'm in Brooklyn now. Flatbush. 170 East 35th Street, at Church Ave. In 1977 there was a blackout in New York and that night I felt an overwhelming desire to say something to society. Me and Kenny [Kris' brother] was there in the apartment, waiting for my mother to come home. The lights go out and everybody was breaking into stores, stealing TVs, cars are crashing into each other. It's complete madness. And I remember this weird feeling. Wanting to say something right out of the window, something that would stop the people from looting and robbing. When my mother came home that night I said: "Mom, why are they doing this?" And she said: "When there is no light, there is chaos." And I never forgot that. It just struck me. I saw people reducing themselves to savages, if I can use that term. And I didn't like it.

So I started writing poetry, from that day forward. Poems about social injustice and about how I felt about living in Brooklyn at that time. I would write them to my mother and she would grade them for punctuation and grammar. Not so much on content [laughs]. That was my second break into hip-hop.

By then of course block parties were prevalent, mix-tapes were out, live tapes. You'd go into a basketball court and somebody would have a big box and they'd be blasting a homemade tape of someone kicking rhymes over "Love Is The Message" [by MFSB] and "Sing Sing" [by Gaz] and all these breaks. I fell in love with it at that point. I knew what rap was and I knew what MCing was, and I just wanted to be a part of that. I was growing up in that.

I didn't link my poetry and MCing together back then. Back then hip-hop had other components to it. For instance I was a master Skully player. It's a street game that you play with bottle-tops and you go from one to thirteen knocking out other tops along the way. Soda can tops, or milk carton tops or whatever. I mean, that was as big as breaking or graf or MCing back then. It was huge, and so was double-dutch. It was all just part of the culture. You didn't separate anything. MCing was a different kind of poetry, a different mentality.

In 1977 my poetry was just to my mom. It was my first attempt at making words rhyme. I don't remember explicitly what my early poems were. My first record, "Advance," although there are three MCs on it – Jerry Levi (Levi 167), and MC Quality also – I wrote the record. I had three verses and I gave them each one and took the last verse. That rhyme that Levi 167 says was the closest to my earliest poetry. It went: "Every generation after every generation / The American nation / Still hit with starvation / The quick sensation / Can only lead the mind to destructive creation." That was the type of poetry that I started writing in 1977. Later, rhythm and color and style were given to it. Some of the words are even the same. That might have been right after the blackout. Most MCs keep their first rhyme in their head. It's like their seed rhyme, for all their other rhymes.

NO TURNING BACK

Then rap music came out, around 1979. Fatback Band had a 45 out on Spring Records. My mother copped that for us. "King Tim III, Personality Jock." I was ecstatic, I was like: "Those guys are finally doing what the streets is doing." And a few months later "Rappers Delight" [by the Sugarhill Gang] came out and at that moment I made my mind up. "I am an MC, that's it." Sometime around 1980 I linked up with a crew in Brooklyn, we didn't even have a name for the crew. I was called Larry G [Kris' given first name is Lawrence]. Kenny wasn't into any of this at the time, he was studying to be a basketball player. And there was this guy named Money Mike and a guy named Neville T and me, Larry G. And we put together rhymes and routines and that type of thing. We used to rhyme over Dr. Jeckyll & Mr. Hyde and the whole Sugar Hill catalog. Those records used to come out every week and we were there like clockwork, purchasing all of them. That wasn't really even much of a start, more of an influence.

What crystallized it for me was in 1984, maybe 1983. I was at a group home in the Bronx. By now I had left home, I told my mother: "I'm an MC, I'm going to study philosophy." She was pissed off, thought I was crazy, since I had dropped out of school. I was probably about 17 years old. And everybody was rappin' in this group home, beating on the tables to make a beat, and people would kick their rhymes. But I had put MCing on hold during this whole time, because I had hooked up with this guy named Zore who was down with this crew DB, Down to Bomb. He turned me on to graffiti art, and I got *hooked*. We used to go down to the 2 and the 5 yard, the Jerome Avenue layups, 6th Avenue, in the Bronx. Later I would go to the bus yards on Tremont Ave in the Bronx. And I made a little name for myself. I wrote KRS.

THE NAME, THE BOMBING

My name Kris started as a joke, as a pun. When I had left home I had spent maybe a year on the street and then I went into a shelter. The Men's Shelter, down on East Bowery. And down there the Hare Krishnas used to come down and feed the homeless. And just before they'd start they'd say that if anyone wants to help feed the homeless they would get a free book, the *Bhagavad-gita*. And I was gassed, because I was studying philosophy in the public library, so I was like: "Wow, the library ain'tgot the *Bhagavad-gita*, so let me get that." I'd offer to help and I'd hang out with them and they'd tell me all about reincarnation and the divinity of Krishna. And I'd go back to the shelter and everybody'd start laughing at me, and my nickname in the shelter became Krishna. I couldn't tell them that calling me the name of a Hindu god was bad, they wouldn't understand. That's like calling me Allah or Yahweh. I couldn't escape it, so I took it on as a name.

When I left the shelter and went into the group home, the Bureau of Child Welfare system found out that I was too young. So I ended up at Covenant House for under 21 year-olds. From there -- where I met Just-Ice, by the way -- the Bureau asked me my name and where my parents were and I told them that my name was Krishna Parker. And that became my name, Kris Parker.

Once Zore opened my whole mind to this world of graffiti, I started writing KRS and bombing Soundview and Bronx River [Projects] and that's when I got into hip-hop for real. When I'd go around to Bronx River to see Afrika Bambaata in the Bronx River Housing Projects throwing parties. Stevenson Park. I actually caught Red Alert and the Jazzy 5 doing "Jazzy Sensation" [sings part of song] in the park one night. Other people started writing KR and KS and KRESS, so I started to add the ONE. Which isn't a new thing, to put "One" after your name.

By the end of my Group Home stay I was 20 and rap had exploded by then. And I had this skill. I went to the School of Visual Arts, for about three months. It was a wasted opportunity, because the Bureau of Child Welfare was paying for my education. Somewhere around 1984 I'm bombing KRS-One, rap is big, Run-DMC, LL, Whodini. Those groups were the epitome of rap music, nothing like what you have today. Run-DMC were the messiahs when they were out. The epitome. Period. Taking their lead, I picked up the mic.

METAPHYSICS, MARTIANS AND MORALITY

My poetry at that time was heavily into religion and philosophy, while I was in the group home. A lot of Metaphysics. But poetry wasn't a priority. Once I got into graffiti art I just got engulfed in that. Then after that phase I picked up the pen and the mic again. And it happened kind of haphazardly, battling other MCs in the group home. And by doing that, I realized that I had some talent.

When I said my rhymes other people would look at me like I was a Martian, because I was talking about nuclear war, police brutality and stuff like that, back then. I was bringing in all the philosophy that I was reading, and Biblical stuff, too. Morality. Ethics. Especially after 1982, when Melle Mel came out with "The Message." My style of rap was crystallized at that point. I knew exactly what I was going to do. I would somehow try to add a Biblical twist to what he was doing. In battles it was ruthless, because I would rhyme like the Bible, with 'Thou" and "Thy" and it would give the appearance of being in an authoritative position. I didn't know that at the time, it was just my style. By that time I was 20 and figuring out what I was doing. So I went back to my original love: MCing.

I got kicked out of the group home on my 20th birthday, in 1985. I went to the YMCA for three months and after that I was supposed to get a job. Of course I jerked all the money and wasted my time and they kicked me out of the Y, so I was homeless again. So I went back to the Third Avenue Men's Shelter on the Bowery and they shipped me and a bunch of other guys on a school bus up to 166th Street and Boston Road in the Bronx.

ENTER: SCOTT LA ROCK

I was in this shelter and about two months after that walks in this new social worker, with a briefcase and everything. And we knew that he was a nerd, he was not part of the cool clique. I went to him to get subway tokens, to jerk the money or whatever. The shelter used to give you two tokens [per day] and you'd sell them, go and buy some herb or some OE [Olde English] 800, or some Chinese food. So I went to this guy, Scott Sterling, and we started arguing over these tokens. We went back and forth with this until I finally said: "You're one of those handkerchief-head house negroes, tap-dancing for the white establishment. You ain't got nothing to do with us black folks, you're a sellout!" And he stood up, all angry, and said: "You don't even know me. You don't know who I am!" And he started saying: "All you homeless blacks who want to sit on your ass, you're lazy and you're wasting your life." And we went back and forth. I was the lazy homeless guy and he was the sellout. We argued for about an hour until security kicked me out of the office.

Then about a week later, I went to Ced-Gee's [from Ultramagnetic MCs] house. He had a 4-track in his house. I met him through another graffiti artist named Funkmaster, who used to write with a guy named Pre-Sweet. They were bombing all over the Bronx. They were a crew, TR, The Rascals. They were an older clique. Funkmaster was a security guard in the shelter, so he'd hear us rhyming and he took us over to Ced's spot. We'd all be piled in there, and then two weeks went by and in walked Scott Sterling. And I'm like: "Yo, how'd your nerd ass get in here, with all us MCs, us true hip-hoppers?" and he's shocked, he's like: "You homeless,broke-ass, no future... how are *you* here?" So we went into the corner after he heard me rhyme and we both sat there feeling pretty stupid. That started our friendship.

Scott asked me to come down to Broadway International or Broadway RT is what it became. Broadway Repertory Theater. On 145th and Broadway. So, lo and behold, I get into this place and it was like Moses in front of the burning bush. It was an epiphany. First of all, it was my first club experience, ever. I get there, all dirty, I get in for free and people are dancing and the clothes are outrageous and people are breakin' and doing the Whop. It was like walking into another world.

And I look to see the source of the music, and it's Scott Sterling. I was blown away. I was humbled and embarrassed.

I went up to the DJ booth and some big security guy blocked me. Then Scott gave a nod and the hand disappeared and I get a chance to walk into the DJ booth. Back then the DJ booth was sacred. He gave me drink tickets, I got some rum & cokes and I'm feeling great. He was scratchin', people are screaming for every record he plays. We went back to the shelter and I was like: "That is *it*. That's me, that's it. I have no other purpose in life."

So Scott would just invite me down and I'd go there every week, for a month or so. And one time this MC group was up there and Scott was in the booth. And the record he was playing kept skippin', so the group was getting messed up and they blamed Scott, even though it was their DJ's fault. So I'm like: "You're dissin' *my* DJ?!" Scott had never said he was my DJ or anything like that. But I felt such an allegiance to him, he was Morpheus in my world. So I jumped on-stage and smashed all five of these MCs. We went line for line and of course I had all these styles backed up in my head for years. So I battled and smashed them. I don't even remember who it was. We were all just locals. And that's when Scott was like: "Yo, we gotta make this a group." And he called the group the Boogie Down Crew. It was really more like a gang. It was me and Just-Ice and ICU, Jerry Levi [Levi 167] from the Shelter, this guy named Castle D. He knew MC Quality, who would eventually introduce me to Ms. Melody. And Scott used to DJ for the breaking crew called BIA – B-Boys In Action. So all of us got together as the Boogie Down Crew. There were about 20 of us at the end of the day, with friends and all.

EARLY DAYS ON WAX

Out of that group we recorded this demo called "**Advance**" [by Scott La Rock & the Celebrity Three], with these lyrics that I had written, three verses that I used to say by myself. After that, Scott took us to a place called Zakia Records. He knew about them from Eric B. Scott and Eric were close friends, they used to buy gold together. They'd buy these big chains, and I used to dis Scott with that, like: "What are you doing?" But that was him. We was so different, it was like night and day. So we signed this record to Zakia, "Advance," and we didn't get no money. I wonder to this day if Scott got any money. I remember what I got out of the deal was a pair of blue Air Jordans. And I was happy and satisfied. So it came out and it didn't really do anything, but it was out and we had a record and it felt good. By then I was going to the Roxy [club]. The Roxy was a whole other experience unto itself.

As for the Boogie Down Crew, Levi 167 became a crackhead, Castle D – who wasn't really part of the group, but was a side MC and used to travel with us – he went to Philly and robbed someone and went to jail for like two years. One day we just didn't see him anymore. MC Quality's mother felt weird about her being in an all-guy group. We were definitely the first Fugee-type group, with two guys and a girl.

After that first group didn't work out, me and Scott went to Sleeping Bag and met with a guy named Will Socolov. This was one of the greatest record companies ever. No one ever got paid anything, you got paid in marijuana. But it was a great label. We learned about them from Just-Ice. One day he left the shelter and never came back. And next time we heard him it was "La la la la la LaToya," with the original DMX. And we knew it was him. So we went over there [to Sleeping Bag] to try and get the same deal. We came out on Fresh Records [Fresh is a part of Sleeping Bag] as a group called **12:41** and the song was "**Success is the Word**," using the Gilligan's Island theme. Of course we got no publishing, nothing, maybe we got our names credited on the record. The group was named from the time when we finally finished mixing the record. It was really that simple.

So the 12:41 record came out and Mr. Magic spun it one time on WBLS. The clubs were spinning it a little. A guy named Kenny Beck produced the record, who was a pretty big dance producer back then. He put his brother in the group, and it was me and Scott with him. It was the only time that Scott ever really rhymed on a record, his only MC appearance. Except for the end of "Dope Beat." We showed up, he [Will Socolov, assumedly] gave us $200 each, we rapped on it and signed something that took all rights away. And that was it. Will and Ronald Resnick [from Sleeping Bag / Fresh] were great. I really love those guys, even though no one ever got paid. Just-Ice got paid. He'd go up there every week and they'd just give him money.

Then we got rejected by Will Socolov. He said he didn't have the room to sign us as artists. We went over to Spring Records and Van Silk was doing A&R there. By then we had our demo, with "Advance," "Success Is The Word" and I had just recorded a demo of the record that would become "Elementary" and also the song "Criminal Minded." We took those songs everywhere. We recorded those songs in a studio on Broadway and I think 79th Street. It was a little set-up in somebody's house and was about $25 an hour to record. There was one other song on the demo, I can't remember the name. It never came out, anyways. We took the demo to Spring, Polygram, Sony, everywhere. And everyone rejected us.

ROCK CANDY AND B-BOY RECORDS

One day we was walking home to the Bronx from Manhattan, we had no money, we had just came back from Tommy Boy, who also dissed us. They were on 96th Avenue and we walked from there to the Bronx. So we were walking across the Willis Avenue Bridge and Scott had a newspaper and he sees an ad on the back of it: "Rock Candy Records and Filmworks, looking for new talent." So Scott calls them up on a pay phone and they said to come right over. So we went over and met Jack Allen, Ray Wilson and Bill Kamarra. And they said: "Let's do it. You can have your own label, we'll put you out." They were in the Bronx, 132nd Street and Cypress Ave. We thought we was large.

By then, in 1986, we were calling ourselves Boogie Down Productions. Because we said we would never be MCs, we'd be producers. Because we thought that no one wanted to hear conscious rap, and no one wanted to hear hardcore thug stuff either. The party-style rhyme is what was prevalent back then. We wanted to start a label and get some other acts. So I drew the label logo while Scott was talking to those guys [at Rock Candy]. The little b-boy character holding the radio. I did that with a pen, on a piece of paper. So B-Boy Records was born, it was just me and Scott.

With contracts, Scott didn't actually know what he was doing, but he knew more than me. I was just green. With Rock Candy we signed a contract that signed away all our rights [laughs]. Before we started with these Rock Candy guys, they put a demand on us. They wanted us to make an anti-crack record. And I'm all for it, because I've always been socially conscious. I was running around calling Ronald Reagan a drug dealer and people thought I was crazy. So we did this record called "**Crack Attack**," which was our contribution to fighting the crack epidemic. They put it out and it didn't go anywhere.

ON THE ATTACK: "SOUTH BRONX"

There was an engineer named Frankie D who worked at Power Play Studios in Queens. And Rock Candy had us go into Power Play to re-record stuff from our demo. I did "Elementary" and Frankie liked our stuff and wanted us to meet with Mr. Magic. Even though we had a label, we went back and tried to meet with Mr. Magic, by basically bombarding his session. And he was working, so he was like:"Get outta here!" Then Frankie D must have played him something when we were gone and he came back and said: "I played it for Mr. Magic and he said it was wack." We we was like: "What? Are you crazy? MC Shan is wack, not me." And I went home and wrote "**South Bronx**."

I performed it for Scott, he played the "Funky Drummer" and started in on the song and it blew his mind. So we ran over to Ced-Gee's house and were like: "Yo, Ced, we need that SP-12 [sampler]." Keep in mind that at that time Ced-Gee was the only person in the Bronx with an SP-12 and he was the absolute man. So he lent us the sounds, the kick, the drum, the snare, the hi-hat. Scott took his records over to Ced and Ced sampled them and made the beat for "South Bronx," and Scott did the drums and Ced chopped it up. I wasn't paying no attention to the beat, it had no significance to me at all. I was strictly about the lyrics.

So we went to this studio in Queens for $25 an hour and recorded it in two hours. $50 on 8 tracks, one take. I must have practiced it once and then recorded it, because Scott was like: "All I got is $50!" I think the guy at the studio kept the master and gave us a cassette of it, and we ran out of there.

Scott was on his way to see Mr. Magic with the song, and he ran into Marley Marl. Scott was such an entrepreneur that his whole plan was to go to Mr. Magic and say: "OK, we'll do a track dissing you and then Shan can come out and dis us." Back then the answer records were real big, with Shante and UTFO and Spyder-D and Sparky-D. We went to them [Marley and Magic] because they was the kings of the battle record. But Marley was the one Scott met with and Marley basically said: "We don't need you, we're the Juice Crew." So we pressed the song up and put it out on B-Boy. We took D-Nice down to that same studio in Queens and recorded "**The P Is Free**" [D-Nice does human beatbox on the original track]." That was another one-take record.

In between this time, in 1986, I had met Ms. Melody, who lived in Brooklyn. And I was living in a freezer under the offices of B-Boy Records. They had a garage that had a freezer, like a walk-in meat freezer. Two people had actually died in there, had suffocated, so they couldn't do anything else with the building. I was still homeless at the time, and was going from house to house. ICU's mother had given him an apartment in Millbrook Projects, so he asked me if I wanted to stay with him, but my pride wouldn't let me stay there continuously. So if I was at the Roxy too late and couldn't get in the shelter, I'd crash at ICU's, or at Ced-Gee's or sometimes at Ms. Melody's. But I said to Bill Kamarra [of Rock Candy] that I wanted money to get an apartment. He said "No, but you can have the freezer downstairs." So I took it. It was either that or be in the street. I remember I had to keep a big brick by the door because if the door slammed I would suffocate and die. So I kept the door open and slept on 16 crates put together with a mattress made out of clothes and newspapers. And that's where I was staying when "South Bronx" came out.

I remember that I went to Latin Quarter, which had just opened, and Red Alert had already been battling Mr. Magic – Red on Kiss 98 and Magic on WBLS. They had a record out called "Duck Alert" [by Marley Marl] that was dissin' Red [and Chuck Chillout], calling him Red Dirt [KRS imitates part of "Duck Alert"]. So Scott, who was friends with Red Alert, gave him "**South Bronx**." And of course on that record I had shouted out Red Alert, I had brought back the history of the Bronx, the Zulu Nation, the Rocksteady Crew. This was street history that I was chatting off. So Scott brought a test pressing of the record to the Latin Quarter and Red Alert threw it on, and that place erupted. I've never felt a chill in my body like that. Everybody stopped dancing and just looked up at the DJ booth. Red Alert played it three times, one right after another, without even mixing it. He'd just pick up the needle and play it again. And I remember Just-Ice turned to me and said: "You got a hit, you out the shelter now." The record started getting really big in the clubs.

I used to go to the clubs and nobody knew who I was. At the time Scott La Rock was the biggest name, like "Scott La Rock and that 'South Bronx' song." No one could even pronounce my name. It was such a weird name for people. As Roxanne Shante said, it sounded like a wack radio station! And that it did [laughs]. Scott was rising in prominence and I was happy because for me Scott was Morpheus, and I would do anything for him. I was like: "You're the one that saved me." So I was basically defending my DJ everywhere we went, which was a prominent theme of that era. We became the kings of the Latin Quarter, we could do no wrong there. And that place was huge, too. If there was a "Class of 1986" or what is called The Golden Age, then the Latin Quarter was the school. That was the place that housed the "Class of 1986."

I remember somewhere along at this time I got a job mopping floors at a children's nursery in Brooklyn. $25 for each time I mopped the floor.

I'd do it twice a week and if I got lucky I'd get to do it three times a week. And I was happy. I'd take the train down there, and catch a quick [graffiti] tag along the way, of course. One day while I was mopping, "South Bronx" came on the radio and I was buggin', with that mop in my hand. I had just put the Mop-N-Glo down and the record came on. And the chill went through my spine again. But I still didn't realize the impact of it. It was a huge hit record. Red Alert played it on Kiss.

ON THE ATTACK, PART TWO: "THE BRIDGE IS OVER"

From there on out, Scott started to ask Rock Candy for money. We started getting $600, and I would get $300. At least I was told we was getting $600. And out of that $300 each we had to give D-Nice $50 or $100 out of what we made. Three weeks later after we was on the radio, MC Shan answered with "Kill That Noise." And that hit *hard*. I heard that [imitates Shan's voice] and I was like: "Whaaat?" When that came out, Mr. Magic played it on a Friday night and by that next Friday I had "**The Bridge Is Over**." I wrote the beginning part [sings "Come on in the dance, with a spliff of sensi..."] first, after we met Mr. Magic. But I threw it aside, 'cause I said: "Nah, nobody's gonna mess with this style." Then I wrote "South Bronx." But then when Shan answered us I said: "Let's do this."

So I ran back to Ced-Gee and said: "Yo, Ced, let's get this on." So Ced came down to this studio on 47th Street between 8th and 9th Avenues, a place called A&R Recording. And we recorded "The Bridge Is Over" in 45 minutes. It was crazy. Ced was buggin' that I did it in only one take. I didn't pay no mind to it because in my mind you was always one take. To this day I'm like that. I did the beat for that song, I played the piano, too. Scott had nothin' to do with that record. It was like a surprise, I was tryin' to do it for him. Scott was somewhere else, probably out buying gold with Eric B [laughs]. I remember Ced-Gee sampled "Eric B Is President" [which Marley Marl had helped produce], the kick and the snare. We threw it in the SP-12 and I did the beat [he imitates beat, "boom boom bap bap, boom bap..."]. Not too much brainwork for that one. It didn't take too much talent.

At the time there was a record by Super Cat called "Boops" and it had the bassline I wanted, so I had the piano that was free in the studio. It was a real piano, and I played it live, one take, for the whole song. If you listen to the original [of "The Bridge is Over"] there's so many mistakes, like at the beginning. That's just me tuning up, trying to get my timing together. We laid the beat down one time, then I played the piano one time, then I got on the mic and recorded the whole record one time. And Ced-Gee mixed it one time. The only overdubs were where you hear the kicks and snares double up. Ced did that live, while we were mastering it [laughs]. Ced's overdubs went directly to the master at the same time! I made a cassette of it, came back and gave it to Scott and he was blown away. He gave it to Red Alert and Red played it off the tape, and it was just *on* in New York City.

After that we started to get flack, people said we was just a battle group, that we couldn't write actual songs. Because that's all that we was doin' at the time. "The Bridge Is Over" came out by itself, but when it came out as a single, we went back in and did a clean radio version to it. Instead of: "Shante's only good for steady fuckin'," it became "pumpin'." We had shout outs at the end of the record. Those were added later. Then we recorded "**A Word From Our Sponsor**" [which came out as the b-side to "The Bridge Is Over"].

"MANY PEOPLE TELL ME THIS STYLE IS TERRIFIC"

After "The Bridge Is Over," MC Shan never responded and neither did Marley or Mr. Magic. That was pretty much the end of the battle. So we was going around battling other crews. That was our thing, that was what we did. And I had a style that's mostly forgotten now. I had a quick style, like when I said: "That's it, that's all, solo, single, no more, no less" [on "Poetry"] and that was new.

The whole idea of hip-hop reggae was new, too. I mean, Run-DMC did the first rap/reggae collaboration with "Roots, Rock, Reggae," so historically they had that record, with Yellowman. But it still wasn't what we was doin'. They were rapping and Yellowman was doing his Jamaican patois. My style was to incorporate Jamaican patois language over hip-hop beats. Oh, man, the damage we used to inflict on these groups, it was just crazy. We'd go into these clubs and they'd set up the battle and I would just start rhyming, and it wasn't just the Jamaican lyrics. It was *how* we battled. We battled like a Jamaican sound system. You played one record, then you'd rewind, and the crowd would go crazy. I had the biggest record out in 1986 and here I come with this cocky, arrogant attitude. I was the Teacher, so in each battle I was scolding the MCs. I was teaching them how they were wack and why they needed to get better. It was just an unstoppable style.

But the battle MC reputation bothered me and Scott. Probably me more, because I was the writer. I was like: "Yo, I got songs." But Scott said that nobody wanted to hear messages. He said that to me early on. He knew we had to come out with the hardcore style, as we called it back then. So I started writing about themes that appealed more to the street. In a way, around 1986 and '87, Run-DMC, LL, Fat Boys and others had gotten so big that there was a whole other audience that was being alienated. These people respected those artists, but those artists also weren't considered "street" any more. They had videos and were on MTV.

THE ALBUM: *CRIMINAL MINDED*

We appealed more to that alienated audience, the audience that felt that rap was getting too commercial. So I wrote this album called ***Criminal Minded***. The purpose of the album was to attract a thug type audience, so we could teach them later on. That was the whole point. We wanted to make intelligence a cool thing. And so we wrote up these records that I personally didn't think was too hardcore. In fact I kind of thought that *Criminal Minded*, the album, was corny, when we finished it. I said: "Man, we're gonna get dissed for this. I mean, 'Listen to my nine millimeter go bang'? Who's going to listen to this?" No one at that time was even thinking about that sing-song kind of style back then. The closest was Doug E Fresh & Slick Rick. They, too, were battle MCs, and that was what you did when you battled. You took a familiar tune, which was also a Jamaican thing, and you turned it into a battle kind of thing. So I said: "I'm going to go from writing records to writing *songs*," and I wanted to position myself as the teacher of hip-hop. I wanted to start to distance myself from being just a battle MC.

We touched up the original "**Criminal Minded**" song from our demo.We had "**Elementary**" touched up, too. The beat may have changed or maybe Scott added some cuts. We completed the *Criminal Minded* album at Power Play in Queens in about two weeks. We didn't have time to be in the studio, loungin'. We got to the studio on time. And we just kicked out the rest of the songs: "**Poetry**," "**Super Hoe**," the new version of "Criminal Minded." When the album came out, I guess I had never realized that it was an album. That was just not part of my mentality. I thought that the album was corny. After all those battle records we did, here I am now, making myself into an artist. I thought I was throwing away a very comfortable position that I was holding in the hip-hop community at the time. It was like facing your fears. You want to go, but you don't. I was recording tracks, I didn't think about an album. Scott's the one who named it *Criminal Minded*.

On the original vinyl for the album, there's a typo, and "**Dope Beat**" was actually called "Hope Beat." Scott La Rock and Ced-Gee brought in the AC/DC sample on that one. I don't know which one of them actually did it, but Scott was heavily into rock. He was a big Led Zeppelin fan, he had everything they ever did. He had all the AC/DC stuff, Iron Maiden, Whitesnake. He'd rock that right along with P-Funk. To this day I don't know why AC/DC didn't sue us for that song [which samples "Back In Black"]. That's all samples. I'm probably incriminating myself, but nothing on *Criminal Minded* is cleared.

It was Scott's idea to remix "**The P Is Free**." He did it with Ced-Gee. Scott was big into reggae, too, just like I was. I think he took Michigan & Smiley's "Dangerous Diseases," which was a huge record back in the '80s [Kris imitates chopped/stuttered beginning of song]. That intro is what makes me think it was Ced-Gee, because that was more his style. I wasn't there when that beat was made. I think the lyrics are mostly the same as the original version.

I always loved the track "**Super Hoe**." That night up in Rochester [mentioned in song] was crazy. And Scott La Rock *was* the Super Hoe. We were completely opposite as people. I'm this shy, reserved seminary student. I was even afraid of girls, I was definitely not the player type, and I'm still not. And Scott was the ep-i-to-me [over-enunciates it] of the player type. I was basically just making fun of him on that track, and he was just laughing in the studio. [Kris sings chorus]. WDKX is a real radio station in Rochester, NY, and I think Scott had slept with one of the DJs or somethin'. He was famous for that.

Rochester was our first paid gig outside of New York City. The first time we traveled to a place to do a show. But we got there and didn't get paid, and we were stranded. The promoter ran off with the money. And somehow Scott got this girl, who I think worked at WDKX, and that's how we got a place to sleep and something to eat the next morning. She might have even paid our way back, or drove us back or something. That was probably the first time that men were referred to as hos, in that song. Scott was proud to be a ho. That record was a celebration of our opposite-ness. We respected each others' position. In a way, we balanced each other out.

THE ALBUM COVER: 9MM GOES BANG

The cover of the album was pretty crazy. Some of that artillery [Kris and Scott are armed with various weaponry, including guns and a hand grenade] we already had, and the rest of it was from this ex-Marine. Like the grenades and the shoulder rounds. On a side note, we used to get our guns in the Bronx from ex-military people, who would come there with brand-new guns, and we used to buy from them. That's part of a whole other book, if you decide to write it. *The Origin of Guns in the Ghetto*. But there was this ex-Marine guy that the Rock Candy guys knew. They brought him in. Every day back then we was packin', with 38s and whatever. We had all kinds of 45s and so on. And we'd go on the roofs of the projects and shoot at cans. That stuff I was wearing, and the grenades and the guns on the table, that was all this ex-Marine's stuff. The gun I was holding was mine, and I think the gun that Scott was holding was ICU's. I can't remember exactly.

We wanted the most shocking album cover that we could find, and that was what it ended up being. We wanted to set a precedent that we was real, this is real, this is where hip-hop is going. From fantasy to reality. And that's exactly what happened. I wouldn't say that we were the only ones, because Eric B & Rakim's *Paid In Full* assisted that image as well, and Schoolly D was out of control, with "P.S.K." That was a huge record back then. But in terms of pictures, posing, how you posed, Eric B and Rakim on the cover with the Dapper Dan jacket and the big gold, that's how you came to the club. We were all part of the same movement that wanted to show the street mentality.

We wanted you to think that we was the most ruthless crew on the face of the Earth and if you even thought of battling us, you was gonna get a buckshot. And we suffered for that, too, in a lot of different ways. To this day I'm not proud when people say that *Criminal Minded* was the beginning of gangsta rap. That's not something I put on my resume. But it was true. No one else was coming out like that, or did what we did.

R.I.P. SCOTT LA ROCK

And then we suffered, because on August 26, 1987, Scott La Rock gets a call from D-Nice that some guy was threatening to kill him or shoot him. Because D was allegedly talking to this guy's girlfriend. Scott said: "Let's squash this beef. You can't run all your life." So Scott went over to where the beef was, in Bronx River Houses. Scott showed up and actually squashed the beef with D-Nice and this guy. But then somebody starts shooting from across the street, out of a window. They was ambushed. The Jeep was packed with people, but only Scott got hit, behind the ear.

I was in Brooklyn then – me and Ms. Melody was renting a house in Canarsie – and I got the call from D-Nice, he was screaming on the phone. "They shot Scott, yo, it's fucked up! Oh god, they shot Scott!" I thought he was kidding, 'cause D-Nice was a jokester. Then he started cursin' at me and I knew it was real. I got in a cab and went all the way up to the Bronx, to where Scott was staying at the time. He was staying with this girl named Dee Dee. And she was there and was hysterical. So we jumped in another cab and went to the hospital. I don't remember which one, it was on Grand Concourse. I didn't even want to go upstairs. I was deeply immersed in metaphysics and spiritual thought and I said: "Nope, I'm going to remember him alive. I don't even want to put the image of Scott being dead in my memory." And I stayed downstairs. I remember that MC Serch [from Third Bass] was the first person I saw on the scene there.

I remember later on in life, Serch asked me why I had a smile on my face on that sad day. And it was because I was like: "He's in a better place now. We are now going to win. Because half the crew is in the spirit realm and the other half of the group is on Earth. We can't lose now." No one knew what I was talking about, no one cared. It was grief and there was finger-pointing.

The city was in an uproar, it was all on the news. I remember Connie Chung, she came and said [imitates uptight female voice]: "Don't you think that your album cover incites violence?" And I was like: "No, this is how people are livin' every day. Does John Wayne incite violence?" So afterwards I had to answer all these questions about violence.

It was wild because we had already started to write *By All Means Necessary* [Boogie Down Productions' second album]. I had already written [the songs] "Stop The Violence" and "My Philosophy." Scott wanted to cut up "Sister Sanctified" [by Stanley Turrentine, sampled on "My Philosophy"], and I had those rhymes. I had just battled Melle Mel at the Latin Quarter and I was trying to turn those rhymes into "Still #1." So we was already doing this other album because the point was to come out like the thug and then turn back and say: "But wait, you can go from this to that."

LOOKING BACK

When I look back on *Criminal Minded* now, first of all I'm very proud of it. It's probably one of the only records I'll ever be remembered for. But if you don't know KRS-One, that was the beginning of what's now called gangsta rap. It wasn't gangsta rap then, it was basically telling the reality of the street. That's all it was supposed to be. We wanted to pose with guns because that was the reality of the streets at the time. If the reality of the streets at the time was the Mr. Softee ice cream truck, we'd have posed in front of that. We was trying to tell our story, and the mainstream didn't hear you unless you were shocking. So if there's anything to come away from it, I would say that you would have to look at *Criminal Minded* all the way up tomy latest release, *Spiritual Minded*. To go from being immature to being mature. From boys to men.

Today we take rhyme styles for granted. On *Criminal Minded* those rhyme styles you hear were original. They hadn't been heard before. The album had originality and we lack so much of that today. It seems that if one rapper comes out with a style, 20 others come after him. Hip-hop now, what it has become, is just not what we intended it to be. When *Criminal Minded* came out, Big Daddy Kane had his own style, Rakim still has his own style, Kool G Rap, Biz Markie. We've lost cultural continuity because hip-hop has gone from being a culture to being a product. And that's one of the things I've devoted my life to, to correct it.

If there's anything to convey to the public, in my opinion we cannot allow corporate America to validate us and to dictate what hip-hop is andwhat hip-hop isn't. And *Criminal Minded* was that stake in the heart of corporate America at that time. All respect to Run-DMC, LL, Whodini, Fat Boys and Kurtis Blow. But when they were doing it, they was called sellouts in the streets. They was the mainstream rappers, they was MC Hammer. And we were pretty much fighting against that. That's what *Criminal Minded* stood for. It stood for Hip-Hop Kulture, with a K. It was like: "You think this way, but blaw!, it's *this* way." We was conscious of what we was doin'. It wasn't a mistake.

And we weren't the only ones. There was the Class of 1987. You have to include Eric B & Rakim's *Paid In Full*, too, because they're really the same album. It was all one album, and it was Biz Markie's *Goin' Off*, Big Daddy Kane's *Long Live The Kane*, Public Enemy's *Yo! Bum Rush The Show*, too. These albums were collectively one album, and we all picked a different topic to address, from the streets. We all hung out together. We sampled Eric B & Rakim's drums to make "The Bridge Is Over." Those were Marley Marl's drums. Even though we were battling at the time, there was still this family thing going on. And big up to all the Juice Crew, because without them I could not exist, literally. If

Shan and Marley hadn't answered, I would not have had all the other records I've done over the last 15 years. If Shan had not followed the rules of hip-hop, it would have been different. But the rules are that if you respect the rapper that is challenging you, then you answer the challenge.